# Religion in the Ancient Mediterranean World
## Part III

## Professor Glenn S. Holland

THE TEACHING COMPANY ®

PUBLISHED BY:

THE TEACHING COMPANY
4151 Lafayette Center Drive, Suite 100
Chantilly, Virginia 20151-1232
1-800-TEACH-12
Fax—703-378-3819
www.teach12.com

ISBN 1-59803-036-1

# Glenn S. Holland, Ph.D.
## Professor of Religious Studies, Allegheny College

Glenn S. Holland is the Bishop James Mills Thoburn Professor of Religious Studies at Allegheny College in Meadville, Pennsylvania. Born in 1952 and raised in Los Angeles, California, Professor Holland received his A.B. in Drama from Stanford University in 1974. After several years as a writer, Professor Holland entered Mansfield College at the University of Oxford and received a master's degree from Oxford in Theology in 1981. The same year, he entered the Divinity School of the University of Chicago; he received his Ph.D. in Biblical Studies, with a concentration in the works of St. Paul, in 1986. His dissertation was later published as *The Tradition That You Received from Us: 2 Thessalonians in the Pauline Tradition* (Tübingen: J.C.B. Mohr [Paul Siebeck]: 1988).

Professor Holland has written on many topics, including the use of classical rhetoric as a means of analyzing the letters of St. Paul and frank speech as a philosophical, political, and literary virtue in ancient Hellenistic culture. He was a co-editor, with John T. Fitzgerald and Dirk Obbink, of a collection of essays on Philodemus, an Epicurean philosopher of the 1$^{st}$ century B.C.E., *Philodemus and the New Testament World* (Supplements to Novum Testamentum 111, Leiden: Brill, 2004). Professor Holland is also the author of *Divine Irony* (Selinsgrove, PA: Susquehanna University Press, 2000), a study of irony as a person's adoption of the divine perspective on events in the human world, with special attention to Socrates and the letters of the apostle Paul. The professor is a contributor and assistant editor for the award-winning multidisciplinary journal *Common Knowledge*, published three times a year by Duke University Press.

Professor Holland has taught in the Department of Philosophy and Religious Studies at Allegheny College, a traditional four-year liberal arts college, since 1985. It was there that he developed, over many years, the course of lectures that is now *Religion in the Ancient Mediterranean World*. The course has proven to be one of Professor Holland's most popular classes and has introduced many of his students to the academic study of religion. The professor was awarded the Thoburn Chair in Religious Studies in 1992 and the Divisional Professorship in Humanities at Allegheny College in

2003. He is also active with the Allegheny College Chapter of Phi Beta Kappa and has served as both its secretary and president.

Professor Holland and his wife, Sandra, an elementary mathematics teacher, have two grown sons, Nathaniel and Gregory.

# Table of Contents
# Religion in the Ancient Mediterranean World
# Part III

# Religion in the Ancient Mediterranean World

**Scope:**

This course of 48 lectures is an introduction to the religious cultures of the ancient Mediterranean world, from the earliest indications of human religious practices during the prehistoric era to the conversion of the Roman Empire to Christianity in the 4$^{th}$ century of the Common Era. The course examines what we can recover of the religious activities of prehistoric human beings before considering in depth the religious cultures of the great ancient civilizations of Egypt, Mesopotamia, Syria-Palestine, Greece, and the Roman Empire. The emphasis throughout the course is not only on the rituals and mythology of a civilization's official religious culture but also on the beliefs, practices, and yearnings of the common person. The course content is derived in part from primary literary sources that speak about these different religious cultures in the voice of the believer. Comparisons among the different religious cultures will reveal what is unique about each and what ideas, practices, and aspirations appear to be typical of all human religious communities. The course is presented in 4 parts of 12 lectures each.

The first part of the course introduces the subject and addresses the fundamental question "What is religion?" With an understanding of religion as beliefs and practices that express a community's relationship to the sacred, it becomes possible to investigate prehistoric religious cultures on the basis of their physical remains. The course will trace the development of religious practices in the transition from the Paleolithic and Mesolithic eras to the Neolithic era and the beginnings of the first great Near Eastern civilizations. The first of these civilizations to be considered is Egypt, the most straightforward example of an ancient polytheistic religious culture developed in relative isolation from the rest of the world. Because of the richness of the sources and the clear points of focus of Egyptian religious culture—the sun, the Nile, and the king—it is possible not only to reconstruct official Egyptian religious practices and mythology but also to gain some sense of the concerns and sentiments of the common people.

The second part of the course shifts the focus to the other great center of ancient Near Eastern civilization, Mesopotamia. Here, a series of city-states, kingdoms, and empires held sway in succession over the centuries, and the people felt some unease at the power and willfulness of the gods. But Mesopotamia has also left religious literature that brings those gods to life. The course pays particular attention to the creation stories, stories about Ishtar, the impetuous goddess of love, and the first epic poem, the story of the hero Gilgamesh. Points of contact between Mesopotamian religious literature and more familiar biblical literature lead to a consideration of the different concepts of divinity in the ancient Mediterranean world and introduce the religious cultures of Syria-Palestine, especially that of ancient Israel. Here again, despite Israel's distinctive history as a people and a nation and its concern with one God, certain recurring religious ideas and practices, such as prophecy, are seen to reflect more widely spread phenomena common to ancient Near Eastern civilizations.

The third part of the course begins with prophecy as a response to the political and religious crises that arose in the kingdoms of Israel and Judah with the threat posed by the Mesopotamian empires of Assyria and Babylon. Faith in the one God proved particularly resilient, as the experience of exile in Babylon led the prophets of Judah to assert all the more emphatically the uniqueness of the God of Israel. By comparison, the religious cultures of the Aegean Sea made a virtue of diversity. The physical remains of the Minoan civilization of Crete offer some intriguing clues to Minoan religious culture, and the ruins of Mycenaean cities on the Greek mainland provide only glimpses of a world much better known through Homer's *Iliad* and *Odyssey*, themselves products of the succeeding Greek Dark Age. With the rise of Greek civilization and the autonomous city-state during the Archaic era, the pantheon of Greek gods and goddesses begins to assume its familiar appearance. The classical age of the 5th and 4th centuries B.C.E. saw the height of Greek civilization, as well as philosophical and literary reflection on Greek religious culture. After the conquests of Alexander the Great and the spread of Hellenistic culture, mystery religions brought the traditional Greek gods Demeter and Dionysus new prominence as divine patrons who could rescue their devotees from the afflictions of the human situation and fear of the blind power of fate.

The fourth part of the course begins by considering how mystery religions introduced eastern gods, such as Isis and Mithras, into the Hellenistic world. Rome is a prominent example of how a distinctive religious culture is gradually transformed by the incorporation of elements of foreign religious cultures, including those of the Etruscans and the Greeks, as well as by evolving social and political history. Rome came to dominate the Mediterranean world around the turn of the age and continued to accommodate the cosmopolitan expressions of the traditional religious cultures of Greece and the east. The proliferation of religious claims and communities inspired skepticism among the intellectuals of the Roman world, leading to philosophical explanations of religious beliefs and literary attacks against religious charlatans. In this pluralistic context, Jesus of Nazareth appears as a Jewish religious reformer proclaiming a new relationship between the divine and the human worlds. His followers spread a faith based on both his teachings and his person throughout the Mediterranean world, despite official persecution and disagreements among themselves over the proper understanding of who Jesus was and what he taught. The Christian movement's resilience under persecution and its appeal to the religious needs and concerns of the Roman world eventually led to its triumph over traditional Roman religious culture under the emperor Constantine, although the traditional religious culture survived and manifested itself in new ways. The concluding session considers the ways in which the religious cultures of the ancient Mediterranean world are most foreign to our own and the ways in which they appear to have expressed the enduring religious yearnings of all humanity.

# Lecture Twenty-Five
# Classical Israelite Prophecy

**Scope:**
After the reign of Solomon, the nation of Israel split into two parts, Israel with its capital, Samaria, to the north and Judah with its capital, Jerusalem, to the south. Both nations flourished in the absence of a regional military power, but the rise of Assyria threatened all the nations of Syria-Palestine. The religious policies of both Israel and Judah were determined by the king and the priesthood, reflecting not only the traditional worship of the Lord but foreign religious influences, as well. The prophets represented an independent voice of religious authority that often came into conflict with official religious practice and political policies. Amos presented a prophetic voice that challenged social injustice in Israel, while Isaiah of Jerusalem urged trust in the Lord, rather than military alliances in political matters. Both prophets emphasized the Lord's love for his people and his faithfulness to his covenantal promises.

## Outline

I.  The political situation in Israel and Judah after the reign of Solomon led to a variety of religious practices in both nations, only some of them consistent with later orthodoxies.

   **A.** The united monarchy of Judah and Israel broke into its component parts during the reign of Solomon's son Rehoboam (r. 928–911 B.C.E.).

   1. The people of the northern territory of Israel felt oppressed by Solomon's practice of requiring forced labor from them but not from the people of Judah.
   2. In the eyes of the northerners, Solomon was a foreign monarch ruling them from a foreign capital and demanding worship in a foreign temple under foreign priests.
   3. The north rebelled against David and Solomon and finally broke away during Rehoboam's reign, under the leadership of Jeroboam (r. 928–907 B.C.E.).
   4. The northern kingdom had a series of short-lived dynasties until Omri (r. 882–871 B.C.E.), who made Israel militarily and politically secure.

5. Judah continued to be ruled by David's dynasty and engaged in frequent warfare with Israel.

B. Both Israel and Judah flourished in a period marked by the absence of a major world power in the Near East between about 1250 and 850 B.C.E.
   1. After the fall of the Hittite empire, while Egypt was preoccupied with internal problems, Syria-Palestine was free of external domination.
   2. A number of native kingdoms arose and developed, including Edom, Moab, Ammon, Sidon, Aram-Damascus, and the Philistine kingdoms.
   3. These kingdoms fought among themselves or formed alliances; they survived until the Assyrian encroachment on Syria-Palestine in the 9$^{th}$ century B.C.E.
   4. From that time on, the political fortunes of both Israel and Judah depended on the actions of the Assyrian kings as allies, opponents, or conquerors.

C. After the kingdom divided in 928 B.C.E., the people continued to worship the Lord in their own territories according to their ancestral traditions.
   1. Judah continued to worship at the Jerusalem Temple but also at other altars dedicated to worship of the Lord located elsewhere.
   2. Israel worshiped at the traditional cultic sites of Dan and Bethel, as well as other altars dedicated to worship of the Lord.

D. Both Israel and Judah incorporated the worship of foreign gods in various ways.
   1. The worship of a foreign god might be practiced by resident aliens.
   2. Women of the king's harem would bring their own gods and religious customs with them.
   3. Official worship of a foreign god might be introduced as a sign of allegiance to a foreign nation as ally or as conqueror.
   4. Religious orthodoxy was determined by the political and religious authorities as custodians of the religious culture of Israel and Judah.

**E.** The most common source of conflict between the authorities and the prophets was their different ideas of what the Lord demanded of his people.

    **1.** Political leaders were concerned with how best to respond to external threats and how to ensure the nation's security.

    **2.** Like most of their contemporaries, the religious authorities believed that the primary religious duty of the people was to obey the king and support the national cult.

    **3.** The prophets proclaimed that the primary duty of both king and people was obedience to the Lord in moral action, as well as proper worship.

    **4.** The prophets represented an independent, self-authenticating voice of religious authority.

**F.** The conflict: Was the will of the Lord expressed by the actions of the king and the priests or by the words and actions of the prophets?

    **1.** The prophets tended to represent either a rejection of royal authority in favor of divine authority or an evolving monotheism.

    **2.** The idea that the Lord alone should rule over Israel represented dissatisfaction with the political compromises that are a part of nationhood.

    **3.** Henotheistic belief in the Lord as the only God for Israel was expressed in terms of the Lord's incomparability and strength, leading to a nascent monotheism.

    **4.** The prophets tended to be theological idealists, claiming in any and all circumstances that the best policy was adherence to the word of the Lord.

    **5.** Prophecy did not inevitably lead to conflict, because some prophets focused attention on the sins of foreign nations that oppressed God's people.

**II.** Both Amos of Tekoa in Israel and Isaiah of Jerusalem in Judah provide examples of the conflict between the prophet and the governing authorities.

**A.** Amos is the earliest of the prophets whose oracles are preserved in a book.

1. Amos was from Judah, but his prophetic ministry in Israel reflects the religious perspective of Israel.
2. Amos probably prophesied beginning around 750 B.C.E., during the reign of Jeroboam II, whose loyalty to Assyria ensured him a long and prosperous reign.
3. Jeroboam's reign also saw a widening gap between the rich and the poor in Israel as a result of social injustice.

**B.** Amos appears to have received his prophetic calling through a series of visions.
1. Amos distances himself from both official and guild prophecy.
2. Amos's only recorded appearance is at the shrine at Bethel, where he prophesied against Jeroboam and predicted exile for the people of Israel.
3. Some of Amos's visions are recorded in Amos 7–8, when he sees everyday objects that convey a symbolic meaning of judgment from the Lord.

**C.** Amos's first oracle is a series of attacks on Israel's traditional enemies.
1. Each of these attacks follows the same formula.
2. In each case, Amos lists the sins of the nation and the punishment that will result.
3. Amos initially presents himself as a nationalist prophet but then pronounces judgment against Israel in the same terms.
4. Israel is condemned for sins against the poor, but the punishment will lead to forgiveness.
5. Amos's message is moderated by the enduring relationship between the Lord and Israel.

**D.** Isaiah was the first of the three great classical prophets, with Jeremiah and Ezekiel.
1. Isaiah apparently spent his entire life in Jerusalem and may have been an official court or cult prophet.
2. Isaiah was married and had at least two sons to whom he gave symbolic names.
3. Isaiah's career covered about half a century, from about 740 to 676 B.C.E.
4. During his ministry, Isaiah gathered disciples who preserved his prophecies.

**E.** One of Isaiah's most well known prophecies was given to Ahaz of Judah around 735–733 B.C.E.

    **1.** Pekah of Israel and Rezin of Aram-Damascus threatened to attack Judah if Ahaz did not join their anti-Assyrian alliance.

    **2.** Isaiah's first prophecy (7:1–9) assures Ahaz that the two enemy kingdoms will fall to Assyria.

    **3.** The second prophecy (7:10–25) provides reassurance with the sign of Immanuel.

    **4.** In the second prophecy, Isaiah tells Ahaz to take the Lord's covenant with David seriously and to trust in his power.

    **5.** The prophecy refers to a young woman who is pregnant and will bear the child Immanuel; she may have been one of the king's wives.

    **6.** The prophecy says that before the child knows right from wrong, Israel and Aram-Damascus will be gone.

    **7.** The child will eat curds and honey, divine food that will help him grow quickly.

    **8.** In spite of this prophecy, Ahaz made an alliance with Assyria, bringing Judah under Assyrian control.

    **9.** The legacy of the prophets is their affirmation of the Lord's faithfulness toward his people, based on his covenantal promises to Israel.

    **10.** Conviction in the Lord's faithfulness sustained the religious faith of the people after the fall of Israel and Judah.

**Essential Reading:**

Henry Jackson Flanders, Jr., Robert Wilson Crapps, and David Anthony Smith. *People of the Covenant: An Introduction to the Hebrew Bible*, pp. 303–321, 339–347, 355–376.

Siegfried Hermann. *A History of Israel in Old Testament Times*, pp. 187–262.

Joseph Blenkinsopp. *A History of Prophecy in Israel: From the Settlement in the Land to the Hellenistic Period*, pp. 80–118.

2 Kings 9–25.

Amos.

Isaiah 1–39.

**Supplementary Reading:**

John H. Hayes and J. Maxwell Miller, eds. *Israelite and Judaean History*, pp. 381–434.

Klaus Koch. *The Prophets*, Vol. 1: *The Assyrian Period*, pp. 36–76, 105–156.

**Questions to Consider:**

1.  What were likely to be the political and religious consequences of an alliance with a military power such as Assyria?

2.  Is it possible to combine successfully theological idealism and political realism? Which must accommodate itself to the other? Why?

# Lecture Twenty-Five—Transcript
## Classical Israelite Prophecy

In the last session, we considered the early development of prophecy in Israel and Judah, which appeared in mostly three overlapping forms: guild prophecy, official prophecy, and independent prophecy.

In this session, we will discuss what is often called "classical" prophecy in Israel and Judah—that is, the prophecy represented by the so-called "writing prophets" who had books named after them during the monarchies, and their ministry during the monarchies.

Now, the political situation in Israel and Judah after the reigns of David and Solomon led to a variety of different religious practices in both nations, both Israel and Judah, and only some of these religious practices were consistent with later orthodoxies.

After the reign of Solomon, the united monarchy that had been pulled together by David at the southern territory of Judah, the northern territory of Israel—that united monarchy broke apart and broke into its component parts once again during the reign of Solomon's son, Rehoboam. Rehoboam reigned from 928 to 911 B.C.E.

The people of the northern territory of Israel had felt oppressed by Solomon's practice of requiring forced labor from them. He had a corvée, as it was called, of laborers from the territory of Israel who were pressed into groups each month to do work on the king's various projects.

However, Solomon did not require forced labor from the southern territory of Judah. That sort of corvée was not imposed on them, and this led to a great deal of resentment against Solomon from those in Israel.

Generally speaking, Solomon was a different sort of person from those in the north, and it was very easy for northerners to consider Solomon a foreign monarch—that is, a Judahite monarch—who was ruling them from the former capital, the former Jebusite city of Jerusalem, and he was demanding a form of foreign worship in a foreign temple—that is, worship in a temple, rather than in the tabernacle—and this worship was being conducted under foreign priests, people like Zadok, a Jebusite priest who was the high priest during the time of David.

Solomon, then, would be regarded as a foreign monarch ruling from a foreign capital, demanding worship in a foreign temple under a foreign priesthood and, therefore, not a king who demands the loyalty and the religious support from the people from the north.

In fact, the north rebelled against David a couple of times, and then it rebelled again against Solomon; the north was only able to break away successfully from the kingdom of Judah during the reign of Rehoboam, the son of Solomon. After the north broke away, after Israel declared itself an independent nation, it took as its king Jeroboam, who had led a revolt against Solomon, and Jeroboam I, as it happened, and he reigned over Israel from 928 to 907 B.C.E.

Now, the northern kingdom had a series of short-lived dynasties until the time of Omri. Omri, you remember, is the father of Ahab. Omri reigned from 882 to 871 B.C.E., and Omri was the one who was able to consolidate the power of Israel, who was able to expand its territories to their greatest extent; it was he who established a capital in Samaria the nation of Israel, and it was he who made Israel militarily and politically secure.

Judah, in the meantime, continued to be ruled by David's dynasty, and the kings of Judah and the kings of Israel engaged in frequent warfare. Both nations, of course, regarded themselves as the true people of God, the rightful inhibitors of promises made to Abraham and the covenant established with Moses at Sinai.

Now, both nations of Israel and Judah arose and flourished in a rather peculiar period of time in the ancient Near East. This was a period that was marked by the absence of any major world power, between about 1250 and 850 B.C.E. This was before the rise of Assyria and after the fall of the Hittite empire. This was a very unusual situation in the Near East, not to have a major world power exerting its influence over Syria-Palestine.

After the Hittite empire fell in Asia Minor, Egypt was primarily occupied with its own internal problems and, therefore, did not seek to reach out to foreign conquests—first of all, in Syria-Palestine. As a result, the ethnic peoples of Syria-Palestine were, for awhile, free to develop their own autonomous kingdoms, and it was during this time when Syria-Palestine was free of external domination that a number of native kingdoms arose and developed, and this included not only Israel and Judah, but also Edom, Moab, Ammon, Sidon, Aram-Damascus, and the various kingdoms of the Philistines.

Now, these kingdoms sometimes fought among themselves. Sometimes, they formed alliances, like nations will in any territory, but they survived more or less intact until the encroachment of the Assyrian empire on Syria-Palestine, which began in the mid-9th century B.C.E. From that time on, the political fortunes of both Israel and Judah depended on the actions of the Assyrian kings. Sometimes the Assyrian kings were their allies; sometimes they were their opponents; and finally, in the case of Israel, the Assyrian kings became their conquerors.

With the rise of Assyria, though, the era of independence for the kingdoms of Syria-Palestine was gone forever, and one could argue that autonomy was not gained until the post-World War II era in the modern era.

Now, after the kingdom established by David and Solomon divided in the year 928 B.C.E., the subjects of both kingdoms continued to worship the Lord, and, of course, they did so in their own territories according to their own ancestral traditions. Judah continued to worship at the Jerusalem Temple, but most of the time, during the kingdom of Judah, its subjects also continued to worship the Lord in other shrines, in other shrines dedicated to the Lord; they were called *bamoths*, or "high places."

Now, many biblical scholars and Bible readers understand the *bamoths* as pagan altars, but the word merely means "altar"; it does not designate the god to whom it was dedicated. In fact, the word *bamoth*, referring to altars, refers to sites where clearly the Lord is being worshiped. At the same time, since these elders were located away from the supervision of the priests of the Jerusalem Temple, it's entirely possible that they were, at times, influenced by foreign religious practices, as well, but there is no direct correlation between the designation "*bamoth*," or "high place," and the imputation of some sort of foreign worship.

Meanwhile, Israel worshiped at traditional cultic sites, particularly Dan and Bethel, but they also had other altars dedicated to the worship of the Lord, the so-called "high places," the "*bamoth*s," and, again, these were possibly subject to foreign religious practices.

Now, in fact, it appears that both the kingdom of Israel and the kingdom of Judah incorporated the worship of foreign gods in various ways. Now, we usually think of this as some sort of wholesale turning of the people's affections to some foreign god—but, in fact, there were many different ways that a foreign god might gain influence, either officially or unofficially.

For example, there might be worship in either Israel or Judah of a foreign god by resident aliens—that is, people from other nations who continue to worship their own gods while either living in Israel or Judah, just as any nation has representatives of other nations living within it and carrying out their traditional practices. These sources of traditional practices would include the worship of foreign gods.

This was also the case with the women of the king's harem. The women of the king's harem would come from other nations, and they would bring their gods with them, and they would bring their own religious customs with them. The historian of Samuel and Kings blames Solomon for allowing his wives to worship their own gods as part of their practice in the harem.

Now, of course, not all of these foreign wives were as devoted to their own gods as Jezebel proved to be. As I've said, her devotion to Ba'al-Melqart was practically evangelistic and led to a lot of problems for Israel.

Official worship of a foreign god might be introduced as a sign of allegiance to a foreign ally, or as a conqueror. This happened to both Assyria and Babylon. That is, the gods of Assyria, once Assyria established hegemony over Israel, had its gods worshiped in Israel, a sign of allegiance and loyalty. If you worship the god, you're not likely to mess with those the god protects. This also happens during the dominance of Babylon in Judah. Worship of a foreign god, then, can be a political action that affirms loyalty to another nation.

Of course, there were also unofficial religious practices that were not sanctioned by either nation's kings or priesthoods. These would be what we call "folk religion." Expressions of folk religion were from possibly foreign influence, or possibly superstitious accretions from other religions, all sorts of things that might happen that we have no trace of in the official records.

In any event, it's important to remember that "religious orthodoxy"—and perhaps we should put that in star quotes— "religious orthodoxy"—at any given time, this was determined by the political and religious authorities. In other words, what was correct religious practice was defined by the king and by the official priesthood because they were the custodians of the religious culture in their own nation—whether Israel, Judah, or some other nation. The idea that the king or the priesthood would somehow be at odds with the intentions of the gods was unprecedented in the ancient Mediterranean world.

It was this power of the king and the priesthood to define the religious culture of the nation that was the most common source of conflict between the political and religious authorities of Israel and Judah on the one side, and the prophets who spoke on the Lord's behalf on the other. The political leaders, after all, were concerned with how best to respond to external threats, and internal conditions. They were concerned with what wars to fight, what alliances to form, how best to ensure the nation's security, and this carried over into the religious sphere. What religious practices and religious accommodations would best ensure the nation's security?

The religious authorities were, themselves, government functionaries, and generally they share the concerns and the points of view of the political leaders—not at all an uncommon phenomenon even in our own time. Moreover, the religious authorities believed that their primary responsibility was the proper maintenance of the worship cult of the Lord, or the proper maintenance of the temple in particular. Their responsibility was to supervise the cultic worship of the Lord throughout the nation, and particularly in Jerusalem. This was all done to ensure the welfare of the people, and to ensure the well being of the king and of the country.

Like most of their contemporaries, the religious authorities in Israel and Judah believed that the primary religious duty of the people was to obey the king and support the national cult—in other words, to put their trust in the king and in the priesthood, to ensure that all was well between the nation and the Lord.

However, the prophets—the prophets generally spoke from a very different point of view. They believed that the primary duty of both king and people was to be obedient to the Lord in the ways that the prophets maintained were right. The primary duty of the king and the people was to be obedient to the covenant, to show their obedience and loyalty to the Lord in specific moral and social actions, as well as proper worship. In other words, the relationship of the Lord was not based on a kingdom, or on a cult—that is, a group of ritual actions—but rather, on an entire mode of living, on an entire way of life. The prophets presented themselves as independent and, to a large extent, self-authenticating voices of religious authority, but they were not necessarily beholden to the interests of the king or any other religious authority, and they formed something of a counterbalance and a challenge to official religious authority.

This was the conflict. Was the genuine will of the Lord expressed by the actions of the king and the priests of the temple, or was the genuine will of the Lord expressed by the words and actions of the prophets?

Now, of course, this question was made more difficult by the fact that prophets tended to represent a nonconforming view of national religion. Either it was based on a traditional rejection of royal authority and in favor of the divine authority of the Lord, or it was based on an evolving monotheism—an evolving conviction that the Lord alone was the one and only God of the whole creation.

The notion that the Lord alone should rule over Israel was older than the monarchy itself, and it became an expression of dissatisfaction with the political and religious policies and compromises that are a necessary part of royal nationhood. Idealists are not happy with the pragmatics that are part of politics.

Henotheistic belief in the Lord as the only God for the people of Israel and Judah to worship was exemplified by Elijah, for example, Israel, and this was expressed in terms of the Lord's incomparability and in the Lord's strength as Israel's defender; this and time led to a nascent monotheism, as the Lord was exalted over all other gods.

Moreover, as I said, the prophets tended to be theological idealists. They claimed in any and all circumstances that the policy was a single policy, adherence to the word of the Lord they proclaimed, that the best policy was always to trust in the Lord. If you obeyed the Lord, the Lord would reward you. If you obeyed the Lord, the Lord would deliver Israel or Judah from their enemies; so, in any international crisis, the best thing to do was to be loyal to the Lord and trust in him to pull you through.

The conflict between political realities and theological idealists almost always resulted in a defeat for the idealists—although, in this case, it was the idealists who wrote the histories. The Bible reflects the point of view of the idealists, rather than the politicians and the realists.

Prophecy did not inevitably lead to conflict, of course, because some prophets—I'd like to mention Obadiah, Nehum, and Habakkuk, for example, usually considered minor prophets in some ways—these prophets focused attention on the sins of foreign nations that oppressed God's people, and they were much less concerned, if concerned at all, with the unfaithfulness of the people of Judah or Israel themselves.

Now, as far as the classical writing prophets are concerned, both Amos of Tekoa in Israel and Isaiah of Jerusalem in Judah provide examples of this conflict between the prophets and the governing authorities, although they do so in different ways.

Amos is the earliest of the prophets whose oracles have been preserved in a book, and his prophecies addressed the state of social justice in the Israel of his day. Amos was from Tekoa, which is a town due south of Jerusalem, in the territory of Judah, but his prophetic ministry took place in Israel, and his prophecies reflect the religious perspectives of Israel.

Amos probably prophesied beginning around 750 B.C.E., during the reign of Jeroboam II of Israel, and this would make Amos an older contemporary of Isaiah of Jerusalem—so their lives overlapped. Jeroboam was a descendent of the usurper Jehu. Jehu had been anointed by the cycle of the profit Elijah, and once he had gained power by slaughtering of the members of the Omride dynasty, he was the one who first brought Israel under the power of the Assyrian empire.

Jeroboam's loyalty as an Assyrian vassal ensured him a long and prosperous reign, but his reign saw a widening gap between rich and poor in Israel as a result of social injustice. This injustice, combined with the rise of Assyrian power, led Amos to declare judgment on Israel and to warn of its impending decline.

Now, Amos appears to have received his prophetic calling through a series of visions. Amos says at the outset, when he defends himself against attack, that he is "a shepherd, a dresser of sycamore trees," and he specifically denies that he is either a prophet or one of the sons of the prophets. We find this in Amos, chapter 7, verses 14–15. He distances himself both from official prophecy and from guild prophecy—which, as I've indicated, was probably regarded with a certain amount of suspicion at this point.

Amos's only reported appearance was at the shrine of the Lord in Bethel, in Israel. Here, he prophesied against Jeroboam and predicted exile for the people of Israel. This, naturally, aroused the ire of a priest of the shrine at Bethel; his name was Amaziah. He told Amos to go away and not prophesy.

Some of Amos's visions were recorded in Amos, chapter 7 and chapter 8. This is an instance of visions where the prophet sees some everyday object—a swarm of locusts, or a basket of fruit, or a plumbline against the wall—and sees in that thing that is actually there a deeper symbolic meaning that carries a message of judgment from the Lord.

The first oracle proclaimed by Amos is actually a series of attacks on Israel's enemies, and he lifts Damascus, Gaza, Philistia, Tyre, Edom, Ammon, Moab, and Judah. In each case, the form of the attack is the same, introduced in the same formula. "For the three transgressions of"—name your enemy here—"and for four, I will not revoke the punishment." For example, then: "For the three transgressions of Philistia, I will not revoke the punishment."

In each case, Amos lists the sins of the nation and the punishment that will result at the Lord's hand, and this is delivered in the first-person as the Lord speaks: "So I will"; "I will." In each case, the final judgment on the nation is exile and destruction by war, or destruction by fire.

Amos, so far, presents himself as a nationalist prophet. He proclaims condemnation on Israel's enemies and concludes with condemnation of Judah and Jerusalem because this was Israel's closest neighbor and closest rival, and, in fact, he condemns Jerusalem and Judah in the same terms that authors from Judah attacked Israel and Samaria with.

Then, though, Amos pronounces judgment against Israel itself using the same formula with "For the three transgressions of Israel, and for four, I will not revoke the punishment." Israel was condemned for sins against the poor that pollute religious practice, but in this case, the expected judgment was tempered with a sense of longing for reconciliation between the Lord and his people Israel. The punishment in this case was chastisement, but not destruction.

Although Amos speaks out against the religious practices of his day, his message is moderated somewhat by the sense that there is an enduring relationship between the Lord and Israel that will not be broken.

Now, in Judah, Isaiah of Jerusalem was the first of the three great classical prophets. The other two are Jeremiah and Ezekiel. They are great classical prophets because their influence was felt both during their own time, and then throughout the subsequent history of Judah, as reflected in the biblical texts.

Isaiah apparently received his prophetic call in the last year of the reign of Uziah of Judah, about 740 B.C.E. If he were around 20 years old then, he would have been a boy during the time of Amos's ministry. Like Amos, Isaiah received his message in visions, and he describes some of those visions.

Isaiah seems to have spent his entire life in Jerusalem, and it appears that he had very easy access to the court and to the temple—so he may have been a member of an aristocratic family, or it's possible that he was an official prophet, a prophet of the court or the temple. I would personally lean towards the temple.

Isaiah was also married, and he had at least two sons who were probably born in 735 B.C.E. and in 734 B.C.E., and in a prophetic action, he gave those sons prophetic, symbolic names. The first was Shear-jashub, whose name means, "A remnant will return," and the other was Maher-shalah-hash-baz, a name meaning "Speedy spoiled quick booty"—in other words, "The spoil will come quickly," and booty will be taken, a very difficult name to get through school with, I should think.

Isaiah's career covered about half a century, from about 740 B.C.E. until about 676 B.C.E. This included the reigns of Jotham, Ahaz, and Hezekiah as kings of Judah. During his ministry, Isaiah apparently gathered a group of disciples, and these disciples preserved his prophecies by memorizing them and passing them down in an oral tradition over several generations.

Now, Isaiah gave one of his best-known prophecies in the period 735 to 733 B.C.E., at a time when Ahaz of Judah was being pressured to join an anti-Assyrian alliance with Israel and Aram-Damascus. Pekah of Israel and Rezin of Aram-Damascus were forming an alliance against Assyria, and they wanted Judah to join them, and when Ahaz decided not to join them, Pekah and Rezin threatened to attacked Judah and remove Ahaz if he decided not to join them in the alliance against Assyria.

Now, Isaiah's first prophecy in the situation appears in Isaiah, chapter 7, verses 1–9, and it assures Ahaz that Pekah and Rezin are no more a threat than are "smoldering stumps of torches. Their light has almost gone out." In other words, their kingdoms would soon fall to Assyria.

The second prophesy in the situation, which is much better known, appears in chapter 7 of Isaiah, verses 10–25; this provides reassurance for Ahaz with a sign from the Lord, the sign of Immanuel: "God is with us." In this prophecy, Isaiah calls on Ahaz to take the language of the cult and of God's covenant with David seriously, and trust in the Lord's power instead of political actions. There's a reference to a young woman who was pregnant. This was most likely a member of Ahaz's court, possibly one of his own wives, and the child's name ensured continuation of the Davidic dynasty because "God is with us."

The prophecy has an additional component. Isaiah said that before the child would reach the age of discernment and would know right from wrong, Israel and Aram-Damascus would be gone. Isaiah referred to the child as eating curds and wild honey. In the ancient Near East, curds and wild honey were divine food, the food of the gods, similar to ambrosia and nectar in the Greek context. This was intended to help the child grow quickly, but even on the special quick-grow food, those who would threaten Judah would be gone before the child would know right from wrong.

In spite of this prophecy, Ahaz sought political rather than divine protection. He made an alliance against Israel and Aram-Damascus with Assyria, thereby bringing Judah under Assyrian control for the first time.

Obviously, the legacy of the prophets was not their ability to carry the day in a given situation. Their legacy is the affirmation of the Lord's faithfulness towards his people, based on the promises made in the covenant between the Lord and Israel at Sinai, and the earlier promise made to Abraham, and the later promise made to David.

It was the conviction in the Lord's faithfulness that sustained the faith of the people after the fall of Israel and the fall of Judah; it was this conviction of the Lord's faithfulness that transformed the national religion of two small states of Syria-Palestine into a faith that has endured to the present day.

In our next session, we will look at the religious crisis that surrounded the destruction of Jerusalem, and the exile of many of its people to Babylon. We will see how the prophets made sense of this disaster, and in doing so, reaffirmed the Lord's faithfulness and loving concern for his people.

# Lecture Twenty-Six
## Israel's Great Crisis

**Scope:**
The last years of the monarchy in Judah were shaped by the imperial ambitions of Assyria, Egypt, and Babylon. Despite a few periods of peace and prosperity, Judah finally fell to the Babylonians, and its aristocracy was sent into exile. During this period, the prophets spoke to the people's hopes and fears, blaming the fall of Judah on the nation's own lack of faithfulness to its covenant with the Lord. Jeremiah and Ezekiel both proclaimed this message, but after the fall of Jerusalem, both adopted a new message of hope and reconciliation. After the Babylonian empire fell to the Persians, the Judahite exiles were allowed to return to their homeland. Second Isaiah preached a message of comfort and restoration based on an overt monotheism. The prophet Haggai encouraged those who returned to Jerusalem to rebuild the Temple and obey the covenant to ensure the Lord's blessing on their community.

## Outline

I.   The last years of the Judahite monarchy were overshadowed by the imperial powers of Assyria and Babylon.

    **A.** In Israel, usurpations and shifting alliances led to the nation's conquest by Assyria and the fall of Samaria in 721 B.C.E.

        **1.** Jehu overthrew Omri's dynasty, made himself king, and submitted Israel to Assyria.

        **2.** The Assyrian alliance led to peace and prosperity under Jeroboam II, but a series of usurpations and kings with short reigns weakened Israel.

        **3.** After Tiglath-Pileser III died in 727 B.C.E., Israel rebelled against Assyria.

        **4.** Assyrian armies laid siege to Samaria, until the capital fell to Sargon II in 721 B.C.E.

        **5.** About 27,900 Israelites were deported and replaced by foreign nobility, who served as imperial administrators for the Assyrians.

    **B.** Judah had a similar history of obedience and rebellion with Assyria and Babylon throughout the 7th century B.C.E.

1. Ahaz voluntarily became a vassal to Assyria when he was threatened by Israel and Aram-Damascus.
2. Hezekiah rebelled against Assyria in 705 B.C.E. by withholding tribute but lost his entire kingdom except Jerusalem.
3. Hezekiah's son Manasseh restored the alliance with Assyria and enjoyed a long and prosperous reign.
4. Judah rebelled again under Josiah, who like Hezekiah, reformed religious practice to emphasize national identity.
5. In the last 20 years of its existence, Judah shifted loyalties between Egypt and Babylon six times, with disastrous results.
6. In 587 B.C.E., Jerusalem fell to the Babylonian king Nebuchadnezzar, who deported the nobility to Babylon.

C. Jeremiah's prophetic ministry took place in the midst of Judah's national crisis.
   1. Jeremiah's prophetic call was an interior experience reflecting the tension between his message and his sympathy for his people.
   2. Jeremiah endured hardships and condemnation in proclaiming his message.
   3. After Jerusalem fell, Jeremiah began to proclaim a message of hope and reconciliation.

II. The fall of Jerusalem was an unparalleled calamity without apparent remedy and demanded a theological response.

A. The fall of Jerusalem was a political and military disaster but also a blow to Judah's religious ideas.
   1. The fall of Samaria to the Assyrians left Judah reassured that it was dear to the Lord, while Israel had been punished for its sins.
   2. The fall of Jerusalem, however, removed the benefits the Lord had conferred on Judah: the land, the king, and the Temple.
   3. The means of renewing the covenantal relationship, the sacrificial cult, had been destroyed.
   4. There were two possible theological conclusions: The Lord had been unable to prevent the disaster or had himself brought it about.

5. If the people were to continue to worship the Lord, they had to accept the Babylonians' conquest as a just punishment from the Lord for Judah's sins.

6. It fell to the prophets to make sense of the people's experience of exile as a prologue to reconciliation with their God.

**B.** Ezekiel's prophetic message among the exiles understood the fall of Jerusalem in terms of Judah's sin and offered hope for reconciliation.

1. Ezekiel was part of the first wave of exiles to Babylon in 597 B.C.E. and acted as their spiritual leader.

2. For the first part of Ezekiel's prophetic career, his primary subject was the fall of Jerusalem; for the second part, it was hope and restoration.

3. Ezekiel's inaugural experience was his vision of "the wheel in a wheel," the throne-chariot of the Lord that allowed him to be wherever his people were, even in exile.

4. Ezekiel proclaims that God's people presumed on their elect status, trusting that the Lord would always protect them.

5. Instead of a punishment, exile had been a blessing, because those in exile escaped the siege and fall of Jerusalem.

6. Ezekiel's vision of the Lord's throne-chariot shows that God is accessible to his people in exile; thus, the possibility of their redemption remains.

**III.** After Nebuchadrezzar, the fortunes of the Babylonian empire rapidly declined, setting the stage for the exiles' return.

**A.** After a struggle over the succession, Nebuchadnezzar was eventually succeeded by Nabonidus, who abandoned Babylon to live in an oasis.

1. His son Belshazzar presided in Babylon over a worsening economic and military situation.

2. The Persians under Cyrus invaded Babylon and took power in 539 B.C.E.

**B.** These events provide the historical context for the prophecies of "Second Isaiah," the author of the oracles in Isaiah 40–55.

1. These chapters stand apart from the oracles of Isaiah of Jerusalem by virtue of their historical setting, their message, and their lyrical beauty.
2. Second Isaiah was apparently a disciple of Isaiah who was also a prophet in his own right and proclaimed the word of the Lord to the exiles.
3. In an atmosphere of despair, Second Isaiah prophesied and revived hope that the Lord would restore the nation's fortunes.

C. Second Isaiah's message is comfort at the end of exile, set in the context of the people's sin.
1. Comfort is possible only because the people have been punished, as the Lord offers renewal of the covenantal relationship.
2. The basis of the comfort is the Lord's sole sovereignty of the earth and his faithfulness.
3. The Lord's glory, power, and incomparability are expressed through images based on his works in creation.

D. In Second Isaiah, a manifest monotheism is proclaimed in rejection of polytheism and idol worship.
1. Second Isaiah satirizes idolatry by equating the idol with the god it represents.
2. This satire is probably consistent with some common polytheistic practices.
3. Second Isaiah's monotheism is illustrated by the ways in which the Lord displays his sovereignty over the cosmos, including fulfilling his word.
4. The idea that the Lord proclaims, then fulfills his word apparently inspired the first written records of prophetic oracles by Isaiah of Jerusalem and Jeremiah.
5. Second Isaiah proclaims the Lord as God of the whole world, including foreign nations and their leaders.

E. Persian policies toward subject peoples were generous in regard to native political and religious traditions.
1. The Persians allowed native aristocracies to reside in their own territories under the authority of Persian political authorities.

2. The Persians also allowed their subjects to worship their own gods, provided they entreated their gods for the king's welfare.

3. In Second Isaiah's oracles, the return to Judah from exile would be the Lord's "day of salvation," when the Lord would reestablish his covenant with the people.

4. But when they returned to Judah, the exiles found a ruined land and people who wanted to join them in a renewed community.

5. Tensions developed and the question arose: What had become of the Lord's promises?

F. Haggai's prophetic ministry addresses this question in the light of God's covenantal relationship with his people.

1. Haggai may have been one of the returnees or he may have lived in Judah all his life.

2. His prophecies reflect traditions that see the Temple as the essential link between the Lord and his people.

3. Haggai was confident that reconciliation with God could be precipitated by reconstruction of the Temple.

4. The people had put off rebuilding the Temple, but Haggai argued that rebuilding the Temple would bring prosperity.

5. Only a renewed Temple cult could ensure the Lord's presence and protect the people.

6. But Haggai also calls the people to forsake sin so that cultic worship can again be effective.

7. In this respect, Haggai is consistent with earlier prophets who said that the cult was effective only if it was supported by the people's obedience.

8. The community of returnees rebuilt the Temple in response to Haggai's prophetic message.

## Essential Reading:

Henry Jackson Flanders, Jr., Robert Wilson Crapps, and David Anthony Smith. *People of the Covenant: An Introduction to the Hebrew Bible*, pp. 380–429.

Siegfried Hermann. *A History of Israel in Old Testament Times*, pp. 263–297.

Joseph Blenkinsopp. *A History of Prophecy in Israel: From the Settlement in the Land to the Hellenistic Period*, pp. 153–224.

Isaiah 40–54.

Jeremiah 1:1–4:4, 26, 36.

Ezekiel 1–7.

**Supplementary Reading:**

Klaus Koch. *The Prophets*, Vol. 2: *The Babylonian and Persian Periods*, pp. 80–151.

**Questions to Consider:**

1. What are the connections among sin, punishment, repentance, and renewal in religious ideas about the relationship between the human and the divine worlds? To what extent are those same connections in operation in human relationships?

2. Why did the idea of returning to Judah have such a powerful hold over the exiles in Babylon, even though many of them had never been there and their nation was no longer independent?

# Lecture Twenty-Six—Transcript
## Israel's Great Crisis

In our last session, we considered the historical context of the conflict between official, political, and religious authorities, and the great prophets of Judah and Israel. In this session, we will look at the theological repercussions of the greatest calamity to befall the Lord's people in their history, the destruction of Jerusalem, and the later exile.

The last years of the Hebrew kingdoms were overshadowed by imperial powers based in Mesopotamia, and those powers were seeking to extend their influence through the Fertile Crescent into Egypt, the great center of ancient civilization.

In the northern kingdom of Israel, a series of usurpations and a series of shifting alliances led to the nation's conquest by its erstwhile ally, Assyria, and the fall of Samaria in the year 721 B.C.E. As we've seen, an Israelite general, Jehu, revolted against Omri's dynasty, and he slaughtered all of the princes of Omri's dynasty, made himself king, and immediately allied himself with Assyria against Aram-Damascus, the traditional enemy of Israel.

Then, the Assyrian alliance led to a relative period of peace and prosperity. We saw the example of Jeroboam II, who was a successful king over a prosperous kingdom, but was warned by the prophet Amos about the neglect of the needs of the poor.

After the reign of Jeroboam II, a series of further usurpations and short reigns of the various kings again weakened Israel. After the Assyrian king Tiglath-Pileser III in 727 B.C.E., Israel rebelled against Assyria and gambled that the new king would be too busy to attack Israel, and if it did, Egypt would provide support for Israel. However, the gamble failed.

Assyrian armies conquered Israel and laid siege to the city of Samaria, its capital—laid siege for three years. Finally, the capital fell to the Assyrian king Sargon II in the year 721 B.C.E. After the fall of Samaria, about 27,900 Israelites from the top layers of Israelite society were exiled, and deported into another Assyrian territory. They were replaced in Israel by the nobility of one of

Assyria's other conquests, to serve as imperial administrators for the Assyrians.

Now, the southern kingdom of Judah had a similar history of disobedience and rebellion with Assyria, and then with its imperial successor, Babylon, happening throughout the 7th century B.C.E. King Ahaz of Judah, as we've seen, made a voluntary vassalage for Judah to Assyria and the empire of Assyria. Soon after it was threatened, Judah was threatened by an alliance of Israel and Aram-Damascus.

With Assyria allied with Judah, the Assyrians soon conquered both Israel and Aram-Damascus, Judah's chief political rivals. This was considered to be a good thing in Judah, but after Sargon II died in 705 B.C.E., Hezekiah of Judah rebelled against Assyria by withholding tribute, and also by eliminating Assyrian influence from the worship of the people of Judah, refocusing worship in a henotheistic manner on the worship of the Lord alone.

However, the Assyrians retaliated, attacking Judah, and reduced Hezekiah's kingdom to the rump state of the city of Jerusalem. Now, Hezekiah's son, Manasseh, reversed that situation. He restored the alliance with Assyria and, as a result, enjoyed a long and prosperous reign as an Assyrian ally, although the historian of Samuel and Kings condemns his policies.

Judah rebelled again under the king Josiah, and Josiah, like Hezekiah, reformed religious practices to emphasize the national identity of Judah, but Josiah was killed when Egypt moved into Judah to defend a faltering Assyrian empire against the attack of the Babylonians. In the last 20 years of its existence, Judah shifted loyalties between Egypt and Babylon six times; that's a little more than once every three years, and each time there were disastrous results, as a series of kings were deposed by the Egyptians or by the Babylonians.

The end for Judah finally came in 587 B.C.E., when Jerusalem fell to the Babylonians under Nebuchadrezzar, and Nebuchadrezzar, as the Assyrians before in Israel, deported the nobility of Judah even as many Judahites fled south to Egypt.

Now, the prophetic mystery of the prophet Jeremiah took place in the midst of this national crisis for Judah. Jeremiah's prophetic call is recorded in the first chapter of the book of Jeremiah, and it appears to be an interior religious experience, and the interior experience that Jeremiah undergoes as his prophetic call reflects the tension between his message and his sympathy for his people, the people of Judah.

Jeremiah is told in this experience that he has been set apart from before his conception to be a spokesperson for the Lord's word, and, therefore, Jeremiah could not refuse this ministry, but Jeremiah, like Moses before him, initially shrinks from his commission—but again, like Moses, he is reassured, and like Moses, he is given the gifts necessary to do his job. Although the nation of Judah will be attacked and will fall, Jeremiah himself will be able to withstand all the impacts against him. He will be like a bronze pillar and will be able to withstand whatever his enemies bring against him.

Throughout the book of Jeremiah, the difficulties of Jeremiah's prophetic ministry are emphasized, because he must proclaim the impending fall of Judah as the Lord's punishment for its sins, and although he recognizes the people's sins and realizes they must be punished, he is also sympathetic to them and feels the pain and the anguish of Judah.

Jeremiah did, in fact, endure many hardships as a result of his prophetic ministry. He was condemned for proclaiming the message that the Lord had given him to proclaim, and, notably, this happened in the situation with the official prophet Hananiah, in Jeremiah, chapter 28, a situation I referred to before.

At one point, in fact, Jeremiah refused to speak the Lord's message any longer, and he held the Lord's word within him, instead of proclaiming it and letting it out, but he soon experienced such physical and emotional pain that he again proclaimed the word. He could find relief from his pain only by prophesying.

After speaking words of condemnation and punishment for most of his prophetic career, after the fall of the city of Jerusalem in 587 B.C.E., Jeremiah began to proclaim a different message, a new message, a message of hope and reconciliation for the people of Judah. He even went so far as to buy a piece of land as a prophetic action—to buy a piece of land in Judah, to indicate that the exiles would, in time, indeed return to Judah, and, in time, that deed to the land would have value again. In fact, we can understand Jeremiah's entire prophetic ministry as a kind of prophetic action, an illustration of both Judah's struggle and its hope.

Now, it's important to understand that the fall of Jerusalem to the Babylonians in 587 B.C.E. was an unparalleled calamity for the people. It was an unparalleled calamity in the history of Judah, and it had no apparent remedy, and because it was an unparalleled calamity, it demanded a strong theological response. A theological response was necessary because the fall of Jerusalem was not only a political disaster and a military disaster, but it was a killing blow to many of Judah's most cherished religious ideas.

Now, when Samaria fell to the Assyrians in 721 B.C.E., Judah was left with the reassurance that Judah was dear to the Lord, and that the Israelite capital had fallen because the Israelites had sinned against the Lord by rebelling against David, by rebelling against the Jerusalem Temple, and so, Judah remained reassured and perhaps complacent about its place in the Lord's affections. When Samaria had fallen, it had fallen because of the sinfulness of Israel.

However, the fall of Jerusalem in 587 B.C.E. removed all of the benefits the Lord had conferred on Judah through the Sinai covenant and the covenant made with David. It removed the land of Abraham and the Sinai covenant, it removed the king promised by the Davidic covenant, and it removed the Temple. The Temple was the means of reconciliation between the Lord and Judah, and it was gone.

There seemed to be no means, then, no chance of renewing the covenantal relationship between the Lord and Judah because the means of repairing that covenantal relationship, the sacrificial cult, the animal sacrifices that made up for the sins of the people—that was gone. It had been destroyed along with the Temple, and so not only had the relationship between the Lord and Judah been destroyed, but apparently there was no way of renewing, of re-establishing, that relationship through the sacrifices of the Temple. This was what made the fall of Jerusalem an unparalleled calamity in the history of the people.

In the face of this kind of catastrophe there were really only two possible theological conclusions: either the Lord had been unable to prevent this from happening because the gods of the Babylonians were stronger than the Lord, or the Lord himself had been the one who brought about the disaster on the Lord's people. That meant that if the people were to continue their national religion and continue to worship the Lord, they had to accept the idea that their own unfaithfulness was what had led the Lord to allow the Babylonians to conquer Judah as a punishment for the people's sins.

In other words, events had apparently validated the prophets' call to repentance, and called people to recognize their responsibility for what had happened. The prophets had called the people to follow the covenant, and according to the prophets, they had failed to do so. As a result, the Lord allowed Jerusalem and Judah to fall.

Now, it fell to the prophets to make sense of the experience of exile and at least establish the possibility of some sort of reconciliation with the God of Israel and Judah, some sort of reconciliation with the Lord, some re-establishment of the equilibrium and harmony between the people and the Lord that had been part of the covenantal relationship.

Ezekiel was really the first prophet to come to terms with the fall of Jerusalem, and to deal with the problems of restoration in a more graphic manner, if you will, and a more thorough way than did Jeremiah. Ezekiel's ministry was among the exiles, and he attempted to make sense of the fall of Jerusalem in terms of Judah's sin, but also, later, to offer the hope of reconciliation with the Lord, as Jeremiah also had.

Now, Ezekiel was a priest of the temple, and as such, he was part of the first wave of exiles from Judah to Babylon. This happened in 597 B.C.E., about 10 years before the fall of Jerusalem. Ezekiel apparently acted as a spiritual adviser to this first wave of exiles, made up exclusively of the royal family and various political aristocrats and religious authorities of the nation of Judah.

For the first part of Ezekiel's career, from about 593 to about 587 B.C.E., his primary subject was the impending fall of Jerusalem; then, the second part of his prophetic ministry, after the fall of Jerusalem, concentrated on hope and restoration for the people and the city of Jerusalem itself.

Ezekiel's inaugural prophetic experience was a vision that has become famous, primarily through a folk song. He had a vision of a "wheel in a wheel," way in the middle of the air. What Ezekiel described was a series of wheels inside each other, and four living beasts that were surrounding these wheels. There was something like a throne in the midst of these wheels.

There was light. There were beings of light. There was the appearance of someone sitting on a throne; that was described primarily in terms of minerals and metals, and there was the idea of light and of speed, the idea that these four living beasts could take this apparition wherever it wished to go in less time than it takes to think about it, with the speed of thought.

This wheel within a wheel, with the rather vague, difficult to describe figure in the middle of it, surrounded by lights like flaming torches—this image seems to summon up the idea of the Lord's throne, but it is a throne where the Lord's presence is localized, where the Lord's presence resides, which is also a chariot—both a seat but also a mode of conveyance. This throne-chariot allows the Lord to be present with his people wherever they may be, and to be present with them immediately.

In other words, this throne-chariot represents the presence or the glory of the Lord. Usually, this was believed to reside in the innermost sanctuary of the Jerusalem Temple, and you'll remember that the power of the various gods of the ancient Near East was believed to be localized, to be localized in their temples, and their power radiated out from that location.

Here, however, the Lord's presence is not confined. Ezekiel saw the Lord's throne-chariot, in fact, leaving the Temple in Jerusalem at one point, and instead, coming to Babylon, where the exiles of Judah were located. In other words, the Lord was present wherever his people would call upon him. He was not restricted to the Temple in Jerusalem, and the Lord's presence among the exiles, in Babylon in particular, indicated that the religious future of the nation resided with those exiles and not with the leaders who remained behind in Jerusalem.

Ezekiel proclaimed that God's people had presumed upon their status as the Lord's elect. They had trusted that the covenant, the Temple, and the Davidic dynasty would protect them from all harm, no matter how they behaved. These were proofs of the Lord's care for them, but they did not, in fact, fit in with their own disobedience of the Lord's covenant; so, they trusted in various proofs of the Lord's care, rather than their own obedience to what the Lord commanded as the basis of the relationship.

Some in Judah apparently blamed the exiled aristocracy for the nation's problems, but according to Ezekiel, those in exile in Babylon were, in fact, the fortunate ones because they escaped the prolonged siege and the eventual fall of the city of Jerusalem. Ezekiel's vision of the Lord's presence in Babylon showed that God was accessible to his people even in exile, so the possibility of redemption and reconciliation with the Lord always remained open.

Now, after Nebuchadrezzar, the fortunes of the Babylonian empire rapidly declined, and the stage was set for the return of Judah's exiles to their own country. After a struggle over the succession, Nebuchadrezzar was eventually succeeded by Nabonidus, who abandoned Babylon itself to live instead in an Arabian oasis.

His regent in Babylon was his son, Belshazzar, and Belshazzar presided over a worsening economic and military situation as the nation of Medea gained control of major trade routes and began, along with the nation of Persia, to dismantle Babylon's imperial holdings.

The Persians and their king, Cyrus—known to history as "Cyrus the Great"—invaded Babylon, and a revolt by the priests of Marduk toppled Nabonidus and handed power to the Persians in 539 B.C.E., making Cyrus, essentially, master of the world and the "king of kings," as was his official title.

Now, these events provide the historical context for the prophecies that scholars call "Second Isaiah"; in other words, the prophet who spoke the oracles that appear in the book of Isaiah in chapters 40–55. These chapters, attributed to the prophet Second Isaiah, may be distinguished from the oracles of Isaiah of Jerusalem by three factors: they are set in exile, rather than in the kingdom of Ahaz; they are concerned with a message of reconciliation, rather than a message of punishment and condemnation; and they have a lyrical, poetic beauty that sets them apart from the other prophecies.

Second Isaiah was apparently a follower or disciple of Isaiah of Jerusalem, who is also a prophet in his own right, and he proclaimed the word of the Lord to the exiles of Judah in Babylon. Second Isaiah prophesied in an atmosphere of despair because the exile of the people had continued for almost 50 years, and Second Isaiah's prophecies revived hope that the Lord would soon restore the nation's fortunes.

Second Isaiah's core message of comfort at the approaching end of the exile is set within the context of the people's sin, which led to the exile and destruction in the first place. At the very beginning of his prophecies, in Isaiah, chapter 40, verse 1, the prophet says, "Comfort: 'Oh, comfort my people,' says your God. 'Speak tenderly to Jerusalem, and cry to her that she has served her term, that her penalties paid, that she has received from the Lord's hand double for all her sins.'" This is Isaiah, chapter 40, verses 1 and 2.

Comfort is now possible, according to the prophet, only because the people have been punished, and now the Lord offers reconciliation and renewal of the covenantal relationship. The basic form of the covenant is apparent in that first verse: "'Comfort my people,' says your God," echoing the basic covenantal affirmation: "You shall be my people; I shall be your God."

The basis of the message is the conviction that the Lord alone is God, sovereign over the entire earth and all its people. The Lord is faithful, in contrast to the frailty of human beings. The Lord's glory, power, and incomparability are expressed through a series of images based on his mighty works of creation and his creative power; his creative work implies his sovereignty over the entire cosmos.

In fact, in Second Isaiah, we finally find a manifest monotheism that is proclaimed in direct rejection of polytheism, and more specifically, a rejection of the worship of idols. In fact, the prophecies of Second Isaiah include a satire on idolatry, and the practice of worshiping idols—and, in fact, Second Isaiah mocks the idea of worshiping something that cannot defend itself—something that can rot or topple over—and thereby equates the idol with the god it represents. If the idol can rot, then the god can rot.

Now, of course, this is a misrepresentation of the use of idols, but it is consistent with certain common polytheistic practices, including—

as we have seen in Egypt—the washing, the dressing, and the symbolic feeding of idols. So, although the idol is not the same as the god, the idol is always treated as if it were, in some way, the god, and to that extent, Second Isaiah, here, hits home.

Second Isaiah's overt monotheism is also illustrated by the way the Lord displays his sovereignty over the cosmos. He is the one who creates and gives counsel to humanity. It is he who reveals himself in his acts in history. It is he who helps those in need, and it is he who declares his intentions—and later, brings them to fulfillment. This idea of the Lord first proclaiming, and then fulfilling, his word seems to lie behind the first written versions of prophetic oracles in the cases of Isaiah and Jeremiah, where the writing is proof, or a record, of what the Lord has said before it is fulfilled.

Second Isaiah, then, proclaims the Lord as God of the whole world, including the foreign nations and their leaders, the one and only God that exists. As a result, Second Isaiah is able to call Cyrus "the Lord's anointed," the first use of the word "messiah," meaning, "anointed one," in the Hebrew Bible. In other words, Cyrus is chosen, like David, to fulfill a particular role in accomplishing the Lord's will among his people. That's in Isaiah, chapter 45, verse 1; Cyrus as the Lord's anointed, a clear declaration that the Lord controls all the nations and all of its peoples because it is the one and only God of the cosmos.

Now, in fact, Persian policies towards its subject people were considerably more enlightened than those of the Mesopotamians had been in regard to native political and religious traditions. The Persians allowed native aristocracies to reside in their own territories under the authority of Persian political figures, and the understanding was that any attempts at rebellion against their Persian overlords would be ruthlessly suppressed.

The Persians also allowed their subjects to worship their own gods according to their ancestral traditions, provided that they also entreated their gods for the welfare of the king of Prussia. In Second Isaiah's oracle, the return to Judah from exile would be the Lord's "day of salvation." That term appears in Isaiah, chapter 49, verse 8. This would be the day when the Lord would set right the destruction that took place on his day of wrath, and he would re-establish his covenant with the people in peace.

In fact, though, despite the fact that the people did return to Judah, the return was considerably less glorious for the exiles than Second Isaiah had predicted. The exiles found themselves in a ruined land the majority of them had never seen before. Moreover, it was not devoid of inhabitants. The people of the land who had been left behind by the Babylonians had continued to live in Judah, and they now wanted to join with the exiles to form a renewed community, and there was tension between these two groups over who was the proper group to take over authority of the land—those who had been exiled, or those who had stayed in Judah.

When tensions developed, then, the question and the situation of the returnees to Jerusalem led to confusion over what had happened to the prophecies pronounced through Second Isaiah. What had become of God's promises pronounced through Second Isaiah?

Another prophet, Haggai, in his prophetic ministry, addresses this question, as well as the situation of the returnees to Jerusalem, and he does so in the light of God's continuing covenantal relationship with his people. Now, we have no way of knowing whether the prophet Haggai was one of the exiles who had returned to Jerusalem about 520 B.C.E., or if he was somebody who had lived in Judah all of his life, but his prophecies do reflect Temple traditions, especially the ones that idealize and celebrate Temple worship, as well as the idea of the sacrificial cult in the Temple as Judah's primary link with the Lord their God.

Haggai was confident that reconciliation with God and the restoration of the welfare of the nation could be precipitated by a single act: the reconstruction of the Jerusalem Temple. Now, the people had put off rebuilding the Temple because their own economic situation was very unstable, and they wanted to wait until conditions improved, but Haggai, on the other hand, maintained that only a rebuilt Temple could ensure prosperity and the Lord's blessing for the people. Only a renewed Temple cult could ensure that people would prosper because his presence, according to Haggai, all abided in the Temple, and that it was the Lord's presence that brought protection and blessing.

However, Haggai also asserted that the Temple alone, the Lord's presence alone, would not ensure well being. He, like the other prophets, called the people to cleanse themselves from sin, to adhere to the obligations of the covenant, so the cultic worship could again be effective in maintaining the relationship between the Lord and his people.

In this respect, then, Haggai was consistent with the pre-exilic prophets who said that the cult would be ineffective if it was not supported by the people's covenantal obedience. In fact, the community of the returnees joined together, listened to Haggai, and did rebuild the Temple—although it did not approach its former grandeur. That would have to wait until the Temple was almost entirely rebuilt by Herod the Great at the turn of the age.

Now, the problem of evil, and the Lord's complicity in the ills that befell his people, continued to present a major theological problem. In our next session, we will look at two responses to the problem of evil: in the book of Job, and in the apocalyptic literature that looks for vindication for God's people at the end of the age.

# Lecture Twenty-Seven
## Syria-Palestine—The Problem of Evil

**Scope:**
Although polytheistic and henotheistic religions can blame evil on conflicts between gods, monotheistic religions must reconcile belief in an all-powerful and morally perfect God with the existence of evil. In the religious culture of post-exilic Judah, evils that befell the nation were usually understood as punishment for sin. But in other cases, the cause of suffering was more obscure. Apocalypticism maintained that the present world order is under the control of forces hostile to God and looked forward to the Lord's vindication of his people at the end of the age. A belief in an afterlife later arose out of belief in retributive justice for martyrs and their persecutors. Ecclesiastes puts aside retributive justice and presents all human endeavors as "vanity" in the face of death. The book of Job deals extensively with the problem of innocent suffering but ultimately advises acceptance of the Lord's inscrutable will.

## Outline

I. The existence of evil is the primary theological problem for a monotheistic religion that posits a single all-powerful and morally perfect deity.

   A. Basic to all religious belief is the conviction that one will receive benefits from the sacred realm in keeping with one's behavior.

      1. Religious activity is a means of maintaining harmony between the human and the divine worlds, including exchange of benefits.

      2. Religious activity reflects the belief that worship and sacrifice will lead the gods to return blessings in equal measure.

      3. If certain forms of behavior are pleasing to the gods, they will accept those who please them and reject others.

      4. In wisdom literature, retributive justice decrees that those who do good will receive good from the gods, and those who do evil, evil.

   B. The existence of evil may be easily explained in polytheistic or henotheistic systems.

1. In polytheistic systems, the gods have competing interests just as humans do, and they often work at cross-purposes with each other.
2. In a henotheistic system, the god worshiped may be hampered by other gods who temporarily afflict his people.

C. A monotheistic religious culture must explain the problem of evil in terms of a single god who is both all-powerful and righteous.
   1. The problem is: "If God is God, he is not good; if God is good, he is not God."
   2. Either God's power or his righteousness is called into question by the existence of evil.
   3. Explanation for the problem of evil is *theodicy*, from the Greek for "God is in the right."

D. As the religious culture of Judah developed an overt monotheism during and after the exile, the need for theodicy arose.
   1. Second Isaiah explained the fall of Jerusalem and the exile as punishment for Judah's sins.
   2. The same idea was expressed by the historian who wrote Samuel and Kings, who attributes the downfall of Israel and Judah to sin.
   3. But after the exile and return to Judah, the fortunes of the community did not improve, despite several religious reforms.
   4. Hopes for divine deliverance and independence from foreign dominion were continually frustrated.
   5. This, along with the fact that the good were not always rewarded nor the evil punished, raised the problem of evil.
   6. This problem led to two related phenomena in response: the hope for an end to history expressed in apocalypticism and the questioning attitude of skeptical wisdom.

**II.** Apocalypticism is the expectation that, at some point, God will intervene in human history and bring it to a halt to save his people.

   **A.** Apocalypticism considers the current age to be dominated by forces that oppose the Lord and oppress his people.

      **1.** The forces that oppress Israel are identified with cosmic evil that opposes God.

      **2.** Those who obey the Lord suffer at the hands of the wicked but will receive their reward in the new age.

      **3.** The principle of retributive justice remains, but its implementation is postponed until the end of the age.

   **B.** Apocalypticism is, in many ways, a natural outcome of Israelite religious ideas.

      **1.** The people of Israel understood their history as a history lived out in relationship to the Lord.

      **2.** The prophets tended to depict historical events as visible manifestations of the Lord's work.

      **3.** As expectations for the restoration of Israel were continually frustrated, the hope for vindication was recast in supernatural terms.

      **4.** Israel's tradition about the day of the Lord's vengeance was now understood as the Lord's direct intervention into history to make Israel the center of the world.

      **5.** Zechariah 14 depicts a final battle when the Lord intervenes and establishes Jerusalem as the place where all the nations will worship the Lord.

   **C.** Apocalypticism is expressed in the presentation of historical events in mythic terms as steps in a progress toward the end.

      **1.** Apocalyptic literature typically presents a vision experienced by a revered figure of the past.

      **2.** The vision reviews recent history in symbolic terms as a vision experienced by the person of the past as his or her "future."

      **3.** Apocalyptic literature is typically concerned primarily with the events leading up to the Lord's victory over the forces of evil.

   **D.** A later form of theodicy related to apocalypticism is belief in a life after death.

1. This belief arose in response to a king of Syria who outlawed Judaism and killed those who refused to submit.
2. Martyrdom raised the problem of how God would reward those who suffered and died for their faithfulness.
3. Belief in retributive justice led some to postulate that divine recompense could come after death for the very good and the very evil.
4. Life after death necessitated resurrection, because the Jews believed that the self did not exist apart from the body.
5. The idea of resurrection and life after death received only limited acceptance in later Judaism.

III. The problem of evil was also addressed by the literature typical of *skeptical wisdom*.

A. In the Hebrew Bible, traditional wisdom is represented primarily by the Book of Proverbs.
   1. Traditional wisdom is comparable to most of the wisdom works from Egypt.
   2. Traditional wisdom reflects practical common sense and belief in the principle of retributive justice.

B. Skeptical wisdom, by contrast, questions the entire human enterprise of attempting to discern the Lord's intentions.
   1. Skeptical wisdom shares the prophetic perspective that the Lord is beyond human knowledge and known only by what he chooses to reveal.
   2. In Ecclesiastes, the questioning of retributive justice is part of a pessimistic view of human existence in the face of inevitable death.
   3. The refrain "All is vanity!" reflects the conviction that death makes human striving meaningless.
   4. Ecclesiastes argues that the best thing one can do is enjoy what life offers while it lasts.

C. The problem of evil receives its most thorough examination in the Book of Job, where it appears in the form of innocent suffering.
   1. The problem of evil was usually posed in terms of the prosperity of the wicked.

2. In Job, a rich and thoroughly righteous man is subjected to a series of misfortunes.
3. Three friends argue with Job that his sufferings prove he must be guilty of some sin.
4. Job asserts his innocence in reply and demands to know why he suffers.

**D.** The audience knows from the outset why Job suffers: The Lord has made a wager with Satan.
1. The wager is an attempt to test Job's fidelity to the Lord when he is not rewarded for it.
2. The prologue to Job provides the audience with a heavenly view of Job's situation.
3. The audience possesses knowledge unavailable to Job and his friends, emphasizing human ignorance of divine actions.

**E.** Job's protestations of innocence alternate with his wish to confront God and his friends' arguments that he must be guilty of sin.
1. Job argues that he is innocent and, thus, should not suffer, while his friends argue that he is suffering and, thus, must be guilty of sin.
2. Both parties subscribe to the simple equation that good behavior produces blessing while wickedness produces punishment.
3. Both parties also believe that the reasons for God's actions are transparent to human observers.

**F.** God's reply makes Job aware that he is in no position to understand or judge God's actions.
1. Instead of answering Job, God points to all the marvels of creation whose full purpose only God understands.
2. God asks Job a series of rhetorical questions that demonstrate that God—not Job—is the source of all knowledge and power.
3. In response, Job keeps silence and "repents" for presuming to judge his creator.
4. God commends Job and rebukes his friends, who did not speak justly of God as Job did.

**G.** The epilogue of the book returns to the storytelling atmosphere of the prologue.

1. God fully restores Job's health and fortunes, thereby "making good" his suffering.
2. This conclusion satisfies the ancient idea that one's last state in life determined one's happiness.
3. The restoration of Job's fortunes does not violate the point of the book, because God's motivations remain mysterious.
4. The answer to the problem of evil is left to God and remains utterly unfathomable to human reasoning.

**Essential Reading:**

Henry Jackson Flanders, Jr., Robert Wilson Crapps, and David Anthony Smith. *People of the Covenant: An Introduction to the Hebrew Bible*, pp. 479–492, 499–505.

Ecclesiastes.

Job 1–7, 32–42.

**Supplementary Reading:**

Glenn Holland. *Divine Irony*, pp. 59–81.

Sarah Iles Johnston, ed. *Religions of the Ancient World: A Guide*, pp. 59–70.

James C. Livingston. *Anatomy of the Sacred*, pp. 247–272.

**Questions to Consider:**

1. Is religion inevitably based on the belief that worshipers will receive a divine reward in some form for their beliefs and actions?

2. Apocalypticism presents the state of the world as hostile to God and his people; how may this view be reconciled with the fundamental conviction that God created the world, declared it good, and continues to rule over it?

# Lecture Twenty-Seven—Transcript

## Syria-Palestine—The Problem of Evil

In our last session, we discussed the reaction of the prophets to the fall of Judah and the exile of the nobility to Babylon—and then, later, to the return to Judah under the Persians. In this session, we will consider the more general problem of evil in monotheistic religion by considering different theological solutions that arose in the years after Judah's exile.

Now, the existence of natural and human evil in the world is the primary theological problem for any monotheistic religious culture since it posits a single, all-powerful, and morally perfect deity. Basic to all religious belief and activity is the conviction that one will receive benefits from the sacred realm that are in keeping with one's ritual and moral behavior.

As we've seen, all religious activity is a means of maintaining balance, harmony, and equilibrium between the human world and the divine world, and part of that harmony, part of that balance, is the exchange of benefits. Religious activity reflects the belief that benefiting the gods through worship and sacrifice will lead the gods, in turn, to give benefits back to their devotees in equal measure.

Within the moral communities created by religious belief and activity, there is the further belief that certain forms of behavior are pleasing to the gods, and other forms of behavior are not pleasing to the gods—and so, the gods accept and reward those who please them, and reject others who do not.

In wisdom literature, as we've seen, this idea is codified as the principle of retributive justice. Those who do good will receive good from the gods, and those who do evil will receive evil from the gods.

Now, the existence of evil in the world may be fairly easily explained in polytheistic or henotheistic systems. There, the benevolent intentions of one god might be thwarted by the ill will of another. In polytheistic systems, the gods have competing interests just as human beings do, and the gods often work at cross-purposes with each other; sometimes that has unfortunate results for human beings. In any event, ultimate power does not lie with the gods themselves, but with fate or "the way things are."

In a henotheistic system, there is one god who is worshiped by the community out of the many gods who exist, and that one god has responsibility towards those who worship him, but still, other gods exist; they may interfere with the intentions of the primary god worshiped, and, at least temporarily, they might afflict the people who worship that one god—although eventually, presumably, their god will step in and bring them the benefits they deserve.

In a monotheistic religious culture, though, there is the need to confront and explain the problem of evil in terms of the central conviction that there is a single god, and that single god is all-powerful and also entirely righteous. Put simply, the problem is presented as, "If God is God, he is not good; if God is good, he is not God." Either God's power or his righteousness is called into question by the existence of evil.

As we've seen, any explanation or attempt to explain the problem of evil is called "theodicy," from the Greek term meaning, "God is in the right." Theodicy attempts to explain that God is in the right under any and all circumstances, despite appearances to the contrary.

Now, as the religious culture of Judah developed an overt monotheism as a result of prophetic preaching during the exile, and then after the exile there was also the need for theodicy and the more complete and firm belief in the God, the Lord of Israel, as the one and only God for all creation, the more there was the need for theodicy.

Now, Second Isaiah, who exhibits that overt and manifest monotheism in his own prophecies, explains the fall of Jerusalem and its exile as the Lord's own work, as consistent with both the power and the righteousness of God because it is a form of punishment for Judah's rejection of their covenantal obligations.

We find the same idea expressed by the historian who wrote Samuel and Kings. He pronounces moral judgment on all the kings of Israel and all the kings of Judah, and he attributes the downfall of both of those kingdoms to the disobedience to the Lord and his covenant, but after the exile, after the return to Judah, the fortunes of the exiles in the renewed covenantal community did not significantly improve over time. There were several religious reforms under various leaders, but the hopes for divine deliverance and independence from foreign dominions were repeatedly frustrated. This frustration and the simple observation that the good were not always rewarded and the evil were not always punished provoked theological wrestling with the problem of evil among the people of Judah.

This wrestling gave rise to at least two related, but still distinct, phenomena in the post-exilic period. First, there is a hope for an end to history in apocalypticism, and then there is the questioning of the basic principle of retributive justice and skeptical wisdom that is exemplified by the book of Job.

Now, apocalypticism is the expectation that God will, at some point, directly intervene into human history. God will bring the progress of human history to a halt in a manifestly supernatural way, and at that point, he will step in to save and vindicate his people. In other words, apocalypticism addresses the problem of evil by presenting the present age as an age dominated by forces opposed to the Lord—in other words, forces that oppress the Lord's faithful people precisely because they are faithful.

These earthly forces that oppress Israel or Judah, the Lord's people—these earthly forces are identified with spiritual forces that are opposed to the Lord's sovereignty over the earth. In other words, these earthly forces that oppose God's people are merely earthly manifestations of a greater cosmic evil that sets itself in opposition to God.

This turns the usual understanding of retributive justice more or less on its head. Under the point of view of apocalypticism, those who obey the Lord and are pleasing to the Lord will suffer in the present age at the hands of those who oppose the Lord and who prosper and get their way. Not that the good will receive blessings in the present life, but the fact that the good will suffer in the present life. Not that the evil will be punished in the present life, but that the evil will triumph and dominate the good in the present life.

At the same time, though, apocalypticism has the condition that at the end, the good will finally receive their reward in the new age at the Lord's hands, and, of course, the evil will then be punished.

The principle of retributive justice remains, then, but it is reversed. It is not this world where the good prosper and the evil suffer. Rather, it is in the new age when the good prosper and the evil will suffer. The reward for the good, in this vision, and the punishment for the evil is postponed until the Lord's direct intervention into history, sometime in the indefinite future.

Now, apocalypticism may have some roots in other ancient Near Eastern religious cultures—there's a lot of debate about this—but in many ways, it's a natural outcome of Israelite religious ideas—in other words, the idea of covenantal obedience in Israel and Judah.

The people of Israel, the people of Judah, always understood their history (as a people) as a history that was lived out in covenantal relationship to the Lord. It is the covenantal relationship that establishes the identity of the people, and everything they do as a people is a result of that covenantal relationship. The covenantal relationship is lived out with specific deeds and actions in history. It is, therefore, a history lived out in covenantal relationship to the Lord who is understood as their God and their sovereign protector—both in the earthly realm and in the cosmic realm.

The prophets, especially, tended to depict historical events in mythological terms. They understood history as only the visible manifestation of the invisible work of the Lord. What happened on earth was the unfolding of the Lord's long-term intentions. Specific acts in history are not meaningless acts of violence but are, rather, part of a cohesive story with a development and a progress towards an appointed end.

In the post-exilic period, the expectation that the Lord would restore the fortunes of Israel through historical means was continually frustrated. So, those expectations were thought of more and more, apparently, in explicitly, supernatural terms, by the Lord acting outside of the processes of history, to bring about restoration and reward for his people.

Israel's tradition about the day of the Lord, the day when the Lord would act decisively to deliver and vindicate his people, is now understood as the Lord's direct supernatural intervention to make Israel the center of the world, which is its proper appointed place. We can see this in Zachariah, chapter 14, for example.

Zachariah, chapter 14, depicts a final battle when all the nations of the world attack Jerusalem, and the Lord intervenes in a supernaturally manifest way to win the battle for Israel. Afterwards, Jerusalem becomes the place where all the nations worship the Lord together. The people of Israel become the priests for the whole world, as the Lord originally promised to the people in the Sinai covenant. Those nations that do not worship by coming to Jerusalem suffer or are destroyed.

Now, apocalypticism is most typically expressed through—naturally enough—apocalyptic literature. This is a mythological presentation of historical events as a progress towards the end of the age—again, not meaningless acts of random violence, but a story that has a plot progressing towards an appointed end.

Apocalyptic literature typically presents a vision experienced by a revered figure of the past; so apocalyptic visions are typically placed on the past of the author and the audience, and this revered figure of the past sees history "properly," which is to say that he sees it from the heavenly perspective, and so it is presented in mythic terms, rather than in terms of natural and historical figures.

This vision reviews recent history in symbolic terms, but it is presented as a vision of the "future"—that is, the future vision of this person in the past, but actually the past from the point of view of the audience, and from the point of view of the actual author.

Most apocalyptic literature, then, features a vision of the future that is already accomplished, and it is presented in symbolic, or if you will, metaphorical terms. So, the audience says, "Wow. Look how accurate that prophecy is. Everything that happened has, in fact, been fulfilled except for the last few events," and the last few events, of course, occur when the author is looking into his own genuine future and attempting to decide how the Lord will bring this progress to its appointed end. In fact, those scholars who examine apocalyptic literature are usually able to date it fairly accurately by the point at which this vision of the future becomes wildly inaccurate.

Usually, apocalyptic literature is concerned less with the new situation of God's people—that is, the specific form of their vindication, the specific form of their reward for their good deeds—than it is concerned with the events that lead up to the destruction of their enemies and the victory of the Lord's people because, of course, it is that progress of events leading up to the end, leading up to the reward of the faithful and the destruction of the evil—that is the time of the present from the point of view of the author and the audience.

It is the anticipation of the end that receives the most attention because in those actions leading towards the end, the author and the audience anticipate what is called the "apocalyptic reversal of their fortunes." They look forward to the time when their suffering will end and the vindication and the reward will begin.

Now, a form of theodicy—that is, justifying the Lord's actions—that is related to apocalypticism but actually appears rather later in the history of Israel is belief in a life after death, which seems to first appear among the people of God in the $3^{rd}$ century C.E.

Now, this belief arose in response to severe persecution of the Jews by a Macedonian king of Syria who outlawed Judaism and killed those who refused to submit, and I will deal with this situation in greater depth in a later lecture. The persecution, though, raised the problem of how those who had remained faithful to the covenant to the point of death, and who had died for their faithfulness, could be rewarded because they certainly could not receive any earthly compensation. They were dead. They remained faithful, and they paid the ultimate price for their fidelity to the Lord and to the covenant, and so, the question arose: How will they receive their reward?

This problem seems to have led to a reluctant acknowledgment among at least some Jews that some divine recompense could come after death—that is, in an afterlife—but still, it was believed that that afterlife, for reward or punishment, was restricted to the very good and the very evil.

Divine recompense also necessitated a belief in resurrection—that is, the return to life of the dead body because the Jews believed that the self did not exist apart from the body—so life after death, that life with the body.

Now, it's worth noting again that this idea of the resurrection and an afterlife developed very late in Judaism, about the $3^{rd}$ century B.C.E., and not all theological schools among the leaders of Judaism accepted the possibility.

Now, apart from apocalypticism and a belief in resurrection and a life after death, another result of wrestling with the problem of evil among the people of Israel and Judah was the literature of skeptical wisdom in the TaNaK—that is, the Hebrew Bible—including especially the books of Ecclesiastes and Job.

In the TaNaK, traditional wisdom is represented primarily by the book of Proverbs. Traditional wisdom, as we know, is comparable to most of the wisdom works we have considered from Egypt, most notably the teachings of Amenemopet, from the first millennium B.C.E. You'll remember that it has striking parallels to the book of Proverbs, especially chapter 22, verse 17, through chapter 24, verse 34.

This sort of wisdom reflects common sense. It is based on the give-and-take of everyday life, and it is firmly based on the principle of retributive justice, the idea that if you are pious and hardworking, then your life will go well. A good middle-class ethic.

Skeptical wisdom, by contrast, questions this principle of retributive justice and the entire human enterprise of attempting to discern the Lord's will and intention. Skeptical wisdom, to some extent, shares the perspective of the classical prophets. In other words, skeptical wisdom agrees with the classical prophets that the Lord is beyond human knowledge. The Lord can be known only by what he chooses to reveal to his people.

In Ecclesiastes, the questioning of retributive justice is merely a part of a more generally pessimistic view of human existence, which seems to arise primarily from the inevitable end of death. The refrain in Ecclesiastes is: "Vanity of vanities; all its vanity, and all is vanity in chasing after wind." This refrain reflects the conviction that death makes human striving meaningless. Like the Egyptian Songs of the Harper and the advice given to Gilgamesh during his quest, Ecclesiastes seems to argue that the best thing that one can do is to enjoy life as long as it lasts.

However, the problem of evil receives its most thorough biblical examination in the book of Job. Job is a sustained meditation on the theological problems posed by innocent suffering. Now, usually, in the ancient world, the problem of evil was posed in terms of the prosperity of the wicked, rather than of the suffering of the innocent, which is the way that we tend to pose the problem of evil.

Now, it may be that there was a reluctance to postulate that there was somebody who was so innocent that they did not deserve any suffering at all. I think it's more likely that the ancient world, like our own, shared a widespread resentment of the prosperous and assumed that the prosperous were, more or less, by their very nature, evil. "How else would you become prosperous because we're good and we're not prosperous?"

In any event, in Job, we find a rich and thoroughly righteous man who is subject to a series of misfortunes. He suffers through the deaths of his children; he suffers through the loss of his property, and then he contracts a chronic illness that causes him a great deal of discomfort and suffering.

In his sufferings, as he is apparently scraping his skin disease wounds on the top of a dung pile, Job is joined by three friends, and his three friends argue that his suffering proves he must be guilty of some sin or other. Well, Job asserts his innocence and demands that God explain to him why he, Job, is suffering as he is.

Now, the usual emphasis on the suffering of Job, and the problem of Job, overlooks the fact that the audience for the book knows from the outside exactly why Job is suffering. Job is suffering because the Lord made a wager with Satan. This is the first thing we find out in the book. There is a prologue that takes place in heaven, where the Lord is there and Satan is there as well. The Satan, here, is not yet the eternal cosmic enemy to God. Instead, the Satan, here, appears in his original capacity as the adversary in the Lord's court. When judgment is being made by the Lord, there is a defense attorney—presumably, one kind of angel—and there is a prosecutor, and that is the adversary, the "Satan," which is what the name originally means.

Here, then, the Lord is having a conversation with his district attorney, if you will, the one who brings accusations against God's people—and usually justified accusations—and here, the Satan argues that yes, Job is a faithful man, but the only reason he is faithful is because the Lord consistently rewards him for his faithfulness. The wager between the Lord and the Satan, then, is an attempt to test Job's sincerity—whether he is faithful to the Lord because he is rewarded, or whether, in fact, he is truly faithful.

A prologue of the book of Job, then, provides a heavenly point of view in Job's situation and grants the audience access to the Lord's council chamber—that is, where the Lord makes all of his decisions—and as a result, the audience possesses knowledge from the outset that is not available to Job and his friends. Moreover, the audience knows that Job and his friends can never guess the reality of the situation that lies behind Job's suffering. The audience knows that neither Job nor his friends are going to say, "Hey, do you know what it is? I'll bet you're suffering because God has a wager with the Satan."

In this way, the story itself emphasizes that human ignorance of God's intentions is inevitable. The full range of factors that lie behind the divine will can never be known to human beings, and what motivates the Lord's actions remains a mystery to his people.

Now, the bulk of the book of Job is devoted to Job's protestations of innocence that alternate with his wish to confront God with his apparent injustice and his friends' arguments that Job must, in fact, be guilty of some sort of sin. Both parties, in their own way, uphold the idea of retributive justice. Job argues that he is innocent, and as an innocent man he should not have to suffer. His friends argue that Job is, in fact, suffering, and since Job is suffering, he must be guilty of some hidden sin that justifies his suffering.

Both parties, in other words, subscribe to the simple equation that good behavior produces blessing, while wickedness produces punishment in the form of suffering, and both parties believe that the motivation for all of the Lord's actions are transparent to human beings—in other words, that a human being can look at what the Lord is doing in any given situation, and immediately understand why the Lord is doing this.

God finally makes his reply to Job and to his friends at the end of the book of Job, out of a whirlwind, and God's reply out of a whirlwind puts Job in his place—making Job aware that he is in no position to understand or to judge God's actions, even in regard to Job's own deserving. God, as it has often been observed, does not answer Job directly. Instead, God points to all the marvels of the divine creation. All of these marvels are under his dominion, and all of them have a purpose that only God himself can fully understand.

Therefore, out of the whirlwind, God asks Job a series of rhetorical questions. Many of them begin with, "Who did this?" "Who did this?" "Who did this?" "Who did this?" They are rhetorical questions because in every case, the answer is, "The Lord."

He has another series of rhetorical questions intermingled with these that begin with, "Do you know?" "Do you know?" "Do you know?" "Do you know?" They are rhetorical because in each case, the answer is, "No, I don't know."

For the questions that are asked, then—"Who did this?" "Who did this?" "Who did this?" "Who did this?"—the answer is, "The Lord, not Job." and, "Do you know?" "Do you know?" "No, I don't; only God knows."

In response, then, to God's recitation of the marvels of creation, Job can only keep silent, and he "repents." He doesn't repent for sin because he is innocent, but he repents for the attempt, for the presumption, of judging his creator.

Now, God commends Job, and he rebukes his friends because he says his friends did not speak justly of God, as Job did. Apparently, Job's searching questions are preferable to God over his friends' smug assurance.

The epilogue of the book returns to the storytelling atmosphere introduced in the prologue. God fully restores Job's health and fully restores Job's fortunes, thereby "making good" his suffering. Now, of course, this conclusion leaves aside certain questions, like whether all the losses Job suffers can, in fact, be made good in any real sense. Some of us might question whether new children make up for the loss of earlier children, for example, but the conclusion does satisfy the ancient world's idea that one's last state in life, the way things are at the point your life ends, determines whether your life was a happy one or a cursed one, and since Job ends with his fortune restored, with a large loving family, his life is ultimately a good life of good things and rewards from the Lord's hand for his righteousness.

This happy ending that restores Job's fortunes as a reward for his righteousness might seem to violate the point of the book—in other words, that there's no clear balance between behavior and reward—but, in fact, it's not violate to the point of the book because God's reasons for compensating Job are essentially as mysterious as the reasons why he first allowed Job to suffer. It all becomes a matter of God-ordained will and is not determined by the way that human beings judge things. Ultimately, in other words, the problem of evil in the world is left in the hands of God, and God's will is his own and is utterly unfathomable to human reason.

Now, in our next session, we will turn our attention from the Near East to another part of the ancient Mediterranean world. Now, we will consider religious cultures in the civilizations that grew up around the Aegean Sea and became part of the heritage of classical Greece.

# Lecture Twenty-Eight
## Early Aegean Civilizations

**Scope:**
Settlement in the Greek islands began in the Neolithic era, with Minoan civilization on Crete reaching its height in the early 15th century B.C.E. Despite extensive ruins and intriguing artifacts, its religious culture is almost impossible to reconstruct. Mycenaean civilization arose during the Bronze Age on the Greek mainland, as incursions of Indo-Aryans settled in geographically distinct areas of the Achaean peninsula. Mycenaean civilization is the historical setting for the events of the *Iliad* and *Odyssey*. It is characterized by shaft tombs, fortified building complexes, and a wealth of goods reflecting vigorous trade with the Near East. The civilization declined rapidly around 1200 B.C.E., as much of the eastern Mediterranean sank into a dark age. The religious culture of the Mycenaean era can be generally described but should be distinguished from the culture reflected in later epic poetry.

## Outline

I. The earliest civilization around the Aegean Sea appeared in Crete during the Bronze Age.

   A. The Aegean Sea was easily accessible by ship from the major centers of civilization in the ancient Near East.

   1. The earliest archaeological findings in the Aegean date from the late Neolithic era and include female figurines like those found in the Near East or northern Europe.

   2. Among these female figurines are flat, abstract representations from the Cycladic islands.

   3. The many female figurines suggest some form of goddess worship in connection with the fertility of the earth.

   B. During the Bronze Age, Crete was home to the Minoan civilization centered in Knossos.

   1. The Minoans came to Crete about 7000 B.C.E., living in small farming settlements.

   2. From about 3500 B.C.E., there was a rapid increase in population, leading to larger settlements and new forms of craftsmanship and maritime trading.

3. From about 2000 B.C.E., Minoans began to construct elaborate building complexes, now often called *palaces*.
4. The building complexes are unfortified, indicating that Minoans had little fear of war or invasion.
5. Apart from the public building complexes in the major cities, there were villages and a system of roads protected by guard posts.
6. Minoan civilization reached its height during the first half of the 15th century B.C.E.
7. Many of the island's cities were destroyed by fire around 1470 B.C.E., suggesting an earthquake or the work of invaders.

**C.** It is very difficult to reconstruct the religious culture of later Minoan civilization with any certainty.
   1. The Minoans' written language, Linear A, has not yet been deciphered.
   2. A later written language, Linear B, was used primarily for records and inventories.
   3. We know almost nothing directly about later Minoan religious belief and practices.

**D.** A variety of clues point to what might be examples of Minoan religious belief and activity.
   1. Building decorations of birds, double-headed axes, and bull horns are often interpreted as religious symbols.
   2. A figurine of a bare-breasted woman holding two snakes is usually interpreted as a priestess or fertility goddess.
   3. A mural depicting a figure somersaulting over the back of a bull is often said to represent a religious ritual.
   4. The bull-leaping scene, bull horns, and the mythological figure of the Minotaur are taken as evidence for a sacred bull in Minoan religion.
   5. Minoan religious culture appears to have been concerned primarily with fertility.
   6. Most of what is taken as evidence for religious activity, however, is also open to secular interpretation.

**II.** Mycenaean civilization on the Greek mainland during the Bronze Age combined Indo-Aryan groups into a single culture.

   **A.** The name of the civilization comes from Mycenae, a site excavated by Heinrich Schliemann in the 1870s.

1. Schliemann devoted his life to uncovering the archaeological sites he believed lay behind the stories of the Trojan War.
2. Schliemann unfortunately tended to inflate the significance of his discoveries.
3. Our knowledge of Mycenaean civilization depends on his discoveries, but we must separate archaeological evidence from legendary accounts.

B. Indo-Aryan invaders settled on the Achaean peninsula before the second millennium B.C.E.
   1. The mountains, valleys, and plains of Achaea tended to divide its inhabitants into distinctive autonomous communities.
   2. The new settlers tended to establish fortified palaces on hilltops overlooking valleys near the coastlines.
   3. Most scholars assume that the Indo-Aryans intermingled with or dominated and eliminated earlier inhabitants.
   4. Stories about relationships among the gods may symbolically represent relationships among each god's worshipers.
   5. Mycenaean writings in Linear B include some mention of divine names from later Greek mythology.

C. Many of the most important early discoveries from early Greek culture were tombs.
   1. *Shaft tombs* cut into the rock seem to be characteristic of the Mycenaean era.
   2. One such tomb dating from about 1700 B.C.E. contained 19 bodies and a wealth of precious artifacts.
   3. The artifacts were made of precious materials that indicate an active trade with the Near East.
   4. The tombs show that Mycenaean culture was highly stratified, with a wealthy and powerful elite.
   5. From 1500 B.C.E., burials are found in *beehive tombs*: round, domed, underground burial chambers.
   6. The burial chambers were reached through a long tunnel with a massive lintel and doorway at the entrance.

D. Mycenaean cities from 1400–1200 B.C.E. were dominated by fortified public *palaces*.

1. These building complexes served as refuge in war and for a variety of public functions during times of peace.
2. The building complex included storehouses, pantries, workshops, living quarters, and public rooms.
3. Fortifications made of boulders or blocks of stone are called *Cyclopean*.
4. These fortifications and other evidence testify to a warrior culture resembling medieval Europe.

E. The Mycenaean era ended in a dark age that affected all the civilizations of the eastern Mediterranean about 1200 B.C.E.
   1. What led to widespread destruction of cities and the collapse of empires is unknown.
   2. The marauding Sea Peoples harried the Mediterranean basin in search of land and plunder.
   3. Economic collapse and the fragmentation of established power added to the upheaval.
   4. Even nations that remained stable experienced upheavals that affected their subsequent history for centuries.

III. Mycenaean religious culture poses the same problems as Minoan religious culture on Crete.

A. Divine names familiar from later Greek religion appear in Linear B inscriptions, implying some continuity.
   1. As disparate regions came to form a single Greek culture, their gods, too, became associated in a process of syncretism.
   2. The gods of the different Greek peoples were identified with each other or associated by family or marriage.
   3. Syncretism brought new influences to bear on the entire religious culture.

B. Zeus was originally an Indo-Aryan god of the invading northerners, Dyaus Pitar.
   1. Zeus was a god of the sky and weather associated with different mountains.
   2. Zeus's primary identification was as sky-father, but he served a range of functions indicated by his many surnames.
   3. Zeus had many divine and human female lovers, but his consort and queen was Hera.

**4.** Hera may have been a goddess of earlier Achaeans, because her relationship with Zeus was often difficult.

**C.** At this point, we may make a few statements about the religious culture of the Mycenaean era.

    **1.** Careful and elaborate burial of the dead posits a belief in an afterlife similar to the present life.

    **2.** Gods of the Mycenaean era are generally the gods of later Greece, although their attributes and place in the divine hierarchy may have differed.

    **3.** Worship of the gods involved ritual sacrifice, either in the cities or the countryside, preferably on mountains or in grottoes.

    **4.** The gods, as well as human beings, were already the subjects of a lively mythology.

## Essential Reading:

Robin W. Winks and Susan P. Mattern-Parkes. *The Ancient Mediterranean World: From the Stone Age to A.D. 600*, pp. 36–44.

## Supplementary Reading:

Walter Burkert. *Greek Religion*, pp. 10–46.

Sarah Iles Johnston, ed. *Religions of the Ancient World: A Guide*, pp. 206–209.

## Questions to Consider:

**1.** Minoan and Mycenaean religious culture, like prehistoric religious culture, must be reconstructed on the basis of artifacts without the assistance of written texts. Which problems in reconstructing these religious cultures are similar? Which are different? Why?

**2.** What problems are presented when reconstructing a religious culture, as Schliemann did, in light of legendary accounts of its history? Should the primary business of archaeology be the accumulation or the interpretation of data? Why?

# Lecture Twenty-Eight—Transcript
## Early Aegean Civilizations

In our last session, we talked about the problem of evil in the monotheistic religious culture of post-exilic Judah—the solutions offered by apocalyptic literature on the one hand, and the book of Job on the other. In this session, we will shift our focus to another area of the ancient Mediterranean world and begin our discussion of the civilizations around the Aegean Sea—looking first at the Minoan and Mycenaean civilizations and their religious cultures.

Now, the earliest civilization to originate in the territories surrounding the Aegean Sea appeared on the island of Crete during the Bronze Age. The Aegean Sea was easily accessible by ship from several centers of civilization in the ancient Near East: Egypt, Asia Minor, and the Phoenician cities of Syria. The earliest archaeological findings from the Aegean date from the Neolithic era, and they include female figurines, the kinds of female figurines that are so familiar to us from the Near East and Europe.

Among these figurines are flat, almost abstract representations of the female form, and these are distinctive to the Cycladic Islands. These are islands southeast of Achaea and due north of Crete. The many female figurines surrounding this area suggest some form of earth goddess worship, probably based on the fertility of the earth—with a primary concern for foreign. Of course, this was common in the Neolithic era, as we have seen.

During the Bronze Age, Crete was home to a flourishing civilization that is called Minoan. It is named after the legendary king of Crete, Minos. It was centered in the capital city of Knossos. The Minoans apparently came to Crete about 7000 B.C.E., and they lived at first in small farming settlements. From about 3500 B.C.E., there was a rapid increase in the population, and this was accompanied by larger settlements and new forms of craftsmanship, as well as the introduction of maritime trading.

From about 2000 B.C.E., Minoans began to construct elaborate building complexes at Knossos and other sites, and then, usually, these building complexes were called "palaces," although that's not really an appropriate designation. The building complex at Knossos, for example, is three stories tall. It has rooms of various design and various sizes, and they seem intended for various different functions. These rooms all surround a central courtyard.

The building complex has many very elaborately decorated rooms. Some have frescoes of marine life, or perhaps of nature scenes, and there are repeated decorative motifs in these rooms at Knossos as well.

Interestingly, these building complexes left by the Minoans are unfortified. This indicates that the Minoans had very little fear of war or invasion. Apparently, their weapons were fairly simple, and although they had carts drawn by horses, they do not appear to have had chariots—that is, war machinery.

Apart from the building complexes—these public complexes I've already described in the major cities—there were villages, and these villages were composed of small, well-built houses, and they were connected by a system of roads that were apparently protected by guard posts, but that would be apparently intended for more internal protection than for protection from external enemies.

Minoan civilization reached its height during the first half of the 15th century B.C.E. Indication of destruction by many of the island cities by fire around 1470 B.C.E. suggests an earthquake, or perhaps an incursion of invaders from the mainland; it's hard to know.

Now, despite the wealth of archaeological evidence, is very difficult for us as moderns to reconstruct the religious culture of later Minoan civilization with any degree of certainty at all. Although the Minoans have a language—in fact, a written language that was non-Greek; it survives in a writing system called "Linear A," and there are very few examples of Linear A that survive to the present day. So far, attempts to decipher the language have entirely failed.

There was also a later written language, Linear B, which represents a form of Greek, but it yields little of interest to us in terms of religious culture because it was used primarily for records and inventories. In other words, it appears to have been a business language, rather than a language of religion, history, or science.

As a result of this lack of written resources, we can know almost nothing directly about later Minoan religious beliefs and practices.

We know nothing about the names or nature of their gods, or even anything about their outlook on life in any kind of direct form. What we have instead is a variety of intriguing clues provided by the archaeological evidence, and these clues point to what might have been examples of religious belief or religious activity on the part of the Minoans.

For example, the building complexes, as I have already mentioned, are elaborately decorated, and there often occurs the motif of a bird; birds are symbols of an earth goddess, traditionally. Other common motifs are a double-headed ax and the horns of a bull.

A well-known artifact from Minoan civilization is a small figurine of a bare-breasted woman in a flaring, layered skirt and a headdress; she holds two snakes in her hands, and she holds them aloft. It's often been speculated that this figurine represents a fertility goddess—or perhaps a priestess of a fertility goddess—because, again, snakes being associated with the earth are often symbols of fertility, among other reasons.

In Knossos there is a mural from about 1500 B.C.E. that depicts a male figure who seems to be somersaulting over the back of a running bull, and then there are two female figures on either side, as well. The bull-leaping scene and the repeated motif of bulls' horns and bulls headed elsewhere in the Knossos complex are sometimes cited as indications of a central place for the figurines of the bull in Minoan religion.

Another possible indication is the myth of the Minotaur of Minos, and "Minotaur" essentially means "Minos bull." This was a monster that was half human and half bull. It was believed to have lived in a labyrinth below Minos's palace, and it ate human sacrifices. As we've seen before, the bull was, of course, a common religious symbol for fertility and also for virile power—sometimes representing the virile power of a god, as in the case of the bull 'El in Syro-Palestinian religious culture.

It's possible, then, between these various motifs of the bull to deduce that the bull was a sacred animal in Minoan civilization, and in 1979, archaeologists uncovered some evidence of human sacrifice among the Minoans. So there may possibly be a connection between the bull and blood sacrifice, which remains hidden in some complex way behind the myth of the Minotaur, although that is entirely speculative.

Taken together, then, Minoan religious culture appears to have been concerned primarily with fertility, not really surprising. This fertility was possibly associated with a snake-bearing goddess, or with the figure of the bull, representing female and male principles.

Even so, though, the lightheartedness of the bull-leaping scene at Knossos seems to suggest sport rather than religious ritual, and, indeed, most of the evidence for religious activity in Minoa and Crete is open to secular interpretation, and that pretty much summarizes the problem. There are indications of what might be religious symbols or representations of religious ideas, but they're also open to secular interpretation, and, ultimately, we have no way of being able to be sure, short of being able to decipher Linear A, and assuming that Linear A would provide any direct information about Minoan religion.

At the same time that Minoan civilization appears in Crete, on the Greek mainland during the Bronze Age, the Mycenaean civilization arose. The Mycenaean civilization combined a variety of Aryan and Indo-European ethnic groups into a single identifiable culture and language. The name "Mycenaean" civilization comes from Mycenae, which was—according to mythology—the city of Agamemnon, the legendary Greek king.

Mycenae as a site was first excavated by Heinrich Schliemann, who was also the first discoverer of Troy. He excavated Mycenae in the 1870s. Schliemann was a German archaeologist. His dates are 1822 to 1890, and what motivated him in his archaeological research was his conviction that the legendary accounts of the Trojan War were based on actual historical events, and Schliemann devoted his life to uncovering archaeological sites he believed were at the center of these stories. This was at a time when these stories were thought to be entirely imaginary: the elaborate story of the *Iliad*, the *Odyssey*, the works of Homer, were believed to be based on nothing but poetic fancy. Schliemann, instead, believed that they were based on some kernel of historical fact, and he devoted his life to excavating archaeological sites in search of some of those historical facts.

At the same time, Schliemann was, by his own admission, a braggart and a bluffer, and he had a tendency to inflate the significance of his various discoveries. He would link them to specific mythological sources, or specific mythological heroes, or specific mythological incidents, without any real evidence. So, for example, he would refer to the jewelry that he had found as the "treasure of Helen," or he would refer to a funerary mask that he had found depicting a bearded man as the "mask of Agamemnon," to give them the inflated importance in association with a specific mythological figure.

However, our knowledge of Mycenaean civilization depends very much on discoveries made by Schliemann and, of course, by those others who followed him, but we, as modern scholars, must be very careful to separate archaeological evidence from legend. We take mythology as perhaps only a very slight indication of how things might once have been.

Now, the Indo-Aryan invaders who spoke an early form of Greek established settlements on the Achaean Peninsula. This happened sometime before the beginning of the second millennium B.C.E. Unlike Egypt, or unlike Mesopotamia, where central rivers tended to unite people geographically, in Achaea the mountains, the valleys, and the plains tended to divide its inhabitants, and, as a result, they ended up gathered in more or less autonomous communities with distinctive characteristics.

The new settlers from the northeast tended to establish themselves in fortified palaces that sometimes, of course, overlooked valleys, and these were usually located near the coastlands, thereby providing safety for the inhabitants and defense in time of war, as well as plentiful farming and trade opportunities in times of peace.

Most scholars assume that the Indo-Aryan invaders encountered an earlier native people or peoples and either came to intermingle with them and intermarry, or perhaps dominated and gradually eliminated them. In fact, some scholars see stories about the interrelationship among the gods in Greek mythology as symbolic representations of the relationships among the groups that worshiped each god; so the relationships of the gods would reflect the relationships of the groups that worshiped them—except in a symbolic form, a representational form.

We do have writings from the Mycenaean civilization. These appear on clay tablets in Linear B, and they include occasional mention of divine names that are familiar from later Greek mythology, notably Zeus, Poseidon, and Apollo.

Now, many of the most important early discoveries of Mycenaean culture were tombs, and this should not surprise us. We've seen tombs as great sources of information for prehistoric religion, and especially for Egyptian religious culture.

In Greece, we find distinctive "shaft tombs" that were cut deep into the rock, and these seem to be characteristic of the Mycenaean era—although, even then, they were probably reserved only for the leading families. It's not an easy thing to cut a shaft deep into rock.

One of these tombs was excavated by Heinrich Schliemann. It's a tomb now known as "Grave Circle A," which dated from about 1700 B.C.E. Grave Circle A contained 19 bodies and a wealth of artifacts of virtually every sort. This is where Schliemann found the so-called "mask of Agamemnon," a flat funerary mask of a bearded man's face made of gold.

In fact, the artifacts in this tomb were made of other precious materials besides gold, including lapis lazuli, ivory, and amber—a fairly clear indication of an active trade in luxury goods with the Near East at the time of Mycenaean civilization.

Apart from providing examples of Mycenaean art, this tomb, Grave Circle A, also demonstrates that Mycenaean culture was highly stratified. That is, we know at least that there was a wealthy and powerful elite who were able to secure positions of dominance not only in the present world, but also in the world to come, as demonstrated by the goods that were buried with them in preparation for their future life.

From around 1500 B.C.E., burials are found in what are called "*tholos*," or "beehive tombs." These are round, underground burial chambers that are covered with domes, and a dome is made out of decreasing rings of stones. These burial chambers are reached through a long tunnel, so one reaches a *tholos* through a long tunnel called a "*dromos*," and these tunnels had massive lintels and doorways at the entrance—again, indicating a great deal of care and a great deal of trouble. Although these tombs, the *tholos* tombs, also held treasures for the deceased at some point, those that have been found so far were apparently looted in ancient times, and there's nothing left for modern archaeologists to discover.

From about 1400 B.C.E. to about 1200 B.C.E., Mycenaean cities were dominated by fortified public "palaces"—although, again, the term "palace" is misleading. Once again, these were essentially building complexes, like those in Minoan Crete, but these building complexes are simpler and plainer than the similar building complexes in the Minoan cities. These buildings provided a place of refuge in time of war, and during times of peace, they served a variety of public functions. They seem to have been centers for political as well as economic power.

The building complexes of the Mycenaean era included storehouses for goods, pantries, workshops, living quarters, and public rooms—that is, rooms for public assemblies. Most notable among these is the "*megaron*," which was a circular room with an open hearth at the center and four supporting columns holding up the roof. Most likely, the *megaron* was used as some sort of throne room, or judgment room, in these public assemblies.

There are fortifications in Mycenaean settlements made of unworked boulders—or sometimes huge, rectangular blocks of stone—forming an architectural style called "Cyclopean," and once again, we see the grandiosity typical of Schliemann here. These walls are called "Cyclopean" because the massive walls seem to be the work of giants, like the Cyclops. You could just call them "big stones," but apparently that would not appeal to the sense of the fantastic.

Such fortifications and the political hierarchy that is reflected in the situation of at least some of the tombs of the Mycenaean era, as well as the legendary account of Mycenaean warfare in, for example, the *Iliad*—all of these testify to a warrior culture, and probably a warrior culture that in many particulars may have resembled that of medieval Europe.

Now, the Mycenaean era in Greece ended in rapid decline into a dark age, and this was a dark age not only in Greece, but it is one that appears to have affected all of the civilizations of the Mediterranean world about 1200 B.C.E. Scholars are not clear on what may have led to this widespread destruction of cities, and the collapse of civilizations that followed this period was during this time that the Hittite empire collapsed in Asia Minor and Mycenaean civilization collapsed in Greece.

Certainly, one contributing factor was the incursion of marauding peoples, sometimes called the "Sea Peoples," that harried the civilizations of the Mediterranean basin in search of land and plunder, but it's hard to tell if the Sea Peoples were the cause of this collapse into the dark age, or if they were a result of this collapse into the dark age. It's hard to know if they were the warriors who brought these civilizations to an end, or the warriors who were left dispossessed by the collapse of their civilizations and who decided to set out and pursue new land, new territories, and new power on their own.

These military attacks, then, by people like the Sea Peoples, probably came in tandem with economic collapse. Perhaps there was a widespread agricultural failure or the end of trade by sea. Perhaps the Sea Peoples, as the name implies, were also pirates who preyed on maritime shipping.

There was a subsequent political fragmentation of both established powers and the economic structures that supported them, even nations that continued and that maintained their internal coherence, such as Mesopotamia and Egypt—these saw internal upheavals that forced their attention to turn inward for, in some cases, several centuries.

Now, our attempts to reconstruct the religious culture of the Mycenaean era faces many of the same problems we found in reconstructing the religious culture of Minoan Crete—mostly, again, because of a lack of clear written sources. As we've seen, some divine names familiar from later Greek mythology do appear in inscriptions in Linear B, and this implies some sort of continuity with later religious culture.

As disparate regions of the Greek mainland, as I said—those autonomous settlements in different places—as they came together to form a single culture united on the one hand by trade and by military alliance, and on the other hand by a common language, most likely their gods, too, became associated with each other. Again, this is a process of syncretism—the combination of attributes, rituals, and mythology of one system of gods with another.

As happened as well in Egypt and in Mesopotamia, the gods of the different Greek peoples were identified with each other, or associated by families, or associated as married couples, or sometimes associated as enemies or as conflicting forces.

This sort of syncretism brought new influences to bear on the entire religious culture of the area surrounding the Aegean Sea. The gods and goddesses of the Indo-Aryan invaders were identified with various local powers that had received other names from earlier peoples. They took over the functions, the rituals, and histories of those earlier gods and, at the same time, added their own characteristics to those stories, those functions, and those rituals.

We find a good example of this process in the case of the chief god of ancient Greece, Zeus. Zeus was originally an Indo-Aryan god of the invading northerners, and his name appears to have been Dyaus Pitar. Zeus appears to originally have been a god of the sky and weather, not really surprising.

He is one of those figures that we call a "sky father," which sometimes becomes dominant in ancient religious cultures, and his association with weather is fairly clear because of his tool, if you will, of the thunderbolt, and as a god identified with the sky and with weather, Zeus became associated with different mountains in Achaea, including Olympus, which is in northeastern Achaea. So, Zeus's primary identification was as the sky father armed with a thunderbolt, but he also served a range of other functions, and these functions are represented by the various surnames or second names that Zeus takes. He is commonly known as "Zeus Olympios," Zeus of Olympus, which is where the gods reside.

However, he is also known as "Zeus Gamelios," "Zeus, the patron of marriage," or as "Zeus Alexikakos," "Zeus, the helper in danger;" "Zeus Agoraios," "Zeus, the patron of the assembly," for the public gathering of the people.

Although Zeus was the father of many offspring, and there are many stories about Zeus as the lover of goddesses, and many more stories about Zeus as the lover of human women, despite his myriad of marital infidelities, his consort and his queen was Hera, and Hera appears to have originally been an earth fertility deity. Some scholars, in fact, speculate that Hera was originally a goddess of the earlier inhabitants of Achaea. Here, we would have an example of the god of the invaders becoming associated with a goddess of the native peoples, the indigenous peoples. There is some speculation that the people who worshiped Hera were a people with matriarchal traditions, rather than the patriarchal traditions of the Indo-Aryan invaders.

Hera's relationship with Zeus—Hera the matriarch with Zeus the patriarch—this was often, may we say, a stormy relationship; and yes, the pun is intended, and I apologize, but later on, Hera and Zeus do learn to live peaceably with each other, perhaps reflecting that eventual conciliation between the invaders and those whose land they invaded.

On the basis of the limited written and archaeological evidence, we may make a few general statements about the religious culture of the Mycenaean era, and here, we are helped considerably by the fact that there are written records not of the Mycenaean era itself, but of the succeeding ages that reflect back on the situation of the Mycenaean era. Although we should not, like Schliemann, be entirely dominated by the desire to associate everything we find with the mythology that takes place in the Mycenaean era, it does provide us some sense of what the religious culture may have been like; it provides, if you will, a template for what religious culture might have been like, a template we do not have for Minoa and Crete.

In any event, there are a few general statements we can make about the religious culture of the Mycenaean era. First of all, we have a careful—and in some cases, very elaborate—burial of the dead, and this clearly posits a belief here as elsewhere in an afterlife, and it is an active life, where the tools and even the luxuries of the present life will still be needed to provide similar tools and luxuries in the life to come.

We may speculate with some confidence that the gods of the Mycenaean era were generally the same gods who worshiped in later Greece—although, of course, it seems reasonable to assume that their attributes, and their place in the divine hierarchy, may have been different during the Mycenaean era. For example, some scholars speculate that Poseidon, the god of the ocean, may have had a dominant place in the Mycenaean era that he did not enjoy during the classical era. This would become, first of all, a reality through his association with seafaring—the basis of maritime trade—but also because of his association with horses.

The worship of the gods clearly involved ritual sacrifice. These were either to have happened in the temple sanctuaries of the cities or in the countryside, and in the countryside, mountains and grottos appear to have been the preferred locations for sacrificial offerings.

The gods, as well as human beings, were already the subjects in the Mycenaean era of a vivid mythology, and this mythology continued to grow and develop over the following centuries until, finally, it formed a rich narrative history that served as the inspiration for the earliest literary endeavors in Greece.

In our next session, we will consider some of the attitudes towards the gods in relationship with human beings, in the epic narratives first composed during the Greek Dark Age.

# Lecture Twenty-Nine
# Religious Culture in the *Iliad* and the *Odyssey*

**Scope:**
The Dark Age (c. 1200–800 B.C.E.) saw a drastic decrease in the scale and quality of life in Greece. Writing disappeared, and memories of the Mycenaean era were preserved in oral stories of gods and heroes. Poets told stories afresh with each performance, using stereotyped phrases and images. Homer's *Iliad* and *Odyssey* reflect the religious culture of both the Mycenaean era and the Dark Age. The *Iliad* tells the story of Achilles's refusal to fight during the last year of the Trojan War because of a dispute with Agamemnon. The poem depicts both gods and human beings at war, under the shadow of Troy's fated destruction. The *Odyssey* tells the story of Odysseus's long journey homeward from Troy and his adventures with goddesses, men, and monsters. Both poems depict the gods as humanity's divine overlords, but they betray a preference for human beings, their bravery, and the comforts of home.

## Outline

I. The epic poems of the *Iliad* and *Odyssey* were apparently first composed during the Dark Age.

   A. The Dark Age in Greece (c. 1200–800 B.C.E.) saw a drastic decrease in population and settlements.

      1. Archaeological sites for the Dark Age are scattered and few in number.

      2. Settlements appear to have been isolated from each other and from the rest of the world.

      3. Burials indicate that settlements were small, with structures built of timber and mud brick.

      4. The exception is a burial site at Lefkandi on Euboea, where the remains of a couple were buried with horses and luxury goods.

      5. The general impression of this period is of a very small population scraping out an existence.

      6. Little is known of religious practice at this time, but presumably, many practices of the Mycenaean age continued on a reduced scale.

**B.** Written language apparently disappeared, and stories of gods and heroes were passed on by oral storytelling.

  1. The Greeks of the Dark Age considered the Mycenaeans god-like heroes of a better time.
  2. Poets would compose a story afresh each time it was told; thus, each performance of the story was unique.
  3. The most notable products of the poets of the Dark Age are the *Iliad* and *Odyssey*, traditionally attributed to the blind poet Homer.

**C.** Homer's *Iliad* and *Odyssey* reflect the religious culture of both the Mycenaean era and the Dark Age.

  1. We cannot simply equate the religious beliefs reflected in the epics with those of the Mycenaean era.
  2. At the same time, scholars assert that parts of the epics reflect early religious beliefs not typical of the time the epics were composed.
  3. We will put this problem aside in favor of considering the nature of the religious culture reflected by the poems as they stand.

**II.** The *Iliad* depicts a divine world very much like the world of its heroes.

  **A.** The *Iliad* is set in the 10$^{th}$ year of the war of the Achaeans against Troy.

  1. The *Iliad* is about the anger of Achilles, who withdraws from combat over a dispute with Agamemnon.
  2. Without Achilles, the Achaeans find the war turning against them.
  3. The Trojan prince Hector kills Achilles's comrade Patroclus, prompting Achilles to take revenge against Hector.
  4. The poem ends when Prium, king of Troy, asks Achilles for his son's body, and Achilles returns it.

  **B.** In the *Iliad*, gods and heroes interact as equal members of a society where a few stand out as leaders.

  1. The gods pursue their own interests in helping one side or the other and often rebel against or try to evade the power of Zeus.
  2. At the same time, the gods recognize that they are under the authority not only of Zeus but also of fate.

3. The heroes also have their arguments and often must be appeased by offerings, just like the gods.
4. The heroes seem to regard the gods as supernatural chieftains who are to be served faithfully and obeyed.

C. The goal of the hero's life in the *Iliad* is to gain eternal renown by his feats of valor.
   1. We have already encountered the idea that the best thing for humanity is to enjoy life while it lasts.
   2. But the heroes of the *Iliad* seek to make the most of life by gaining the glory due a mighty warrior.
   3. Homer lists the names and genealogies of the warriors who fall in battle, providing the glory they desire but also reminding his audience of the human cost of war.
   4. Eternal renown is the only reward these warriors seek from the gods; when they die, their souls go "wailing down to Hades."

D. The *Iliad* often shows the gods wielding a direct supernatural influence over human beings.
   1. The Greeks attributed any sort of uncharacteristic behavior to madness, the influence of a god that prevents clear thinking.
   2. The Greeks thought of a person's character as the product of rational thought, because a person always acted according to what he or she believed to be good.
   3. This meant that irrational behavior had to originate outside of a person's character, in other words, with the influence of the gods.
   4. We still talk about love in much the same way, as something that overcomes us from outside.
   5. The *Iliad* portrays a humanity that is under the gods' control yet presents its heroes as fully in charge of their own lives.

III. The *Odyssey* shows different aspects of religious culture in the Mycenaean era and Dark Age than does the *Iliad*.

A. The *Odyssey* is the story of Odysseus and his long journey homeward after the Trojan War.
   1. Odysseus sets out with a fleet of ships, but through a series of adventures, he ends up alone.

2. Odysseus incurs the wrath of Poseidon after blinding the Cyclops, but through constant vigilance, Odysseus eventually escapes all dangers.

3. Odysseus is seduced by a sorceress and a nymph, in turn, but ultimately chooses to return to Ithaca and his wife, Penelope.

4. Once in Ithaca, he finds his home filled with Penelope's suitors and must use his wits and strength to regain his place at home.

**B.** As in the *Iliad*, the *Odyssey* presents the gods as humanity's divine overlords.

1. Poseidon takes revenge against Odysseus, although he knows that Odysseus is destined to return home.

2. Apollo destroys Odysseus's crew after they slaughter the cattle of the Sun.

3. Athena admires Odysseus's craftiness and assists him, sometimes in opposition to Poseidon.

4. When the nymph Calypso keeps Odysseus on her island for seven years, Zeus orders her to let him go.

5. Despite help or hindrance from the gods, it is Odysseus's resourcefulness and guile that finally bring him home.

**C.** At one point, Odysseus travels into the underworld to consult with the shade of the prophet Tiresias.

1. The portrait of Hades in the *Odyssey* has influenced subsequent portrayals of the underworld.

2. The poet presents Hades as a dark, joyless place full of mourning, insubstantial spirits.

3. Odysseus sacrifices a goat, and spirits who drink its blood revive sufficiently to speak to him.

4. The shade of Tiresias provides a prophecy, but Odysseus allows other shades to drink and tell their fate.

5. The shade of Achilles notably gains no satisfaction in Hades from the renown he earned in life.

**D.** Odysseus journeys through a world of wonders in frequent contact with the sacred.

1. All the supernatural beings he encounters prove a hindrance to Odysseus and delay him on his journey.

2. By contrast, human beings are mostly helpful to him, although at home, he faces human foes.

3. Calypso offers Odysseus immortality and everlasting youth, but he chooses to return home instead.
4. Odysseus rejects both the fate of the gods and the fate of the hero, preferring his home and his family.
5. The *Odyssey* finds the value of human life in peace and the pleasures of marriage and raising children.

E. Homer's work played a central role in the religious and literary culture of later Greek civilization.
1. Homer's poems became the primary literature of all educated Greeks.
2. The *Iliad* and *Odyssey* shaped vocabulary and style of Greek rhetoric.
3. Homer's poems also conveyed theological ideas central to later Greek religious culture.
4. Through Homer's poetry, Mycenaean heroes continued to stimulate the imagination of Greek culture.

### Essential Reading:

Homer. *The Iliad*, books 1–6, 22–24.
Homer. *The Odyssey*.

### Supplementary Reading:

Walter Burkert. *Greek Religion*, pp. 47–53.

### Questions to Consider:

1. What are some consequences of the *Iliad*'s concentration on particular human actors at one point in the Trojan War, in contrast to a story about the entire conflict?

2. Odysseus's courage, guile, and physical appearance make him attractive to both human and divine women, and he has prolonged sexual affairs with two of them. How does this play into the main thrust of the epic, which is about the longing for home and marital fidelity?

# Lecture Twenty-Nine—Transcript
## Religious Culture in the *Iliad* and the *Odyssey*

In our last session, we considered some of the earliest civilizations of the Aegean Sea: Minoan civilization on the island of Crete, and Mycenaean civilization of the Greek mainland. In this session, we will discuss the Greek Dark Age, and early Greek religious culture as it is reflected in the epic poems the *Iliad* and the *Odyssey*. Now, the Dark Age was apparently the time when the poems the *Iliad* and the *Odyssey* were first composed and performed, and they reflected memories of the Mycenaean era as a heroic age.

The Dark Age in Greece lasted about four centuries—that is, from about 1200 to about 800 B.C.E., and the Dark Age saw a drastic decrease in the population, and in both the number and the size of settlements. Archaeological sites for the Dark Age, as a result, are widely scattered and very few in number. What settlements there were appear to have been fairly isolated from each other, as well as from the rest of the world, and burials—for the most part—contained no traded goods, indicating isolation.

Burials also indicate that the settlements were small—with the largest including perhaps, under 500 people—and structures in these settlements were built of timber and of mud brick instead of stone. There is an exception, however. This is a burial site at Lefkandi on the large island of Euboea, just off the eastern coast of Attica. It includes the remains of an adult couple, and this man and woman were buried with four horses and a trove of silver and gold treasures. They are buried in a very large burial chamber, and there are other items there that seem to indicate some trade with the Near East.

The chamber itself is made of timber and mud brick, and there are other burials in the area that also seem to indicate some trade at this time with the Near East, but this is only one burial site that has been discovered, and despite this one site—which, at most, indicates the wealth and prestige of this individual couple—the general impression we receive from the archaeological sites of the Dark Age in Greece is of a very small population scraping out an existence.

As a result, we know very little about the religious practices at this time, and there are no cultic sites that have been discovered that are specific to this era. Presumably, though, many of the ritual practices that were carried out in the Mycenaean age continued, although probably on a much reduced scale, both in terms of the activities, the rituals conducted, and in the quality of the offerings made to the gods.

Additionally, during the Greek Dark Age, written language apparently disappeared. We find the end of Linear B, for example, and memories of the Mycenaean era, as well as stories of the gods and heroes, were retained in oral form as storytelling, as poetry. We can imagine that surrounded by the ruins of the Mycenaean era, the Greeks of the Dark Age could easily ascribe to the people who had lived in these cities the glory and the virtue that their own era seemed to lack.

The poets who told the stories of the gods and heroes of the earlier age, in fact, composed a story afresh each time it was told. Because it was an oral composition, it was retold in a different way every time—just as when a person tells a story, he or she invariably changes it each time, or even something that is stereotyped as a joke is changed each time it is told, to fit an audience, and to reflect the person's memory of the story.

The poets, however, used stereotyped phrases and stereotyped images—first of all to help sustain the story, occasionally using a particular motif, or a particular metaphor, or a particular image to give them a moment to think about what they were going to say next—but also to extend and fill out the poetic meter of a story as they told it. So, in addition to the natural tendency to tell a story orally each time it is told, there was also the use of these stereotyped phrases and stereotyped motifs to help the poet compose as he went along.

Each performance, then, of the poem—each performance of the story—was unique to a particular time and place, even when the story was told in the same way. Even when the same story was told in the same way by the same poet, each performance was slightly different.

The most notable products of the poets of the Dark Age are the *Iliad* and the *Odyssey*. Both of these poems are traditionally attributed, of course, to the blind poet Homer, and we can perhaps surmise that the inability of a blind poet to either read or write memorializes the fact that these were oral stories, told as poetic performances from the very beginning. It is a tribute to the original oral composition of these two great epics.

Now, Homer's *Iliad* and his *Odyssey* reflect the religious culture of both their settings in the Mycenaean era, and of the Dark Age in which they were composed. So, we have a combination, most likely, of Mycenaean religious ideas—or the ideas of Mycenaean religious culture, perhaps I should say—and the ideas of the religious culture of the Greek Dark Age, combined and intertwined.

As a result, we cannot simply greet the religious attitudes and beliefs enshrined in the stories with those of the Mycenaean era that serves as the setting of the story, but at the same time most scholars assert that parts of the epics do reflect early religious beliefs and practices that were not typical of the later era when the poems were actually composed. So, there was a combination of the religious cultures of the Mycenaean era and the Dark Age reflected in these epic poems.

In view of the central place that both the *Iliad* and the *Odyssey* hold in later Greek culture, I'm not going to try to untangle the specific aspects that come from the Mycenaean religious culture and the Dark Age religious culture. Instead, I'm going to talk about the nature of the religious culture suggested by the poems themselves, and see what the poems have to say about the points of view of those who composed them.

Now, the *Iliad* depicts a divine world very much like the world of its heroes—in other words, the divine world that is very much like the human world in the way its heroes live and act. The gods as well, like the heroes, become passionately involved in the conflict of the Trojan War, and the gods, like the heroes, are very taken up with concern for the fate of their human favorites.

Now, the *Iliad* is set in the tenth year of the Trojan War, the war between the Achaeans against the city of Troy. The war was initiated when Paris, a prince of Troy, abducted Helen, who was the wife of Menelaus, and took her off to Troy as his mistress.

Menelaus's brother, Agamemnon, was the one who led the Greeks—called, here, the "Achaeans"—to war, but the *Iliad* is not so much about the war itself, its causes and its progress. It is more about the anger of Achilles—Achilles, of course, the greatest warrior among the Greeks. At a certain point, he withdrew from combat, and this happened when Agamemnon, the leader of the Achaeans, claimed a captive woman who rightfully belonged to Achilles.

When Achilles withdraws, the war turns against the Greeks, and the poem depicts the pitched combat in the plains before the city of Troy. However, it also depicts the human and divine drama as either side presses for a military advantage, and we see the scales tipping back and forth between the two sides as one gains an advantage, and then the other.

Achilles's comrade, Patroclus, is killed by the Trojan prince Hector when Patroclus is wearing the armor of Achilles—Hector naturally thinking, therefore, that he has killed Achilles. The death of Patroclus prompts Achilles to rejoin his countrymen, specifically to take revenge on Hector, prince of Troy. Not only does Achilles attack and kill Hector, but as a means of shaming and humiliating his victim, he drags his dead body around the city of Troy behind his chariot. The *Iliad* ends when Prium, the king of Troy, comes to Achilles in the Greek camp to ask for his son's body, and Achilles, deeply moved by the old man's plight, returns Hector's body to his father.

Now, in the course of the *Iliad*, the gods interact with each other and the heroes interact with each other in very similar ways. The gods and the heroes are both, more or less, equal members of a society in which a few stand out as the leaders.

The gods pursue their own interests. They help one side or the other in the Trojan War, and often they rebel against the commands of their leader, Zeus, or at least attempt to get around him. However, the gods also recognize that they are under the authority not only of Zeus, but also of Fate. They are bound not only by the commands of Zeus, but by the unalterable dictates of Fate.

The gods in the *Iliad*, then, are essentially larger, stronger, immortal human beings, and they can intervene in human affairs, but although they are gods, their power has definite limits, and this is revealed over and over in the course of the epic.

What is interesting is that in the *Iliad*, the gods obey Fate not because Fate is unavoidable, not because it has an absolute power, but because to go against the dictates of Fate would be to undo the fabric of the cosmos. It would be to invite chaos to reign once again. Fate is part of the webbing that holds the cosmos together. To violate Fate, to go against its dictates, means that chaos, once again, can break into creation and lead to the end of all things, including the gods themselves.

Like the gods, the heroes of recent Troy also have their arguments with each other as they press for their own advantage, or their own point of view, and the heroes of recent Troy must often be appeased by offerings and entreaties to overcome their anger. This is particularly seen in the case of Achilles. Offerings are made to Achilles to turn aside his anger so that he might return to the Achaean army, and there is beseeching of Achilles to get him to return to the army, to help his fellow Achaeans advance their cause against Troy.

Like the gods, then, the heroes have their own arguments; they receive offerings, and they receive entreaties to change their opinions and their relationships. The relationships of the heroes with their leaders mirror the gods' relationships with Zeus. Often, they go against their leaders or try to get around them. Indeed, it seems as if the heroes regard the gods in much the same way that they regard their own human chieftains. They seem to regard the gods as supernatural leaders, as supernatural chieftains, who are to be served faithfully and whose commands must be obeyed, but like human chieftains, it's also expected that the gods will provide gifts and rewards for their favorites—those who serve the most dutifully and also the most successfully.

There is this interesting parallel, then, between the divine world and the human world of the hero in the *Iliad*. The divine world is made up of individuals with strong wills, with their own powers and with their own intentions, but they do submit to the authority of their chieftain. The human world of the heroes is made up of people with their own strengths, their own powers, and their own intentions—but they, too, submit most of the time to the will of their chieftains.

In keeping with this sense of the hero's integrity, in keeping with this sense of the hero's dignity—in the face not only of his human chieftains, but also in the face of the gods—there is this idea that the goal of the hero's life is to gain eternal renown. This is the point of the hero's life as displayed in the *Iliad*. The hero's desire is to gain eternal renown, specifically, of course, to gain eternal renown for his heroic actions on the battlefield—for his bravery, for his integrity, for his skill in combat.

This attitude that drives the hero on into battle and leads him to support his fellows, rather than to turn tail and flee, reflects the attitude we have already encountered in the Harper's Songs in Egypt, in Gilgamesh, in Mesopotamia, and in Ecclesiastes from Israel: Since all life is fated to end in death, the best thing for humanity to do is to enjoy life while it lasts, to do what is necessary to procure happiness while life lasts, but there is an important difference. In the world of the *Iliad*, in the face of inevitable death, the heroes there are determined to make the most of life by gaining glory, the glory that is due to the mighty warrior.

Homer lists the names of those who fall in battle. He lists the genealogies of those who fall in battle, and in doing so, he provides those heroes with the everlasting glory that they desired and that they deserve. Each hero, or virtually each hero that falls in battle, is a hero whose name, and whose family, and whose background we learn about. On the one hand, this grants those heroes the everlasting renown that is a hero's goal in life. On the other hand, perhaps more poignantly, it reminds the audience of the human cost of war. Each warrior who falls is a man with a family, with a background, with earthly concerns that are cut off when the spear pierces his heart. In fact, eternal renown is the only lasting reward that these warriors can ask of the gods. When they are cut down, Homer tells us that their souls go "wailing down to Hades," the abode of the dead.

Now, the *Iliad* often shows the gods wielding a direct supernatural influence over human beings, and this direct, divine, supernatural influence produces uncharacteristic behavior; it makes the heroes angry, or unusually brave, or leads them into misjudgments.

Now, the Greeks attributed any sort of uncharacteristic behavior to *ate*—that is, to madness or self-delusion, and this was understood as the influence of some god that overwhelmed a person's ability to think clearly. This is because the Greeks thought of a person's character as the product of rational thought. That is, they believed that a person's actions arose from a careful weighing of what he or she knew to be good or evil in a particular situation, and after weighing these things and making a judgment, a person acted in a particular way. So, the way you acted was based on what you knew, either sound knowledge or faulty knowledge.

This same idea, that character was based on knowledge, is characteristic of all of the Greek philosophers in the later eras. Therefore, if character, if action, arises from knowledge, irrational behavior must then, by definition, originate outside of a person's mind. It must be contrary to what that person knows, and, therefore, it must be contrary to that person's character. In other words, it must come from outside, from the gods. The gods temporarily disable a person's good judgment by some irresistible urge to behave in a particular way.

Now we, of course, as moderns recognize the irrational and the unconscious in human thinking, but we still talk about love, in particular, in much this same way. Love, we feel, is something that overcomes us from outside. It produces behavior that would otherwise be inexplicable, and it doesn't really respond to any kind of rational analysis. So, the way that we, in the Western world, talk about love is the way that the Greeks thought about any unusual or uncharacteristic behavior, attributed to *ate*—madness or self-delusion.

The *Iliad*, then, portrays a humanity that is under the gods' control, and yet a humanity that is fully in charge of its own lives. There is this very interesting balance of what we might call the "free will" of the heroes and the divine control that the gods exert over them.

Sometimes, the heroes are driven by divine impulses into mad acts, but as human beings, they remain noble in the face of their fate.

Now, the *Odyssey*, the other epic poem of Homer, comes from this same religious culture that is reflected in the *Iliad*, but the *Odyssey* represents different aspects of that culture in the story of a man making his long way home after the Trojan War. The *Odyssey*, of course, is the story of Odysseus. Odysseus was an Achaean warrior who is better known for his guile and his cleverness than for his prowess in battle—although he was a very good warrior—and his long journey homeward after the Trojan War makes up the substance of the story of the *Odyssey*.

Odysseus starts out with a fleet of ships, but he has a series of adventures—or perhaps, misadventures—at different landfalls where his ships come to port, and, gradually, his fleet is reduced to a single ship, and before long that single ship has disappeared with his men, and Odysseus continues his journey alone.

Odysseus initially incurs the wrath of the sea god Poseidon by blinding a Cyclops named Polyphemus. After that, Poseidon throws various obstacles in Odysseus's way, thereby prolonging his journey. However, through constant vigilance, Odysseus is able to escape eventually from all of the dangers his journey presents.

Odysseus is also seduced by a sorceress, Circe, and then later by a nymph, Calypso. Ultimately, though, he leaves each of them to return to his home island of Ithaca—where he is a king—and to his wife, Penelope.

Finally, once he is back in Ithaca, Odysseus finds his home filled with Penelope's would-be suitors, and he must use his wits and his strength one final time to regain his place at home.

As in the *Iliad*, the *Odyssey* presents the gods as humanity's divine overlords; the gods dole out rewards and punishments, and the gods must be appeased when they are offended, in order for human beings to escape their wrath. As we've seen, Poseidon works against Odysseus in revenge for blinding Polyphemus, even though Poseidon knows that Odysseus is destined, by Fate, to eventually return home safe.

Apollo destroys Odysseus's crew after the crew thoughtlessly slaughters the cattle sacred to the sun god. Athena, on the other hand, the goddess of practical wisdom, admires Odysseus because he is crafty; he is sly. He makes good plans, and so Athena assists Odysseus. Sometimes, she goes head-to-head with Poseidon, who is something of a traditional rival for Athena.

Similarly, when the nymph, Calypso, keeps Odysseus on her island for seven years, it is Zeus, the king of the gods, who sends his divine messenger, Hermes, to her to order her to let Odysseus go home. However, despite the help or hindrance that Odysseus may receive from the gods—hindrance from Poseidon and Apollo, help from Athena and Zeus—it is still Odysseus's own cleverness, his own resourcefulness, his own guile, that ensures his eventual return to Ithaca.

Before Odysseus leaves Circe's enchanted island, he travels into the underworld to consult with the shade of the blind prophet Tiresias and learn from him what the future holds in store for Odysseus.

Now, the portrait of Hades in the *Odyssey* has influenced most subsequent portrayals of the underworld, but it also recalls for us, at least, other journeys into the underworld in other ancient Mediterranean literature. Like portrayals of the underworld in the Mesopotamian literature, for example, the poet presents Hades as a dark, joyless place—full of warring, insubstantial spirits.

When Odysseus goes down into the underworld, he sacrifices a ram and pours out its blood on the ground. Spirits approach him and are able to drink the blood—that is, the life force of the ram, and in doing so, they revive sufficiently to speak to Odysseus and to talk about their situation in Hades.

Once the blind seer Tiresias has drunk the blood of the ram, he provides a prophecy for Odysseus, but he also prompts other shades in the underworld to approach him and to drink the ram's blood so that he may discover their fate. One of these is the shade of Achilles, and we learn after Achilles drinks the ram blood and speaks with Odysseus that Achilles takes no satisfaction at all in the eternal renown he has gained in life now that he is dead, and Achilles in effect says that he would rather live as a slave on earth than rule in Hades.

Now, Odysseus journeys through a world of wonders, where each landfall brings him into contact with the world of the sacred—with gods, with monsters, with nymphs, with sorcerers, with all sorts of marvels. Although some of these supernatural beings are benevolent, most are not; even those who are benevolent, like Calypso for example, prove a hindrance in some ways to Odysseus because they delay him on his journey home.

By contrast, the human beings Odysseus encounters on his journey are, for the most part, helpful to him—although, of course, once he gets home, he faces a host of human foes, as the suitors for Penelope's hand oppose him and prove an obstacle.

One of the interesting episodes in the *Odyssey* is that Calypso offers Odysseus divine status. In other words, she offers him immortality and everlasting youth of the sort the gods enjoy, and she offers him a place as her consort in a setting of everlasting pleasure. This is the very thing that the demigod hero, Heracles, suffered to achieve: some sort of immortality, some sort of place among the gods.

Calypso offers it willingly to Odysseus: immortality, everlasting youth, a beautiful nymph as his consort in a setting of everlasting pleasures. Odysseus rejects it. Odysseus rejects godhood to return to his place in the human world.

In fact, Odysseus rejects not only the fate of the gods, but also the fate of hero. Instead, his ambition is to return home from the divine world, the world of gods and heroes, to the human world, the "normal" world we might call it—the world of home and family— and the embrace of his wife, Penelope.

The *Odyssey* finds the value of human life not in glory, not in adventure, not in everlasting renown, but in peace and comfort, the pleasures of the marriage bed, and the raising of children—again, recalling that familiar advice of wisdom literature—to enjoy the simple pleasures that life has to offer.

Now, Homer's work played much the same role in the religious and literary culture of later Greek civilization that the King James Bible has played in Western religious and literary culture, at least in English-speaking nations.

Now, Homer's poems were written down in a language that reflected several different Greek dialects, and this became the primary literature of all educated Greeks, much as the King James translation of the Bible into English was once familiar to all educated Britons and Americans.

As a result, the *Iliad* and the *Odyssey* shaped the vocabulary and the style of Greek rhetoric, much as the King James Bible shaped the vocabulary and style of public and private speech in the 18th and 19th centuries in Britain and the United States.

Homer's poems also convey basic theological ideas that became central to later Greek religious culture, just as the Bible's stories have arguably shaped American Christianity much more than doctrinal works, or even the systematic theology of the different churches.

Through Homer's poetry, the idealized heroes of the Mycenaean era, the religious concerns of the Dark Age continued to wield an influence over later Greek religious culture and literature—and so, also, of course, over all of later Western culture.

Now, in our next session, we will look at the Greek religious culture of the age that succeeded the Dark Age—the Archaic Age.

# Lecture Thirty
## Religious Culture in Archaic Greece

**Scope:**
The Archaic Age in Greece (800–480 B.C.E.) saw an increase in population, the renewal of international trade, and the development of the city-state as the primary political entity in the Greek territories. The city-state was governed by a council of its citizens who also served it as soldiers. Although each city-state had its distinctive religious character, certain beliefs and practices united them in a common religious culture. The Greeks shared a pantheon of gods and interacted with them through prayer, dance, music, processions, festivals, and sacrifice. Gods were worshiped in their own sanctuaries, but some sanctuaries attracted worshipers from all over Greece. Similarly, all the Greek territories participated in the athletic contests of the Pan-Hellenic Games every four years. Two poetic works, *The Homeric Hymns* and Hesiod's *Theogony*, grant us insight into some of the prevailing beliefs and attitudes toward the gods in the Archaic Age.

## Outline

I. Greece began to emerge from the Dark Age in the 8$^{th}$ century B.C.E., when its population increased and a new culture developed.

    **A.** The Archaic Age, the period from about 800 to 480 B.C.E., saw the renewal of international trade.

        **1.** Archaeological remains from about 900 B.C.E. include artifacts apparently obtained in trade with other nations, notably Phoenicia.

        **2.** Foreign influences include Egyptian elements in temple design and adoption of the Phoenician alphabet.

        **3.** Population growth led to Greek colonies around the Mediterranean basin.

        **4.** Growth and international contact led to a greater awareness of Greek identity.

    **B.** A fundamental component of Greek society from the Archaic Age was the regional city-state (*polis*) ruled by a council of citizens.

1. Citizenship was based on military service as a *hoplite*, an armored infantry soldier armed with a spear, a short sword, and a round shield (*hoplon*).
2. Landowning farmers who could afford to serve as *hoplites* shared the right to govern the *polis* in council.
3. The *polis* represents an essential equality among citizens, in contrast to those denied citizenship.
4. The *polis* included buildings set aside for governance, public facilities, a marketplace, temples, and the surrounding farmlands.
5. The population of a *polis* ranged from several hundred to a few thousand.
6. There was substantial regional variation among the city-states in governance, public and private activities, and attitudes about life.
7. Each *polis* worshiped particular gods and had its own religious celebrations and festival calendar.

II. Despite this variety, certain religious presuppositions, beliefs, and actions united Archaic Greece in a common polytheistic religious culture.

A. Greek religious culture of the Archaic Age reflected the sense that the sacred and the secular were intertwined.
   1. Because the natural world was alive with the presence of the sacred, every aspect of life had its religious component.
   2. Religious activities were undertaken to maintain social harmony and equilibrium between the human and divine worlds.
   3. All religious activity was public and communal and carried out according to inherited traditions.

B. The Greeks of the Archaic Age interacted with the divine world through specific ritual actions.
   1. Prayers spoken aloud consisted of calling on the god, asserting a claim on the god's good will, and making a request.
   2. Both music and dance were a means of honoring the god and accompanied other forms of interaction with the divine.

3. Processions were a proclamation of divine and human honor with ramifications for the community.
4. The most important ritual action was animal sacrifice, either to accompany a request or as thanks for a benefit received.

C. The focus of ritual worship was the god's sanctuary, the sacred space devoted to worship of the god.
1. The altar was a necessary part of the sanctuary, the site where animal sacrifices could be offered.
2. The altar was separate from the temple, the dwelling for the god's statue and storage space to display votive offerings.
3. The god's sanctuary might also include a sacred grove, dormitories for pilgrims, and dining rooms for private clubs.
4. The location of a sanctuary varied according to the god's realm of concern.

D. Although most sanctuaries were located in the *polis*, some sanctuaries were located in places sacred to the god.
1. The sanctuary of the goddess Demeter at Eleusis attracted worshipers from all over the Greek world.
2. Oracles were usually associated with a specific location, such as the oracle of Apollo at Delphi.
3. The Pan-Hellenic Games united all Greeks in a common religious observance every four years in Olympia beginning in 776 B.C.E.
4. Time was calculated by *Olympiads* of four-year periods, instead of by the reigns of rulers.

E. Because Greece had no religious establishment, religious traditions were communicated by action and by word.
1. Children learned how to perform rituals by watching them performed by others.
2. Traditions about the gods were passed on through oral storytelling, either among individuals or by a poet to a group.
3. Mythic stories taught moral lessons, explained how the world worked, provided a common identity, and revealed the character of the gods.

**F.** Many mythic stories reflect a growing unease about the gods during the Archaic Age and a deepened sense of human insecurity.

   **1.** The famous pronouncement of the Delphic oracle, "Know yourself," was a reminder to know where you fit in to the cosmic order.

   **2.** The gods were believed to be jealous of their divine prerogatives, and they would lash out at human beings who presumed to rise above their station.

   **3.** Divine jealousy, or *nemesis*, was provoked by human success that led to complacency, then to *hubris*, impudent pride.

   **4.** Every human triumph potentially aroused a sense of guilt and raised the possibility of divine punishment.

**III.** Two works of the Archaic Age give a sense of the religious sentiments of the era and the attempt to create a consistent mythology.

   **A.** The two works are a series of songs known collectively as *The Homeric Hymns* and Hesiod's *Theogony*.

   **1.** Both works share the poetic meter employed in Homer's epics, the hexameter, with six metrical units to a line.

   **2.** Each metrical unit consists of a long syllable and two short ones (a *dactyl*) or two long syllables (a *spondee*).

   **3.** This meter, *dactylic hexameter*, was used in most long poetic works by the Greeks and Romans.

   **B.** *The Homeric Hymns*, from the 7th and 6th centuries B.C.E., provide a sense of the gods and the sentiments toward them.

   **1.** Some hymns are poetic renditions of well-known myths.

   **2.** Other hymns list titles and attributes of the gods and the rites and locations sacred to them.

   **3.** Other hymns are primarily songs of praise, similar to the biblical psalms.

   **4.** The hymns vary widely in length and are generally agreed to be the work of many poets.

   **5.** *The Homeric Hymns* represent the poets' attempts to offer new renditions of familiar stories, to honor the gods, and to gain renown.

   **C.** Hesiod's *Theogony* is a poem about the gods' origins that also attempts to systematize the relationships among them.

1. The *Theogony*, from about 740 B.C.E., is the work of a poet from Boetia usually identified as Hesiod.
2. Hesiod's poem bears a resemblance to Mesopotamian and Egyptian theogonies.
3. Hesiod's account tells how Zeus came to be king of the gods and guardian of the cosmic order.
4. His story is full of violence, with acts of incest, castration, patricide, and usurpation.
5. Each generation rebels against the one before it, only to have the next generation rebel against it in turn.
6. Ultimately, Zeus kills his father, Kronos, and marries Hera, who rules with Zeus as his queen.
7. Hesiod then catalogues the gods and demigods, providing a pocket portrait of each.

**D.** *The Homeric Hymns* and the *Theogony* reflect the elaborate mythology and imagery associated with the Greek pantheon in the Archaic Age.
   1. Both works bears witness to the multitude of gods and divine beings representing the realm of the sacred.
   2. *The Homeric Hymns* give a sense of pious regard for the gods and the voice of those who worshiped them.
   3. Hesiod's *Theogony* represents an attempt to bring order to the mythic tradition to create a unified and systematic account of the gods' genealogy.

## Essential Reading:

Jules Cashford, trans. *The Homeric Hymns.*

Hesiod and Theognis. *Hesiod: Theogony, Works and Days; Theognis: Elegies*, pp. 11–57.

Robin W. Winks and Susan P. Mattern-Parkes. *The Ancient Mediterranean World: From the Stone Age to A.D. 600*, pp. 58–74.

## Supplementary Reading:

E. R. Dodds. *The Greeks and the Irrational*, pp. 1–63.

H. D. F. Kitto. *The Greeks*, pp. 64–79.

Sarah Iles Johnston, ed. *Religions of the Ancient World: A Guide*, pp. 210–219.

**Questions to Consider:**

1. Why was the institution of the city-state central to Greek identity and the later development of ancient Greek culture?

2. What are some of the consequences of the belief that human achievements are likely to lead to divine jealousy? In what ways are similar ideas expressed in our own time?

# Lecture Thirty—Transcript

## Religious Culture in Archaic Greece

In our last session, we considered some of the religious attitudes and beliefs reflected in Homer's epic poems the *Iliad* and the *Odyssey*. In this session, we will consider the religious culture of the Archaic Age, a period of robust growth and development that established the basis for the Greek Enlightenment, and for the classical Greek culture.

Now, Greece emerged from the Dark Age beginning in the $8^{th}$ century B.C.E., once the population sharply increased and the shape of later Greek culture began to develop. The Archaic Age begins, therefore, about 800 B.C.E., and it continues until about 480 B.C.E. This was a period that saw the renewal, among other things, of international trade. We have some archaeological remains from about 900 B.C.E. that include artifacts that were apparently obtained in trade with other nations in the eastern Mediterranean, notably the Phoenicians, and this renewed contact is manifested in other, different ways.

For example, some scholars see Egyptian influence in Greece in the design of Greek temples, because like the temples of Egypt, the Greek temples are rectangular, and the roofs are supported by columns. They also see Egyptian influence in the production of standing statuary, with the human subjects presented in more or less static poses, as they were in early Greek sculpture.

The influence of Phoenicia is clear not only in certain archaeological discoveries, but also most clearly in the Greek alphabet, which adapts the Phoenician alphabet to become the basis for written Greek by the year 740 B.C.E.

We have the re-establishment of international trade, then, or at least trade with the other portions of the Mediterranean world, and we have population growth, and population growth led to the establishment of Greek colonies around the Mediterranean basin, again, because Greece is a maritime power. The establishment of Greek colonies outside of the Aegean area itself led to the question of what made a person Greek, and this is a question that persists throughout history in Greek civilization.

Increased growth and international contact led to a greater awareness of what we might call "Greek identity." Later, this results in a clear distinction between Greeks and non-Greeks, the Greeks and the "others," and the others are usually referred to as "barbarians"—in other words, those who do not speak Greek and are not part of the Greek world.

Now, one of the fundamental components of Greek society that begins to appear in the Archaic Age is the *polis*, the regional city-state ruled by a council of its citizens. Citizenship, in this period of Greece, is based on military service, specifically as a *hoplite*; a *hoplite* is an armored soldier who is armed with a spear and a short sword, and who carries a large, round shield called a *hoplon*. Landowning farmers could often afford a panoply of *hoplites*. So, these farmers would share the right to govern the *polis* in councils, and they also shared the responsibility for selecting the individuals who took on the more specialized responsibilities of government.

Now, the *polis* might be governed by a variety of systems, but each *polis* recognized the difference between those people who were citizens, who had the responsibility of the right of government, and the inferior position of those who were denied citizenship. Those who were denied citizenship included, of course, women of all classes, but also slaves, the poor who did not have land, and resident foreigners.

The *polis*, led by a council of citizens, also included buildings set aside for governance, other various kinds of public facilities, workshops for artisans, the *agora*—that is, a common marketplace for the exchange of goods, and temple districts, and they also, of course, shared surrounding agricultural regions. It was these agricultural regions around the *polis* itself whose produce supported the population of the *polis*.

The population of a *polis* might range from several thousand to a few hundred. The largest of the cities of Greece, the largest *polis*, was Athens, which may have had well over 100,000 inhabitants—not citizens, but inhabitants.

There was substantial regional variation among the *poleis*, then, across Archaic Greece. There was variation with respect to governance, the way that the people governed themselves or were governed by others in the *polis*. There was difference in dialect; so there were different versions of the Greek language spoken in different territories and in different *poleis*. There were different public and private activities, and, very often, there were quite different attitudes about life—the meaning and purpose of life, and how it should best be lived in the public sphere.

This variety, of course, was also reflected in religious culture. Each *polis* worshiped particular gods, and each *polis* had its own distinctive celebrations and its own distinctive festival calendar of such celebrations.

Now, despite this variety, there were certain religious presuppositions, certain beliefs, certain ritual actions that united all the people of Archaic Greece, and they shared—in general—a common, polytheistic religious culture. The Greek religious culture of the Archaic Age reflected the common ancient belief that what we moderns identified as the "sacred" on the one hand, and the "secular" on the other, were, in fact, inextricably intertwined. The general religious culture of the Archaic Age in Greece saw the sacred and the secular as intertwined, as more or less inextricable, as part of the same reality.

The Greeks of this period, then, believed that the natural world was alive with the presence of the sacred, and the sacred manifested itself in particular places and in very powerful ways, or in particular beings in very powerful ways—obviously, in spirits, for example, or in gods. Every aspect of life, then, that took place in this world throbbing with the sacred had its religious component. It catered to the sacred nature of reality as much as to the secular nature of reality.

Religious activities were undertaken to establish—or, more often, to maintain—social harmony, but also that equilibrium between the human and the divine world that is the goal of all religious activity. Most often, this harmony or equilibrium was established through actions that acknowledged the superiority of the gods and acknowledged the dutiful position of the human subjects who submitted to the will of the gods.

Virtually all religious activity in Archaic Greece was both public and communal. In other words, a person's life was lived not as the life of an individual, but as the life of a member of a family, or the member of a clan, or as a citizen of a *polis*, or as one of a people. So, in these cases, an individual acts as the member of a group, large or small, that is in relationship to the divine, with the sacred that permeates all of life.

One interacted with the divine world according to inherited traditions, to gain benefits not so much for the individual, but for the community—or at least for one of those small groups within the community. The focus of Greek religion, then, during the Archaic Age, was on the benefits that the gods would bestow upon individuals as members of large groups, not individuals per se.

Now, the Greeks of the Archaic Age interacted with the divine world through specific ritual actions—primarily prayer, dance and music, processions, and animal sacrifice—all familiar to us already from the series of lectures. Prayers were apparently spoken aloud, of course, so the gods could hear you, while the person praying stood with his or her arms spread.

Prayer consisted of calling on the god, asserting some claim on the god's good will, and then making a specific request. So, the gods are invoked rather simply and straightforwardly with a specific request, the way you might ask somebody in your own household for something.

Both music and dance were a means of praising and honoring the gods, and they formed an accompaniment to other forms of divine interaction. So, there might be music and dance accompanying prayer, but certainly accompanying religious processions as part of festival activities.

In fact, processions were often the public face of individual religious activity, a public proclamation of divine honor, but human honor as well, as the humans did obeisance to and worshiped their gods. The processions represented the fact that these public interactions, these individual actions on behalf of the group, had ramifications for the larger community, and those ramifications meant that spiritual benefits were bound not only to those who performed them, but to the groups to which they belonged.

I mentioned animal sacrifice. In the context of Archaic Age Greece, the animal sacrifice was usually a sheep or a goat. Often, the blood was allowed to seep into the ground. The blood and a portion of the meat were offered to the god, and usually animal sacrifice was part of a request for aid from the god—or perhaps as a thanksgiving offering for some benefit received already from the god.

The focus of ritual worship was the god's sanctuary, but this needs to be understood in the larger sense in Greece, just as it is in Egypt and in Mesopotamia. The god's sanctuary is the sacred space devoted to the worship of that god, and that includes the temple, but also, usually, an outside altar—wherever animal sacrifice is performed— and associated buildings and space in a "reserve," we might call it— a space, a territory, a property set aside for the use of the god and the gods' worshipers.

The altar, of course, was the most necessary part of the sanctuary because the altar was where sacrifice was offered to the god, and usually, the altar stood in front of the god's temple. Greek temples of this period were rectangular buildings, and they had stepped foundations—maybe representing the fact that it was necessary to move upward to approach the gods, or perhaps for more practical reasons, to raise them above the level of the street and surrounding ground—but it also carried the idea that the gods were, at least to a certain extent, "higher." You would go up to worship the god. You would go up to offer sacrifice or ask for things in prayer.

Greek temples, then, were rectangular buildings on stepped foundations. Their roofs were usually tiled and pitched, and they were supported by columns. So, you have that familiar triangular tiled roof held up by strong columns, and, usually, the roofs had decorated pediments. That is, the triangular space under the roof was decorated with some sort of scene honoring the god, or it represented some mythological situation reflecting the intentions and the specialization of the history of the god.

The temple was intended to protect the cult status of the god, and, again, this may reflect Egyptian influence—a standing statue of the god if the god is male, and a sitting statue of the god if the god is female—that is to say, a goddess—so that we had standing statues of male gods and sitting statutes of female goddesses.

The temple also provides a place to store and display votive gifts offered by worshipers—that is, various commemorations of benefits received from the god or goddess, offered by the worshipers, those benefited as a sign of their thanksgiving, as a sign of their honor, and also—to a large extent—as an advertisement for the gods' powers.

These votive gifts took on a variety of forms; for example, they might be statues of the god presented in various materials—stone, wood, or metal. They might be representations of body parts that were healed by the god's intervention; you might find a votive representation of a leg, a hand, an eye, an ear, or some other body part that had been healed. Other votive gifts were other, more common, goods—or perhaps some sort of produce from those who had less means to provide gifts of thanksgiving for the god.

All of these votive gifts, though, were placed within the precincts of the temple itself, and they represented not only the benefits that the people had received, but were also an advertisement for the honor and the power—the loving concern, if you will—of the god for his or her worshipers.

The temple could be quite small, in some cases, especially in the countryside, or, in a major *polis*, the temple could be very large—in some cases, large enough to seat several hundred people in an act of worship.

The location of the god's sanctuary in relation to the *polis* also varied. Usually, the location of the sanctuary reflected the god's realm of concern. Gods of the political order, for example, had sanctuaries in the center of a *polis*, while the sanctuaries of some other gods might be located a distance away, somewhere out in the countryside. Although most sanctuaries sacred to the gods were located within the individual *poleis*, some sanctuaries were located in places sacred to the god away from the city, and worshipers went to those temples or those sanctuaries to worship a particular god where that god was most comfortable and most at home.

A good example of this is the sanctuary dedicated to the goddess Demeter at Eleusis. Eleusis is to the northwest of Athens, and this is where the worshipers of Demeter would follow a long trail—called the "sacred way," a highway—to gather from all over the Greek world, to celebrate festivals sacred to Demeter, the goddess of grain. They, therefore, came out of their cities to go to where the goddess was particularly located—a place particularly sacred to her. We will talk more about Demeter in a later lecture.

Divine oracles—that is, oracles that would carry a message from the god, or who could determine a god's will as an answer to a "yes" or a "no" question—these oracles were usually also associated with specific locations; so we have the famous oracle of Apollo specifically at Delphi. It is the location that defines the oracle—in fact, more than with the association of Apollo, so the oracle at Delphi is an example of the sacred space that people had to travel to come to visit when they wished to consult the god.

Delphi was due west from the city of Thebes, and the oracle there was consulted by inquirers for divine insight into both the present—that is, the way things were, and how they were to deal with them—but also for insights into the future.

A very well known central religious festival, the Panhellenic Games, brought competitors, again, from all over the Greek *poleis* to a specific location, Olympia, every four years. This began in 776 B.C.E.

The games were a religious occasion. They were an expression of devotion to all the gods resident on Mount Olympus, and they were important enough so that any wars that might be taking place were suspended for a period of time, to allow the games to take place for all of the Greek *poleis* participating.

In fact, periods of time in Greece, at this time, were calculated in four-year "Olympiads," all reckoned from the year 776 B.C.E. Time was not reckoned according to the reigns of rulers, and this testifies not only to the importance of the games of Olympus, but also to their unifying nature—the fact that they unified Greece sufficiently that all Greeks in all of their scattered *poleis* all kept a calendar based on the same four-year rotation of the Olympic Games.

Since Greece had no religious establishment as such and no ruling class of priests as such, inherited religious traditions were communicated primarily through religious action and by the spoken word. So, children would learn how to perform rituals by watching them being performed by others, or they would take part in community festivals, to learn how and why those festivals were celebrated.

Meanwhile, traditions about the gods and the gods' relationship to human beings were passed on through oral storytelling, and this might happen on an individual basis, as one person tells a story to another—perhaps a father to his son—or it might take a more official and artistic form, as a poet recounted a story to a group. We have found that already in relation to the *Iliad* and the *Odyssey*.

Mythological stories were not only meant to provide information, but to also commonly teach moral lessons. They explained how the world worked, and they provided a sense of common identity for all the Greek people. Additionally, they gave their audience a clear sense of what the gods were like and what constituted humanity's relationship with the gods.

As it happened, many of these mythological stories reflected what we might call a growing unease about the gods in the Archaic Age— that is, a deepened sense of insecurity and helplessness in the face of gods who were sometimes hostile to human beings.

There's a famous oracle, the oracle of Apollo at Delphi, with the phrase, "Know yourself." We sometimes take this as an imperative for self-knowledge: Know whom you are, and know what you are capable of, but, in fact, originally, "Know yourself" was more of a reminder to the Greek person to know where he or she fit into the cosmic order. Another translation might be, "Know your place. Know how you fit in."

This is because the gods were not only superior to human beings, but they were also jealous of their divine prerogatives, and it was believed that the gods would lash out at any human being presumed to rise above his or her station—especially if they rose above their station in such a way that it brought dishonor on a god.

Sometimes, this divine jealousy was moralized as *nemesis*, which is loosely translated as "righteous indignation"—that is, the gods rightly becoming indignant at human presumption—but this divine jealousy was provoked by human success, because human success led to complacency. Human complacency led to *hubris*—that is, "impudent pride"—and then, impudent pride invited retaliation.

One quick example is the weaver Arachne, who decides that her weaving is of such a fine quality that she challenges the goddess Athena to a contest, and what's worse, in the contest, not only is her weaving better than Athena's, but what she makes is a portrait of all the various ways the gods have offended against and wronged human beings; so, Athena turns her into a spider. That's a good example of the divine jealousy that is moralized as righteous indignation. No, Athena is just angry because she lost.

In place of the quest for fame, then, in the Dark Age, we have a fear of forgetting one's place in the cosmic order. Every triumph potentially aroused a sense of guilt because it raised the possibility of punishment from some offended beauty, because, "You're getting above your place."

Now, there are two major poetic works of the Archaic Age that can give us a good sense of the religious sentiments of this era, and they are also an attempt to systemize some sort of consistent mythology. The two works are, first, a series of songs composed to honor the various gods, and these songs are known collectively as *The Homeric Hymns*, and then secondly, the *Theogony*, a poetic work attributed to Hesiod.

Both of these works date from the Greek Archaic Age, and both share the poetic meter also employed in Homer's epics, a meter called the "hexameter," with six feet or metrical units to a line. Each of the metrical units consists of a long syllable followed by two short syllables, a "dactyl," or two long syllables, a "spondee." These two different forms, the dactyl and the spondee, are alternated to provide some variety to a poem.

Usually, this particular meter is called "dactylic hexameter," and this was the meter for most of the long poetic works by the Greeks, and then later by the Romans—not only the *Iliad* and the *Odyssey*, but also Virgil's *Aeneid*. *The Homeric Hymns* also share this meter. They are usually dated to the seventh and sixth centuries B.C.E., and they provide some sense not only of who the gods were, but how the Greeks felt about them—the sense about the gods.

Some of these hymns, such as the "Hymn to Demeter," provide poetic renditions of fairly well known mythological stories, and, in this case, the story of Persephone, Demeter's daughter by the god Hades.

Other hymns are "aretologies," which list the titles and attributes of the gods, as well as the rites and locations that are sacred to those gods. Others describe a god's birth or origins, while others are primarily hymns of praise, similar to some of hymns that we find in the biblical book of Psalms.

The hymns also vary greatly in length—from three lines in the "Hymn to Demeter," to 580 lines in the "Hymn to Hermes." They are generally agreed to be the work of many different poets. Apart from their poetic beauty, *The Homeric Hymns* represent the poets' attempt to charm an audience with a new rendition of familiar stories, or to honor the gods, or even to gain fame for themselves. In the "Hymn to Apollo," we have the line, "Remember me in the time to come." That's in the "Hymn to Apollo," 3:166.

Another major poetic work of the Archaic Age is Hesiod's *Theogony*, a poem about the origins of the gods that also attempts to systematize the relationships among the gods. The *Theogony* dates to about 740 B.C.E., and it's the work of a poet from Boetia on the Greek mainland, usually identified as Hesiod. Hesiod was also the author of the *Works and Days*. That identification is often disputed.

Hesiod's story bears a resemblance to Mesopotamian and Egyptian theogonies we've already discussed, and this may not be, more or less, an inevitable result of the fact that Hesiod's story also begins in chaos, traces the generation of the elder gods, and finally culminates in the stories of the gods who were involved with human activities—so, it has a similar story to tell; it's not surprising, perhaps, that it resembles Egyptian and Mesopotamian stories that tell basically the same story in much the same way.

Hesiod's account is inspired by—and dedicated to—the Muses, the daughters of Zeus, and tells how their father Zeus came to be the king of the gods and guardian of the cosmic order. The story that Hesiod tells is, not surprisingly, full of violence. It recalls, in some ways, the story of Osiris and Seth, another violent story. It recalls the *Enuma Elish*, another violent story, and like them, it's full of violence, incest, castration, patricide, and usurpation.

The first new generations of beings give birth to creatures unlike themselves, and each generation rebels against the one before it—a son killing and displacing his father, only to have his son rebel against him, and displace him in turn. Ultimately, the god Zeus kills his father, Kronos, and marries his sister, Hera, and from that time on, she rules the cosmos with Zeus as his queen.

Once Hesiod has established the origins of the cosmic order, he catalogs the gods and demigods who inhabit it, and he provides a pocket portrait of each of those gods. I will be talking more about the *Theogony* in the next lecture.

For the moment, though, *The Homeric Hymns* and Hesiod's *Theogony* both reflect and elaborate mythology and the rich imagery that are already associated at this time with the Greek pantheon in the Archaic Age.

Both of these poetic works bear witness to the multitude of gods, demigods, and other divine, supernatural beings that represent the realm of the sacred in the Greek tradition. *The Homeric Hymns*, in particular, give a sense of a pious regard for the gods, and they provide the living voice of those who worshiped those gods, as it speaks to us across centuries in these songs.

Hesiod's *Theogony* is less successful as a poetic work, quite honestly, but it represents an attempt to bring order to the inherited conglomerate of mythological tradition, somehow to create a unified and systematic account of the gods that might appeal to a rational person.

Now, in our next session, we will look in more detail at Greek accounts of creation, and we will include an account of the Greek version of the primordial flood.

# Lecture Thirty-One

## Greece—How Things Came to Be

**Scope:**

The Greek story of creation as it is presented in Hesiod's *Theogony* resembles creation stories from Egypt and Mesopotamia. Creation begins when Chaos spontaneously gives rise to divine beings that, in turn, create new beings through sexual generation. Earth and Heaven give birth to the Titans, the Cyclopes, and a race of monsters. One Titan, Kronos, castrates Heaven and becomes king, only to be deposed in turn by his son Zeus. Zeus establishes the cosmic order but has an ambivalent attitude toward humanity, punishing men by creating the race of women. The Greek story of the flood as it appears in a Roman version in Ovid's *Metamorphoses* has many points of contact with the Mesopotamian stories of Atrahasis and Utnapishtim, as well as the biblical story of Noah. Points of similarity and difference in the Greek creation and flood stories provide insight into Greek religious culture.

## Outline

I. The story of creation as it appears in Hesiod's *Theogony* resembles creation stories from Egypt and Mesopotamia.

  **A.** The poem begins with an invocation of the Muses, giving Hesiod's account a flavor of divine revelation.

    **1.** The story begins with Chaos, not associated here with the waters of the sea, as it was in Egypt and Mesopotamia.

    **2.** Gaea, Earth, appears, then Tartaros, the Depths, appears *in* the earth, the foundation for all creation.

    **3.** The third created being is Eros, Love, whose existence is essential to creation by sexual generation.

    **4.** The last cosmic elements to appear are Nyx, Night, and Erebus, Darkness, who give birth to Day and Space.

  **B.** Gaea gives birth to offspring that constitute the natural and divine context for human existence.

    **1.** Gaea bears Ouranos, Heaven; Earth and Heaven are the boundaries of the divine realm.

    **2.** Gaea produces mountains and seas, the first pleasant, the other "barren."

**3.** Finally, Gaea mates with her son Ouranos and gives birth to 12 children, the Titans.

**4.** Gaea and Ouranos next engender the race of Cyclopes, then three monstrous sons whom Ouranos imprisons in the earth's depths.

**5.** Gaea incites her Titan son Kronos to punish Ouranos for this wicked deed.

**6.** Kronos castrates Ouranos and throws his genitals across the earth, engendering the Furies, the Giants, and Aphrodite.

**7.** Night produces offspring, states of mind that oppress human beings or cosmic forces that work against them.

**C.** The story continues with Kronos, now king of creation, and his sister Rhea, who bears him 12 children.

   **1.** Kronos eats each child at its birth because of a prophecy that one of his children would usurp his throne.

   **2.** Rhea hides her 12th child, Zeus, and instead, gives Kronos a stone that he devours.

   **3.** Grown to adulthood, Zeus overcomes Kronos, releases his siblings, and becomes ruler over the gods.

**D.** The rest of the poem lists divinities, their partners, and offspring, with some attention to "how things got to be how they are now."

   **1.** The Titan Prometheus brings fire to humanity and tricks Zeus into choosing the worse portion of the sacrifice for the gods.

   **2.** Zeus punishes Prometheus by chaining him to a rock until the Titan is freed by Heracles.

   **3.** To punish human men, Zeus sends them Pandora, the first woman, who brings a box full of ills for humanity.

**E.** The question arises: What religious ideas are at work in this explanation of "how things came to be the way they are now"?

   **1.** The gods who are involved in the lives of human beings are several generations removed from creation.

   **2.** The gods that now rule are a part of the cosmic order and, thus, subject to forces they cannot control.

   **3.** Since creation, parents are not necessarily the same sort of beings as their offspring.

      **4.** The gods can be ambivalent or even hostile to their own offspring or the offspring of other gods.

      **5.** There is a pattern of hostility between generations, with each new generation rebelling against the previous one.

**II.** The gods' hostility toward humanity reaches a climax with the Greek version of the story of the flood.

  **A.** Book I of Ovid's *Metamorphoses*, a 1st-century C.E. Latin retelling of Roman mythology, provides the Greek story, using the gods' Latin names.

      **1.** Ovid places the story in the context of the succession of world ages that steadily decline from the Golden Age to the Iron Age.

      **2.** Iron Age humanity is characterized by brutishness; thus, the gods decide to destroy humanity.

  **B.** The gods gather in council to decide how to cleanse the earth of the crimes of human beings.

      **1.** Jupiter (or Jove, the Roman equivalent of Zeus) has traveled the earth in disguise and been an eyewitness to the depravity of humanity.

      **2.** Jupiter argues that the crimes of humanity deserve punishment and threaten the stability of the cosmos.

      **3.** The gods wonder what will happen without human beings to bring them offerings, but Jupiter assures them that he will provide a new race of humanity.

      **4.** Jupiter decides to send a flood to inundate the world and drown all human beings.

  **C.** There are points of contact with the flood stories of Atrahasis and Ut-napishtim in Mesopotamia and Noah in Israel.

      **1.** Like the story of Atrahasis, the story of the flood in *Metamorphoses* is part of the longer story of the creation of humanity.

      **2.** As with the Mesopotamian stories, the gods gather in council and give assent to the chief god's plan.

      **3.** As in the story of Noah, humanity is destined for destruction because of depravity, but a renewed human race is planned.

    **4.** Ovid's version is notable for the gods' reluctance to destroy humanity and the careful deliberations among them.

**D.** The flood is sent without any regard for the preservation of humanity beforehand.

    **1.** No human being is singled out before the flood to prepare a means of survival or to save other life.

    **2.** There is no preparation of a boat, no gathering of animals in couples, no saving of possessions or lies to the neighbors.

    **3.** Jupiter sends rain, while Neptune (Poseidon) creates an earthquake to send a torrent to sweep humanity away.

    **4.** Ovid dwells on the effects of the flood and the resulting famine on humanity and animals.

    **5.** One human couple, Deucalion and Pyrrha, survive by chance when their boat runs aground on Mt. Parnassus.

    **6.** Like Noah, the couple is unmatched in righteousness.

    **7.** Deucalion and Pyrrha make landfall in the midst of the flood, which only later subsides at Jupiter's command.

    **8.** As in the other flood stories, the survivors' first impulse after making landfall is to offer a sacrifice to the gods.

**E.** As in the other stories, after the survivors sacrifice, they gain the attention of the god.

    **1.** In the other flood stories, the gods are pleased by the sacrifice.

    **2.** Here, Jupiter discovers that Deucalion and Pyrrha have survived and knows they are righteous.

    **3.** When Jupiter commands the flood waters to recede, they reveal a desolated earth.

**F.** Ovid's story ends in the establishment of a new relationship between the gods and humanity and repopulation of the earth.

    **1.** Deucalion and Pyrrha consult the oracle of Delphi, who cryptically tells them to throw "the bones of your great mother" (that is, stones) behind them.

    **2.** When they do so, the stones slowly turn into human beings.

    **3.** As a result, the human race is now hearty and makes its living from working the soil.

4. The animals are brought back into existence by spontaneous generation.

5. Deucalion and Pyrrha are not the parents of the renewed humanity, as Noah and his wife are.

6. As in the other stories, the flood institutes a new situation for humanity.

7. No mention is made of the fate of Deucalion and Pyrrha, who appear to return to their previous lives but in a new creation.

8. The various flood stories are clearly all related, but what is most significant are the differences between the stories and what they reveal about their different religious cultures.

**Reading:**

Hesiod and Theognis. *Hesiod: Theogony, Works and Days; Theognis: Elegies*, pp. 11–57.

Ovid. *Metamorphoses*, book I.

W. K. C. Guthrie. *The Greeks and Their Gods*, pp. 27–112.

**Questions to Consider:**

1. The story of creation in Hesiod's *Theogony* is in part a story about incest and intergenerational violence. What ideas about the nature of creation and human existence do these stories seem to reflect?

2. What are the consequences of thinking about successive ages of human existence as representing a steady trend downward, rather than a trend upward?

# Lecture Thirty-One—Transcript
## Greece—How Things Came to Be

In our last session, we considered Greek religious culture during the Archaic Age, when the foundations for later Greek society and culture were first established. In this session, we will look at the story of creation as it unfolds in Hesiod's *Theogony* and other accounts, and we will look at the Greek version of the flood.

Now, the story of creation as it appears in Hesiod's *Theogony* covers familiar ground since its narrative, in many respects, resembles the creation stories told in Egypt and in Mesopotamia. The poem begins with an invocation of the Muses; the Muses were the nine daughters of Zeus who inspired artistic creation, and this invocation is not only a formality, but it also gives Hesiod's account something of the flavor of divine revelation. He calls upon these divine figures to help him talk about the origins of the divine and human world.

Once again, we find the story of creation begins in chaos—but chaos, in this case, is not associated with the waters of the sea. You remember that in the creation narratives in Egypt and in Mesopotamia, chaos was represented by the waters of the sea, but here it is not, perhaps because the Greeks were seafarers who respected but did not fear the sea as such.

Next, we are told Gaea, the Earth, appears—not she is born or is generated, but that she appears—and then, Tartaros, the Depths, appears in the earth; so, again, instead of the waters being the fundamental substance of creation, the place where everything takes place—here, the earth appears to be the foundation of all creation.

Gaea is described as: "firm, the standing place for all the gods," and the idea of a firm standing place for all the gods might recall to us the Benben, the little pyramid of earth where Amun stood to create at the beginning of his creation story in the Egyptian tradition.

After Gaea and Tartaros, the Depths, the third created being is, perhaps surprisingly, Eros, Love. In other words, the third created being is the principle of erotic attraction between male and female. Now, this makes a certain amount of sense because this erotic attraction between male and female is essential to the rest of the creative process in the sense that that creative process continues, really eternally, through sexual generation. The last elements to appear from cosmic Chaos are Night, and Erebus—that is, Darkness—and in the first act of sexual generation, Night and Darkness give birth to Day and Ether—that is, Space.

Gaea, Earth, is the mother of all creation from this point on, and she gives birth to a range of offspring that constitute the natural and the divine context for human existence. For example, next, Gaea spontaneously gives birth to Ouranos, Heaven; Ouranos becomes the resting place for the gods, just as Earth is the resting place for human beings. Between Earth and Heaven, we find the boundaries of the divine realm.

Gaea, then, produces the natural features of the Earth and, particularly, those natural features that were most familiar to the Greeks—mountains and seas. On the one hand, the mountains are considered to be pleasant and fertile. They are the realm of nymphs, but the sea, on the other hand, is "barren," because it bears no produce—although, of course, the Greeks knew well that it was alive with various creatures below the surface.

Finally, Gaea mates with her offspring Ouranos and gives birth to 12 children, six male and six female. This is the race of Titans. The last Titan, the twelfth, is a son, Kronos. This, however, is not the end of the offspring of Gaea.

Next, Gaea and Ouranos engender between them the insolent race of Cyclopes. Cyclopes are giants who are also mighty craftsman, and then, there are a series of three monstrous sons, each one with 50 heads and 100 arms. Ouranos is horrified by their appearance, and Ouranos imprisons them in the depths of the earth, in Tartaros, within Gaea. This means that Gaea, instead of being able to give birth to these monstrous offspring, is once again stuck with them.

The womb of the earth is swollen with these monstrous offspring, and Gaea, in her discomfort and in her outrage, incites her Titan sons to punish their father, Ouranos, for this wicked deed that he has committed. But the five Titan sons are afraid of their father, and only one of them—the sixth, Kronos—is willing to take on his father and destroy him.

What Kronos does is to destroy Ouranos by destroying his virile power. Kronos castrates Ouranos with a sickle, and then he throws his father's genitals across the face of the earth. In this way, Gaea is impregnated once again; now, she gives birth to two different varieties of beings: the Furies on the one hand, and the Giants on the other. Then, Ouranos's genitals fall into the sea, and a foam is produced as they hit the surface and sink into the sea. From the foam rendered by the severed genitals of Ouranos, Aphrodite, the goddess of love, appears and arises from the foam. This is an image made very famous by Botticelli's "Birth of Venus."

In the meantime, Night also produces a host of new offspring. Most of them are states of mind that oppress human beings, or in some cases, cosmic forces that will work against human beings. Night, apparently, is not a good friend to humanity.

Hesiod next lists the offspring of the Titans, but the story really continues with Kronos because Kronos is now king of creation, and his sister, Rhea, his consort, is forced to bear his children. Rhea gives birth to 11 children, but Kronos eats each one of his children at its birth, and he does this because of a prophecy given to him. He was told that one of his children would overcome him and usurp his throne as king of the cosmos.

After losing her first 11 children in this way, Rhea hides her twelfth child, Zeus, from the moment that he is born. She hides him from Kronos and instead gives Kronos a stone wrapped in swaddling clothes, which Kronos immediately swallows whole.

In the meantime, the child, Zeus, is hidden on the island of Crete. He is placed under the protection of a group of nymphs, and when the child cries in his infancy, the nymphs make a great deal of noise so that Kronos will not hear him.

Later, once he has grown to adulthood, Zeus does indeed overcome his father, Kronos. He kills him and slits open his belly, and when he does so, much as with the story of Red Riding Hood, his siblings—Zeus's brothers and sisters who were swallowed by Kronos—are able to escape their father's belly. Now, however, they are fully grown, and they join Zeus as the 12 Olympian gods.

This is the story of how Zeus became the father and greatest of all the gods, because he is the one who conquered and overcame his despotic father, Kronos, and now he rules over the gods and over humanity, with his sister, Hera, as his queen.

Now, once Hesiod has established the divine order in Heaven and on Earth in this way, the rest of the surviving part of the poem lists divinities, their partners and their offspring, and a certain amount of attention is given to "how things came to be the way they are now" for human beings.

Hesiod tells us that the great benefactor of humanity in its early years was a Titan, the Titan Prometheus. It is Prometheus who brought fire to humanity from Heaven, and thereby benefits them by providing them with a source of warmth and a means of cooking their food.

It's also Prometheus, the Titan, who tricked Zeus into choosing the worst portion of the sacrificial victim for the gods. He did this by wrapping the portion for the gods in fat, and Zeus said, "Oh, that looks good. I'll take that," and that left behind the meat, the more desirable portion of the victim, for human beings to consume.

Zeus is not happy with Prometheus, as you can imagine after these two offenses against the dignity of the gods, and he chains Prometheus to a rock. Each day, Prometheus is spread-eagled on this rock, and each day his liver is eaten by an eagle. Each night, to make sure that the torture continues, his liver grows back, only to be consumed again by the eagle the following day. This happens continuously until, eventually, Prometheus is rescued by the semi-divine hero, Heracles.

On the other hand, Zeus does not let humanity get away with benefiting from the gifts provided to it by Prometheus, so he decides to punish humanity—which, incidentally, at this point is composed entirely of men. Zeus has the divine blacksmith and craftsman, Hephaestus, make Pandora, a woman whose name means, "all gifts." Pandora is the first woman, and she brings with her to the Earth and to the world of men a box filled with ills for humanity.

Now, Hesiod cannot refrain from arguing at this point that it was not so much the box of ills that was the punishment for humanity, but rather the woman herself. The woman herself is the punishment for man because women love to share men's prosperity, but when bad days come, they are no help to them at all.

On the other hand, Hesiod points out that a single man has no one to care for him when he is sick, and a single man leaves his goods not to offspring, but to some distant relatives. Apparently, Zeus, by creating Pandora, has punished men by putting them into a double bind with regard to women. They can't live with them, and, apparently, they can't live without them. Now, as with any ancient cosmogony, we may reasonably ask what religious motifs and ideas are at work on this particular explanation of how things came to be the way they are now.

First, the gods who are involved in the lives of human beings are not the agents of creation. This is also true, of course, in Egypt and Mesopotamia. The gods who are involved with human beings and human concerns are, in fact, several generations removed from creation, and creation itself is not part of a plan or an intention by the gods, but it is something that just happens, and especially in the account of Hesiod, it appears to happen spontaneously, more or less as a product of natural forces, to the extent that we can talk about "natural forces" before creation begins. There is no apparent reason for the process of creation, though.

Second, and as follows, the gods that now rule the cosmos are not the originators of the cosmos. Instead, the gods that now rule the cosmos are a part of the cosmic order, and, therefore, they are subject to the certain cosmic forces that others are also subject to. Like human beings, they are subject to forces that they cannot control. They are not all-powerful. Their power has very definite limits, in fact.

Third, from the time of creation, parents are not necessarily the same sort or order of beings as their offspring. In fact, the 12 gods born to Rhea and Kronos are the first beings who give birth to beings like themselves. In other words, the gods become mothers and fathers of other gods, but even the gods have children who are not like them. Some of them are demigods and heroes who have one divine parent and one human parent, and we find in Greek mythology that the gods can be ambivalent and even hostile to their own offspring, especially ambivalent and often hostile to the offspring of other gods. We see, for example, that Hera is not at all polite or supportive towards Heracles, the son of Zeus.

Moreover, these stories show us a pattern of hostility between one generation and another. Each new generation in Hesiod's account rebels against and—overcomes—the previous generation. There's a clear pattern of violence, here, violence within these divine families with attacks against fathers, conspiracy between spouses, incest, and incestuous rape. All of this divine violence only makes the human situation seem even more precarious. Since the gods are violent towards each other, they have no reason to love humanity, and, in fact, they have often, in the past, acted against humanity as a whole as well as against individual human beings. The gods are not necessarily friends with humanity.

Now, this same hostility, the same hostility between the gods and humanity, continues into later ages, and it reaches something of a climax with the Greek version of the story of the worldwide flood, the devastating flood that destroys almost all of humanity.

Now, in this case, the fullest account of the flood in the Greek tradition is actually found in a Latin work. It appears in Book one of Ovid's *Metamorphoses*. This is a 1st-century CE Latin retelling of Roman mythology, but this Roman mythology is largely taken over from the Greeks, so I will refer to Ovid's story in the *Metamorphoses* in order to give the account that is very close to the account in the Greek tradition—although I will also use the Latin names for the Greek gods, just to make things clearer, or perhaps more confusing.

Ovid, the Latin author, places the story of the flood in the larger context of the events that surround the creation of the cosmos; he also places it within the context of a succession of world ages—from the Golden Age, to the Silver Age, to the Bronze Age, and to the Iron Age, although the Bronze Age and the Iron Age are also archaeological eras. Of course, Ovid is not talking about these ages in that sense, and this will become clear.

The first age is the Golden Age. This is ruled by Saturn, the Latin name for Kronos. During this time, all of humanity is noble and lives together in peace. The natural world was abundant. It was always springtime, and the earth grew produce spontaneously, so there was no need for men and women to till the soil as farmers.

The Golden Age was followed by the Silver Age, and this was the first of the ages ruled over by Jove, or Zeus. This saw the creation of the four seasons. Eternal spring was succeeded by the four seasons of the agricultural year as they now exist. This also saw, therefore, the first agriculture and the appearance of domesticated cattle, as well as the invention of human shelter, because now, of course, the weather changes during the year, and it is necessary for human beings to keep themselves warm.

Next is the Bronze Age. The Bronze Age saw a fiercer attitude among human beings who were dedicated to warfare, but although they were violent, they were not vicious. Their warfare was violent—but without the kind of hostility towards one another that is typical of later, more corrupt ages.

Finally comes the Iron Age, and humanity during this time was not only vicious, but brutish and ignorant. The crimes of humanity during the Iron Age accumulate until the gods feel the only solution is to destroy humanity.

The gods, therefore, gather in council. They come together in the highest Heaven to hear Jove's condemnation of humanity, and to decide how best to cleanse the earth of the crimes that human beings have committed.

Jove—that is, Zeus—Jove himself has traveled the earth in disguise as a human being, and he has been an eyewitness to the depravity that now characterizes humanity. He says, "You would think that men had sworn allegiance to crime." Jove argues that not only the crimes of humanity deserve punishment, but that they threaten the very stability of the entire cosmos. They are a form of chaos that threatens to metastasize and destroy the entire cosmic order. As Jove says, "The cancer is incurable."

The gods, not surprisingly, support their king, but they do wonder among themselves what will happen to them without human beings to bring them offerings, sacrifices of animals, and other goods. However, Jove reassures them. He says that he will provide a new race of humanity, created by supernatural means, and that this new race of humanity will worship and provide for the gods.

After rejecting destruction by fire—it occurs to Jove that it's possible fire might flare up and consume the whole creation—Jove decides to send a flood to inundate the world, and thereby drown all human beings.

Now, at this point, we can already see points of clear contact with flood stories of the Near East, flood stories of Atrahasis and Utnapishtim in Mesopotamia, and the story of Noah in Israel. Like the story of Atrahasis, the story of the flood in *Metamorphoses* is part of a much longer story of the creation of humanity and the gods' attempt to contain humanity.

As with the Mesopotamian stories, the gods gather in council, and they give assent to the chief god's plan—although we note that the Greek gods anticipate the loss of sacrifices from human beings; this is something that only occurs to the Mesopotamian gods after the fact. As in the story of Noah, humanity is destined for destruction because of its depravity. Its wickedness surpasses all bounds and calls for its destruction by a just god, but—at the same time—the flood is considered to be a means of cleansing, a means of providing for a renewed humanity that is already planned.

Ovid's version of the story is notable for the gods' reluctance to destroy humanity and the careful deliberation that precedes the flood. This is especially so in comparison to the Mesopotamians' story, where the gods seem to be carried off, carried away, by their anger against humanity.

In the story, in Ovid's *Metamorphoses*, the flood is sent without any regard for the preservation of humanity beforehand, and this is probably its most distinctive feature. In distinction to the other flood stories, that is, there is no human being or person singled out beforehand, before the flood, to prepare a means of survival. There is no attempt to save other human life through that person, or animal life through that person, as there is in the other stories we've reviewed; so there is no preparation of a boat, no gathering of animals into couples, no saving of possessions, and no lies to tell the neighbors, as in the Mesopotamian stories.

Jupiter—that is, Jove, or Zeus—sends down rain from heaven to create the flood, while his brother Neptune—that is the Latin name for "Poseidon"—creates an earthquake, and that earthquake sends the waters overflowing the banks, and the torrent sweeps away all humanity and all of humanity's works. Ovid tells us, after the flood, "All was seas without shores."

Unlike the near Eastern stories, Ovid dwells on the effects of the destruction on humanity and animals, not only from the inundation itself, but from the famine that follows it—much more suffering, much more anguish among humanity, here, than in the other stories.

There's one couple—a man named Deucalion and a woman named Pyrrha—who survive the flood by chance. They survive when their boat runs aground on Mount Parnassus, just north of Delphi. This was a mountain that was sacred to Apollo and the Muses.

Like Noah, this couple is unmatched in righteousness. Deucalion, Ovid tells us, is the best and most upright among men, whereas Pyrrha is the most pious among women. Deucalion and Pyrrha make landfall in the midst of the flood. It's only later that it recedes at Jupiter's command. In the other stories, the flood recedes and leaves the survivors' craft stranded on a mountain by the receding waters.

Like Atrahasis, like Ut-napishtim, like Noah, Deucalion's and Pyrrha's first impulse after making landfall is to offer worship in thanksgiving for surviving the flood, and they offer a sacrifice.

Also as in the other stories, after the survivors' act of worship, they gain the attention of the god responsible for the flood. In the story of Atrahasis and Ut-napishtim, the gods are attracted by the sweet smell of the sacrifice, and they prevent the chief god from sharing in the sacrifice because he had prompted them to try to destroy humanity. In the story of Noah, Noah's sacrifice pleases the Lord, and it's a sign of his pious regard for the Lord and his thanksgiving after being allowed to survive the flood.

Here, in the story Ovid tells, Jupiter discovers that only Deucalion and Pyrrha have survived the flood out of all humanity, but Jupiter also knows, as Ovid tells us, that both were guiltless, both are true worshipers of God. Therefore, when Jupiter commands the floodwaters to recede, Deucalion and Pyrrha are the only survivors of the flood—and when the floodwaters recede, they reveal a desolated earth.

Like all the flood stories we've reviewed, Ovid's version ends in a new relationship established between the gods and humanity—

leading, of course, to the repopulation of the earth. Deucalion and Pyrrha seek the will of the gods by consulting the oracle of Delphi—rather surprising, perhaps, in this context that they do not go to the gods themselves, do not interact with the gods—as Atrahasis, Ut-napishtim, and Noah did. They do what any Greek seeking the will of the gods would do, which is to go to the oracle at Delphi.

The oracle tells them to "throw behind you the bones of your great mother." This is one of those somewhat enigmatic pronouncements that were supposed to be typical of the Delphic oracle, but Deucalion and Pyrrha figure it out. They soon realize that when the oracle tells them to "throw behind you the bones of your great mother," the oracle is telling them, in fact, to throw the stones of Earth behind them—Earth, Gaea, being the great mother of all living things.

Thus, this is what they do. As they walk down the mountain, they slowly throw stones over their shoulders, and the stones they throw slowly soften, and they grow, and they turn into human beings. The stones thrown by Deucalion turn into men, and the stones thrown by Pyrrha turn into women. As a result, the human race—as we now know it—is hardy and gains its nourishment as the result of working the soil. In other words, human beings are now fed by their true mother, Gaea, the Earth.

The animals, on the other hand, are brought back into existence not by a deliberate action of the gods, or by human beings, but by spontaneous generation since the Greeks believe that organic life arose from spontaneous actions of the Earth. In this case, the animals appear as the wet Earth warms and dries in the sun, after the flood.

Like Ut-napishtim and his wife, Deucalion and Pyrrha are not the natural parents of the new humanity—that is, the way, for example, that Noah and his wife are the ancestors of all human beings, through their three sons and their wives. As in the other flood stories, a new situation has been instituted for humanity as a result of the flood—although here, the new situation is really more implied than explicit.

Here, the new situation has to do with the new nature of the new humanity. In the other stories, it's a covenantal vow, or in the Mesopotamian stories, a fleeting promise from a fickle god, and in Ovid's story, there is no mention made of the ultimate fate of Deucalion and Pyrrha after the flood, but they certainly are not whisked away, like Ut-napishtim and his wife, to the edges of the world. Rather—like Noah and his wife, and their family—it appears that Deucalion and Pyrrha return to their previous life, but their previous life lived out in the midst of a new creation for which they are partly responsible.

It seems clear that these stories from Mesopotamia, Israel, and Greece are all related in some way, but what is most significant are the differences between them, because these differences tell us a great deal about the religious cultures that spawned them and, therefore, about their ideas about the gods, about humanity, about creation, and about the relationships among them.

Now, in our next session, we will talk about the figure of the goddess in Greek religious culture, and I will concentrate on three figures in particular: the goddess Athena, the goddess Demeter, and the goddess Aphrodite.

# Lecture Thirty-Two
## Greece—The Goddess

**Scope:**
Although goddesses in polytheistic religious cultures often have associations with fertility, most of them develop beyond this primary identity. This is the case in Greece, where goddesses represent a wide range of female activity. Athena, goddess of practical wisdom, is a patron of the arts of civilized society in manufacturing and household crafts. She is also the voice of wisdom in the war council. Demeter is the goddess of the cultivated earth and its crops. She appears primarily in the role of grieving mother in the myth of Persephone and Hades, a story that explains the cycle of the seasons. Aphrodite is the goddess of erotic love and the most beautiful of the goddesses. She is portrayed as an active and generous lover, although she may express her anger by inducing *lover's madness*. These three goddesses indicate the many different ways the Greeks thought about the feminine aspect of the divine.

## Outline

I. Goddesses in polytheistic religious cultures often originate as fertility deities, but their significance extends beyond fertility.

   A. Isis is associated with the fertility of the Nile Valley in connection with Osiris, his death, and return to life.

      1. Isis is a loving wife to Osiris, a grieving widow at this death, and protectress of Horus, the divine Pharaoh.

      2. Isis gradually acquired other associations and power until she was a dominant goddess in her own right.

   B. We see a similar process at work in Mesopotamia with the goddess Inanna/Ishtar.

      1. Inanna's erotic connection with Dumuzi leads, in time, to her dominion over heaven and earth.

      2. Her sexuality leads to her association with natural disasters, the frenzy of battle, and divine retribution.

   C. In Greece, the character of the gods and goddesses developed over time, as one religious culture collided with another.

      1. Some Greek goddesses have little connection with fertility, or those connections are muted.

    **2.** Even goddesses with clear connections to fertility manifest those connections in diverging ways.

**II.** Athena, goddess of the virtues associated with Greek civilization, shows a markedly Aegean character.

    **A.** Athena seems to have originated in Minoan and Mycenaean culture as a goddess of fortresses.

        **1.** The goddess was earth-based and associated with fertility but also with birds and snakes.

        **2.** The goddess was associated with bluffs and the location of fortresses and, thus, also with fortresses and cities.

        **3.** The association with fortresses may explain Athena's identity as a warrior, or she may be related to an Indo-European warrior goddess.

    **B.** Athena was patron goddess of Athens and was associated with cities in general and with the civilized arts.

        **1.** Her role as protective deity of Athens probably stems from an association with the Acropolis.

        **2.** In mythology, Athena's patronage of the city was the result of a contest between her and Poseidon to give the most useful gift.

        **3.** Poseidon created a saltwater spring, while Athena created an olive tree.

        **4.** Athena's gift was deemed more useful, and olive oil became the economic staple for Athens.

        **5.** Athena was patroness of civilization and culture, administrative government, and the family.

    **C.** Athena is also the goddess of the practical wisdom that enables a person to get things done.

        **1.** She sprang from Zeus's head when Hephaestus struck it with a hammer to relieve the god's headache.

        **2.** Athena fosters the knowledge that makes civilized life possible, as both domestic and manufacturing arts.

    **D.** Athena is also a warrior goddess, depicted dressed in battle-gear with a spear and shield.

        **1.** Athena's interest is not in battle itself but in military skill, strategy, and tactics.

        **2.** She was associated with several Greek heroes whom she admired for their strength, skill, and cunning.

**E.** Athena was a virgin goddess, one of only three immune to the power of Aphrodite.

    **1.** Athena's virginity allows her to maintain independence and an equal footing with men.

    **2.** Athena is proud of her beauty and vies with Aphrodite and Hera to be declared the most beautiful by Paris.

    **3.** Even so, Athena does not use her beauty to influence either gods or men.

**III.** Demeter was the goddess of the plowed earth, the goddess of grain, and the patroness of agriculture.

    **A.** Demeter was prominent as a mother but gained that status only reluctantly.

        **1.** She spurned Poseidon's advances and disguised herself as a mare.

        **2.** Poseidon then raped her in the form of a stallion, and she gave birth to twins.

        **3.** Demeter also spurned Zeus, who then had intercourse with her in the form of a bull.

        **4.** Their daughter Kore was Demeter's dearest child.

    **B.** Demeter's cultic importance arose from the myth about Hades's abduction of Kore.

        **1.** When Kore disappeared, a distraught Demeter sought her all over the earth.

        **2.** During her wanderings, the earth became barren and yielded no produce.

        **3.** For a time, Demeter served as a nurse in the household of King Celeus in Eleusis.

        **4.** Zeus sent Hermes to Hades to demand he return Kore, but Hades gave Kore pomegranate seeds to eat before restoring her to Demeter.

        **5.** As a result, Kore could return to her mother for only a part of each year.

    **C.** This story has affinities with other fertility myths in which a goddess mourns the loss of a loved one to the underworld.

        **1.** Eleusis became the primary cultic site for the worship of Demeter and later became a center of a mystery religion devoted to her.

        **2.** Most of the mystery religions had their origins in fertility rituals.

**IV.** The Greek goddess of erotic love was "Golden Aphrodite."

   **A.** Aphrodite was one of the most popular and widely worshiped Greek deities.

      **1.** Aphrodite was related to Near Eastern goddesses whose association with fertility has strong sexual overtones.

      **2.** Aphrodite also shares many attributes with the Indo-European goddess Dawn.

      **3.** Even with these similarities to other goddesses, Aphrodite remains unique in many respects.

   **B.** Aphrodite's association with fertility makes her the source of abundant life, inspiring growth of plants and animals.

      **1.** Aphrodite's connection with the cycle of the seasons appears in stories about the deaths of her lovers Anchises and Adonis.

      **2.** Aphrodite has an affinity for birds and for sweet flavors and fragrances that stimulate sexual desire.

      **3.** Aphrodite is associated with the rhythms that govern organic life and, thus, with cosmic cycles.

      **4.** Despite her chronic infidelity, Aphrodite was also a patroness of the welfare of the family.

   **C.** Chief among Aphrodite's divine attributes was her unparalleled beauty.

      **1.** Her beauty was part of her essence, and because it was divine beauty, it was literally stunning to behold.

      **2.** Aphrodite's essential beauty was unmistakable even when she was in disguise.

      **3.** In art, Aphrodite is typically depicted adorning herself, bathing, or dressing.

      **4.** After the $5^{th}$ century B.C.E., Aphrodite was usually depicted nude in statuary.

      **5.** The goddess is called "Golden Aphrodite," perhaps because gold is bright, is beautiful, and retains its beauty forever.

   **D.** Aphrodite's beauty is the physical manifestation of her powerful sexuality.

      **1.** Aphrodite's nature derives from her origins: She was born from the foam created when Kronos tossed his father's severed genitalia into the sea.

2. Aphrodite is "never-virgin," because she always appears as an enthusiastic participant in sexual acts.
3. Aphrodite actively seeks out and seduces her lovers and is generally benevolent toward them afterwards.
4. Sacred prostitution was practiced at some of her temples, where the women were courtesans skilled in the arts of seduction.
5. As a seductress, Aphrodite is also associated with rhetoric, the art of persuasion.
6. Aphrodite is responsible for the lover's madness that makes a person pursue the object of his or her desire at all costs.
7. Aphrodite uses lover's madness as punishment against those who have dishonored her by shunning love.

E. Aphrodite represents one aspect of what the Greeks considered to be the feminine aspects of the divine realm.
  1. As Athena apparently represents woman as the mistress of practical wisdom and Demeter seems to represent woman as mother, so Aphrodite represents woman as lover.
  2. These roles may represent more extensive theoretical possibilities for female activity than the Greeks are often given credit for imagining.

**Essential Reading:**

Jules Cashford, trans. *The Homeric Hymns*, pp. 5–26, 85–99, 108–113, 133–141.

Ovid. *Metamorphoses*, books V–VI, X.

**Supplementary Reading:**

Walter Burkert. *Greek Religion*, pp. 139–143, 152–156, 159–161.

*The New Larousse Encyclopedia of Mythology*, pp. 107–108, 130–132, 150–155.

**Questions to Consider:**

1. What do these different goddesses say, if anything, about the roles of women in ancient Greek society? How do we reconcile powerful goddesses with relatively powerless women in Greek society?

**2.** In many ways, Athena and Aphrodite seem to represent feminine opposites. Is this, in fact, the case, and if so, what does the contrast between them tell us about Greek ideas about women?

# Lecture Thirty-Two—Transcript
## Greece—The Goddess

In our last session, we discussed two Greek stories about "how things came to be the way they are now," Hesiod's *Theogony*, and the flood story of Deucalion and Pyrrha. Today, in this session, we will consider different aspects of the divine feminine in Greek religious culture, in the persons of three major goddesses: Athena, Demeter, and Aphrodite.

We have seen that although goddesses in polytheistic religious cultures often appear to originate as fertility deities, their dominion and significance usually extends far beyond fertility. Isis, for example, in Egypt, is associated with the fertility of the Nile Valley in association with Osiris, and Osiris's death and return to life leads to that idea of fertility as part of the death and rebirth of the crops.

Over time, though, Isis is also given further responsibilities, including the role as divine protectress of the Pharaoh. Of course, both of these associations—fertility, and protecting the Pharaoh— arise from the central myth of the conflict between Seth and Horus. This includes Isis's role as the loving wife to Osiris, and then as his grieving widow at his death, and then as the nurture and protectress of her son, Horus. Horus, of course, is the prototype of the divine Pharaoh.

Even apart from this myth, though, Isis gradually acquired other associations and powers in Egyptian mythology until she became a dominant goddess in her own right, revered as the Queen of Heaven.

We see a similar process at work in Mesopotamia with the goddess Inanna/Ishtar. Of course, her original association with fertility is very clear, an association with her consort, Dumuzi, but then that association is elaborated and is extended into other divine roles. Inanna's erotic connection with the pastoral god, Dumuzi, leads to her role as the goddess of love and sexual energy, and not merely fertility.

As a result of her association as the goddess of love and sexual energy, she becomes the producer of the dynamic power of life, and because she is associated with the dynamic power of life, she becomes the guardian of the cosmic order where this dynamic life takes place—and, finally, she gains dominion over both Heaven and Earth.

Her unbridled sexuality also leads to another association, her association with prostitution, with trickery, and then later, with natural disasters, with the frenzy of battle, and with the principle of divine retribution—again, all of these rising out of fertility associations in the case of Inanna, but also going far beyond them into a dominion over all aspects of human life and the royal title of "Queen Over Heaven and Earth."

Now, in Greece, of course, the character of the Olympian gods also developed over time, as the religious culture of one people collided with another, and in the process, produced variations among similar gods, but also through a more or less natural process of religious development and mythological evolution, as well.

There are some Greek goddesses with little apparent association with fertility, and there are others who have some association or identity as a fertility goddess, but that lies very much in the remote past. It does not necessarily influence the way the goddesses are classically portrayed. Even among those goddesses with more obvious connections with the earth and fertility, there are variations in how those connections shape the goddesses' identities and how they appear in the mythology.

Let us begin with Athena. Athena is the goddess who, in many ways, exhibits the virtues most commonly associated with the height of ancient Greek civilization, and, in fact, from the very beginning, Athena apparently shows a markedly Aegean character.

Most likely, Athena's origins lie in the Minoan and the Mycenaean cultures that we discussed earlier. As we've seen, it appears that these cultures worshiped a goddess who was a protective spirit of fortresses, and who sometimes assumed the form of a snake. This goddess was "chthonic"—that is, she was an earth-based divinity, and as a result of her association with the earth, she was associated with the principle of fertility and with the agricultural cycle.

However, we also see that this goddess was probably associated with birds, and we may be reminded in this connection with the reappearance of the bird motif in the Minoan building complexes, and, in fact, also associated with Minoan religious culture, we have the figure of the goddess or the priestess who held snakes aloft, as appearing in that figurine that I have already mentioned.

As an earth deity, this goddess was also apparently associated with large rocks, and with rocky bluffs, and, of course, rocky bluffs in Greece, as we've seen, were the location of fortresses because they provided protection and oversight of plains and coastlines. Because this deity is associated with large rocks and bluffs, she is also associated with the fortresses that are built on those bluffs, and because of her association with fortresses, she is associated with palaces, the places where kings reside within a fortress. Ultimately, she is also associated with cities.

Athena exhibits these same connections. She retains strong connections with both snakes and birds in her classical form. Her shield, her *aegis*, is surrounded—or rather depicts—the head of Medusa, who had hair made of snakes. So, there, we have the snake association, and in her classical form, Athena is associated with a particular bird, the owl, which is also a symbol of her wisdom.

We may also postulate that the association with fortresses may explain why Athena is depicted as a warrior goddess—although that warrior aspect of Athena's identity may also derive from her association with an Indo-European warrior goddess.

Now, Athena, of course, was patron goddess of the city of Athens— one of the dominant cities of ancient Greece—but she has a larger association with cities in general and, more particularly, with the arts of the cities, which are properly called "civilized" arts. These are the arts, the abilities, and the skills that allow cities to function.

Her role as the protective deity of Athens probably stemmed from an earlier association of this earth-based goddess with the Acropolis. The Acropolis was the rocky mountain where the Temple of Athena was built behind the city of Athens.

In mythology, Athena's patronage of the city of Athens was something that she gained through a contest, a contest between Athena, the goddess of wisdom, and Poseidon, the god of the sea. The contest was conducted by the city elders of Athens to award the patronage of the city to the god who could provide the city with the most useful gift, and this conflict in the contest between Athena on the one hand, and Poseidon on the other, may be a mythological representation of a conflict between maritime interests and agricultural interests in the city's history.

Poseidon, as the god of the sea, gives a rather water-based gift to the city of Athens, a saltwater spring in the center of the city. Athena, on the other hand, created an olive tree, and this creation of the olive tree reveals Athena's association with nature and with fertility. The city elders of Athens decided that Athena's gift was the one that would prove the most useful to the city, and, in fact, olive oil became the basis of the Athenian economy.

Athena was also the patroness of cities in general and, therefore, of civilization—a Latin word that derives from the idea of "city," or "peoples," and she is also, therefore, a patroness of culture. This means a number of things. On the one hand, Athena is responsible for administrative government—that is, the kind of government that sees to the common business of the city.

Therefore, she is also a patroness of politics because politics are the human interactions that allow government to take place. She is a goddess of justice because one of the primary responsibilities of a city is to administer justice fairly to its citizens. She is a goddess of rhetoric because rhetoric is persuasive argumentation that makes political interaction possible, and so, also, the life of the city.

On the other hand, she has more "personal" functions, if that's the right way to put it, but she is also associated with the family—the person within the family—because the family, in Athena's care, was the basis for good citizenship, and the family and its well-being was the source of civic well-being, the family as the building block that creates the well-functioning city.

Athena, as I've mentioned, was also a goddess of wisdom, and, once again, this is the practical wisdom that enables a person to take command of a situation, or to get things done. It is the wisdom that gives groups of people the ability to work together to create the society and culture of the city, but it is primarily aimed at pragmatic ends—getting things done.

This quality, or this association with Athena, is reflected in her origins in mythology. The story is that Zeus, the king of the gods, suffered one day from a terrible headache, and the pain was so bad and so intense that he finally asked Hephaestus, the craftsman and blacksmith of the gods, to take his hammer and to just give him one right there, in the center of his forehead.

When Hephaestus did this, Zeus's head cracked open, and the goddess Athena sprang full-grown from his forehead. Obviously, Athena is a goddess associated with the thinking capacity of the mind. Therefore, her "mother"—and I put that in quotation marks—the mother of Athena was Metis, "reason," and Athena fosters the sort of knowledge that makes civilized life possible—reasoned life, rational mental activity, and, again, this means not only the conduct of the city and the political and personal interactions of its people, but the arts as well—both domestic and manufacturing—make city life possible.

On the one hand, Athena oversees the making of plows and of the building of ships and chariots, and training horses—training horses to make them useful for human beings and to enable human beings to do things. On the other hand, Athena is also the patroness of domestic arts, such as weaving and the making of pottery—things that enable women to get things done in the home.

Of course, this is part of the business of the ancient Greek city's work, so Athena, again, is a warrior goddess because this, too, is part of the concern for the welfare of the city. Athena is always depicted in art dressed in battle-gear, armed with her spear and shield and wearing a helmet. Unlike Inanna, Athena's interest in war is not in battle per se. She's not interested in the blood lust or the fervor of battle.

What Athena is interested in is military skill, strategy, and tactics, and it is Athena who is present in the war council in the voice of wisdom. As a result of her association with war, strategy, and tactics, Athena was closely associated with several of the Greek heroes, including Heracles, Perseus, and Odysseus. These are heroes she admires for their strength, but also and primarily for their skill and their cunning—in other words, for these heroes' ability to take command of a situation and to accomplish their aims.

Now, at the same time, Athena is a virgin goddess. She is immune to the power of Aphrodite, and this is true of only three goddesses in ancient Greece. One is Athena; another is Artemis, the goddess of wildlife; and the third is Hestia, goddess of the hearth.

In the case of Athena, her virginity appears to be a way of maintaining independence and an equal footing with the men with whom she deals—this way ensuring that her relationships with these men, these crafty and skillful men, are based on mutual respect. Athena is proud of her beauty; she enjoys her beauty for its own sake, and, in fact, she is one of the three goddesses who vie together for the prize of the most beautiful goddess, and the prize of the golden apple from Eris—Athena, Hera, and Aphrodite, who engage in that contest.

However, Athena does not use her beauty to influence either the male gods or men. Instead, her beauty is a reflection of her divine nature, a physical manifestation of her godhood.

Now, a Greek goddess with much clearer and definitive connections with fertility is Demeter. Demeter is the goddess of the plowed earth, the goddess of grain and the patroness of agriculture. Demeter is prominent in the Greek mythology primarily as a mother, and given this prominence, it's perhaps important to remember that Demeter became a mother pretty much against her will, only.

She was wooed by Poseidon, the god of the sea, but she spurned him, and in order to avoid his attentions, she disguised herself as a mare, but Poseidon saw through her disguise and took on the form of a stallion himself and raped Demeter. As a result, she gave birth to twins.

Later on, Demeter also spurned Zeus, but like Poseidon, Zeus took on an animal form and had intercourse with Demeter in the form of a bull. The product of this union was Kore, a Greek word meaning "daughter," and Kore was Demeter's most beloved child.

Demeter's cultic importance arises primarily from her connection with a mythological story involving Hades's abduction of her beloved daughter, Kore. Hades is the god of the underworld. He abducts the young woman and imprisons her in his underground realm.

When Kore disappeared, of course, Demeter was distraught. She looked for her daughter all over the face of the earth. In her grief, Demeter left her hair unbound, the traditional sign of grief. She fasted, refusing to take in food, and she carried torches with her to aid her in her search, so that she could look for Kore both day and night.

During Demeter's wanderings on the earth, she neglected her divine duties, and, as a result, the earth became barren and yielded no produce. For a time, Demeter disguised herself as an old woman and served as a nurse in the household of King Celeus in Eleusis. This is when Demeter cared for Celeus's son, Triptolemus.

At the urging of the gods because they were afraid that the earth would suffer irreparably from the lack of produce, Zeus sent Hermes to Hades to demand that Hades return Kore. Kore is now known by the name of Persephone.

Hermes gives Zeus's order to Hades to return Persephone, Kore, to her mother, Demeter, but before she leaves, Hades gives Persephone pomegranate seeds to eat. Pomegranate seeds were a symbol of marriage, and eating pomegranate seeds, Persephone ties herself in marriage to Hades for all time. As a result, Persephone could only return to Demeter, her mother on earth, for a part of each year, and she spent the rest of the year with her husband in the dark underworld.

The story, of course, explains the cycle of the seasons. This very clear affinity with other fertility mythology we've looked at, where a goddess mourns the loss of a loved one—that loved one has become lost by becoming trapped in the underworld, and, at the end, there is a partial restoration of the loved one, which makes possible the return of the fertile season at the goddess's instigation.

In the case of Demeter, Eleusis, the home of King Celeus, whom she served—Eleusis became the primary cultic site for the worship of Demeter, and, later, Eleusis became the center of a mystery religion that extended throughout the Mediterranean world, and as we will see, most of the mystery religions that originate during the Hellenistic era have their origins in fertility rituals.

However, the Greek goddess with the closest affinities to fertility and a very close resemblance to Inanna as the goddess of erotic love was Aphrodite. Aphrodite's matchless beauty earned her the epithet, "Golden Aphrodite."

Aphrodite probably had her origins in the Near East, and it's worth noting that in the Trojan War, her sympathies were with the Trojans, but at the same time, she was one of the most popular and widely worshiped of the Greek deities.

Aphrodite's birth, if you remember, came from sea foam, and her association with the island of Cyprus argues for Phoenician origins for the goddess because, as you have seen, there was extensive contact between the Phoenicians and the Greeks. This means that Aphrodite would then be related to Near Eastern goddesses, whose association with fertility has these strong sexual overtones.

Aphrodite also shares many attributes with an Indo-European goddess, Dawn, named after the god of the day, and shares with her such attributes as beauty, and association with the sky, and association with light, and an affinity for human lovers. Of course, even with these associations to other goddesses, especially the Mesopotamian Inanna, Aphrodite remains—in many ways—unique and, in fact, decidedly Greek in her character.

As I have said, Aphrodite is a sky deity, so her association with fertility is understood very broadly, to make her the source of abundant life, as Inanna was. She is the one who inspires the growth of plants and animals. She represents the dynamic power of life.

Now, there are some traces of Aphrodite's connection with the annual cycle of the seasons in stories of two of her human lovers. These are the young men Anchises and Adonis, two beautiful young men who are beloved by Aphrodite, and through no fault of hers, they come to bad ends. Both of these stories appear in several variations in the Greek mythology.

Aphrodite, like Athena, has an affinity for birds, but in her case, the affinity is most especially not towards owls, as with Athena, but with doves, birds that we still associate with love. Aphrodite has an affinity for the sweet savor of fruit and the sweet smell of flowers and, in fact, with all of the sweet fragrances that stimulate sexual desire.

Aphrodite is associated with the rhythms that govern organic life, and, as a result, she sometimes appears as a spinner—a spinner whose wheel represents the cycles of life, a spinner who thereby sustains life and growth and governs cosmic cycles, as well as natural ones.

Aphrodite, of course, is chronically unfaithful to her husband, who happens to be the least attractive of the gods, Hephaestus, the divine craftsman and blacksmith, but despite chronic infidelity, Aphrodite was also involved in the welfare of the family. She sometimes appears as a patroness of marriage; that is a specialty of hers, of course, in her sexual aspect, as a guardian of the sexual aspect of marriage. She is associated with families in terms of the welfare of clans and the welfare of children.

Chief among many of Aphrodite's divine attributes, though, was her unparalleled beauty. This was a beauty that surpassed the beauty of all the other goddesses, which was why Eris eventually gives her the golden apple as the most beautiful of the goddesses, apart from the bribe she offers him, of course.

Aphrodite's beauty is unsurpassed because it is part of her very divine essence, part of her very being, and since this is divine beauty, it is literally stunning to behold. I always think of one of those wolves in an old Tex Avery cartoon, who sees a beautiful woman and goes, "Boing!!" This is apparently the kind of effect Aphrodite has on those who see her.

Aphrodite's essential beauty is unmistakable, even when Aphrodite is in disguise. My favorite example of this comes from Book III of the *Iliad*. Aphrodite has disguised herself as an old, withered crone. She wants to encourage Helen to forsake her plans to repent her adultery with Paris, and instead, go back to Paris's bed to do some more adultery. Aphrodite is therefore disguised as a withered old crone, but Homer notes that Helen knew the goddess at once, "the long, lithe neck, the smooth, full breasts, and the fire in those eyes," apparently Homer's idea of a crone.

In art, Aphrodite is usually depicted adorning herself, or bathing, or dressing, and different depictions of Aphrodite in statuary took on traditional forms and emphasized different aspects of her beauty. Often, they have surnames for Aphrodite based on her pose, so that Aphrodite Callipygos is "Aphrodite of the beautiful buttocks."

After the 5th century B.C.E., Aphrodite is usually depicted nude in statuary. This is because unlike Inanna, the divine power and beauty of Aphrodite resides in her own beautiful body and not in any adornments—so she most clearly expresses her essential divine nature when she is unclothed.

As I mentioned, the goddess is often called "Golden Aphrodite," and there may be a number of reasons for this. For one thing, gold is bright. It's beautiful in itself, and it retains its beauty forever. At the same time, gold is associated with persuasion—such as the persuasion of seduction, or persuasion of rhetoric—and we find that notable rhetors or orators in the ancient world were sometimes called "*chrysostom*," or "gold mouth." We know both Dio Chrysostom and John Chrysostome; they're very persuasive speakers.

Gold is also associated in the Greek world with honey, which never spoils, and so, also, with sexual fluids. However, Aphrodite's beauty is only the physical manifestation of her dominant characteristic, the powerful sexuality that sets her apart from all other Greek goddesses. Like Athena, Aphrodite has no real mother, and like Athena, Aphrodite was born full-grown, and like Athena, Aphrodite's nature derives from her origins.

Athena was born from the forehead, the mind, of Zeus. Aphrodite was born from the foam caused when Kronos castrated his father and threw his severed genitalia into the sea, determining Aphrodite's definitive characteristics.

Not only is Aphrodite not ever a virgin, like Athena, Aphrodite is "never-virgin." There's no story in the mythology where Aphrodite is anything other than an enthusiastic participant in sexual acts. Like Inanna, Aphrodite is sexually powerful, but unlike Inanna, she is sexually generous. She actively seeks out and seduces her lovers, but she is generally benevolent towards them afterwards.

Like Inanna, Aphrodite is also patroness of prostitutes, under the title, "Aphrodite the Whore." Apparently, sacred prostitution was practiced in some of her temples, but the women there were not only sexual partners for men, but also courtesans skilled in all the arts of seduction, and as a seductress, Aphrodite is also associated with rhetoric, the art of persuasion, as I've said, "golden speech."

Aphrodite is also responsible for the lover's madness, a form of *ate*, that makes a person ignore all other considerations—family, honor, virtue—because they are in pursuit of the object of their desire. This kind of madness usually has a tragic end in Greek mythology—although occasionally, it doesn't. Occasionally, Aphrodite uses it as a form of punishment for those who have previously dishonored her by spurning romantic love—so she punishes them, ironically, with too much desire for romantic love.

Like Athena and like Demeter, Aphrodite represents one aspect of what the Greeks considered to be the feminine aspects of the divine realm, the primacy of erotic love. Just as Athena appears to represent woman as the mistress of craft and industry, and Demeter seems to represent woman as mother and protector, so Aphrodite represents woman as lover, whose love is of a sort that almost literally makes the world go round.

Although these roles may still seem to us to categorize and limit the scope of women's existence, they do represent far more extensive theoretical possibilities in female activity than the Greeks are often given credit for imagining.

Now, in our next session, we will consider the classical era. This includes the ubiquity of Greek religious culture as it is presented through art, architecture, tragedy, and philosophy.

# Lecture Thirty-Three
# The Classical Era in Greece

**Scope:**
The Classical era in ancient Greece (481-322 B.C.E.) fell between the Persian wars and the death of Alexander the Great, when the Greek city-states, especially Athens, achieved a political and cultural synthesis unparalleled in the ancient world. The radical democracy of Athens was based on the active participation of all its citizens. The Classical era brought a new spirit, often characterized as *humanism*, to architecture, statuary, tragedy, and philosophy. But the primary intention of these endeavors was to glorify the Athenian state and honor the gods who preserved its peace and prosperity. Individuals were important primarily as contributors to the common welfare of the *polis*. Art and architecture exhibited idealized proportions as a reflection of divine order, and tragedy depicted how violations of divine propriety were punished. Philosophy saw human reason as a part of divine nature and pursued the virtuous life based on knowledge of the good.

## Outline

I.  The Classical era is the period between the end of the Persian wars (481 B.C.E.) and the death of Alexander the Great (322 B.C.E.).

   **A.** The Persian Empire extended to western Asia Minor in the 540s B.C.E., including the Greek cities of Ionia.

   **1.** In 499 B.C.E., the Ionians revolted against Persia with some support from Athens, but they were defeated.

   **2.** In 490 B.C.E., an army of 22,000 Persians advanced toward Athens but was routed by an Athenian hoplite army of 11,000 at Marathon.

   **3.** Athens devoted a good amount of its revenues to building a naval fleet of oared triremes.

   **4.** In 480 B.C.E., Xerxes moved into Greece with a large army and naval fleet.

   **5.** A Greek army assembled to meet the Persians but was defeated at Thermopylae, where 300 Spartans remained to delay the Persians' pursuit of the Greek army.

      **6.** With central Greece open to the Persians, the Athenians abandoned their city.

      **7.** The Greek navy attacked the Persians at Salamis, a narrow strait near Athens, and defeated them.

  **B.** After the Persian Wars, Athens became the dominant city-state in Greece and developed a unique political culture.

      **1.** Around 400 B.C.E., Athens developed a radical democracy with full participation in government and debate for all citizens.

      **2.** Most political offices were filled by lot, and a stipend was provided, allowing poorer citizens to hold office.

      **3.** Most decisions were made by majority vote of the assembly of all citizens that met 40 times a year.

      **4.** The body of citizens was now restricted to those free men whose parents were both Athenians.

**II.** Classical culture in Athens brought a particular approach to art and architecture, as well as theatre and philosophy.

  **A.** This approach is often called *humanism*, because it is said to reflect the importance and integrity of the individual.

      **1.** The importance of the human form in classical sculpture emphasizes the individual person.

      **2.** The evolution of tragedy that focuses on the travails of the tragic hero brings a new importance to the individual.

      **3.** Greek philosophy deals with the duties of human beings and the meaning of the ideals they profess: justice, piety, love.

      **4.** These ideas are said to exemplify the new humanism of the Classical era.

  **B.** In fact, the Athens of the Classical era focused not on the individual but on the *polis*, the city-state.

      **1.** The political impulse behind the development of radical Athenian democracy was a sense of Athenian superiority.

      **2.** Athenians believed that they had proven themselves superior to other Greeks and to non-Greeks by their strategy and bravery against the Persians.

3. The focus of virtue was the Athenian state, and an individual's worth was his worth as a servant of the state.

4. The individual who was most venerated was the one who had contributed the most to the common good of the *polis*.

C. Architecture was intended to present the glory of the Athenian *polis* through a building's beauty and proportion.

1. The work of the gods was to impose order on the chaos that threatened to overwhelm creation.

2. In Greece, the divine order of the cosmos was increasingly understood as a function of reason.

3. Order was represented by the beauty of proportion, a function of mathematical reasoning, a form of divine science.

4. The most common examples of classical architecture are the temples of the Acropolis, dedicated to glorifying the gods.

5. As the cosmos was thought of as a well-ordered, rational design, the gods increasingly were thought of in terms of idealized rationality.

D. Statuary idealized the human form as a divine creation of beauty and proportion.

1. Greek statuary had long taken stylized forms, such as the *kouros*, a young man, and the *kore*, a young woman.

2. Stylized forms were retained even as sculptors created more naturalistic images of human beings in standardized poses.

3. The emphasis on the individual human form was secondary to the idealization of the human form.

4. The same idealized human forms were used to represent the gods as literal embodiments of divine order and design.

5. There is less emphasis on the human form *per se* than on using the human form to say something about the gods.

III. Theatre in Greece had its origins and its contextual setting in the festival worship of Dionysus.

A. Every spring saw the Dionysia, four days of performances of poetry, music, and dance in the god's honor.

1. Choruses of 50 members, who both sang and danced, performed dithyrambs, lyric hymns in praise of Dionysus.
2. Tragedies retained a smaller chorus augmented with individual actors who portrayed characters taken from mythology.
3. Comedies presented actors and chorus in lighthearted and usually obscene stories that ended happily.
4. The plays involved the interaction of human beings with one another and with the gods.

B. The tragedies of Aeschylus, Sophocles, and Euripides reflect on individual actions in the context of the *polis*.
1. The leading characters are often members of ruling families whose actions have consequences for their cities.
2. Aeschylus's *Oresteia* trilogy centers on murder, retribution, and purification to restore divine order to Argos.
3. Sophocles's *Oedipus the King* tells how Oedipus discovers the truth about himself while trying to lift at plague from his city of Thebes.
4. Euripides's *The Bacchae* tells the story of Pentheus, who rejects worship of Dionysus and is punished, while his family is exiled from Thebes.
5. In most of these plays, the chorus represents a voice of traditional wisdom and piety.
6. The resolution of many tragedies is less about the fate of the characters than the restoration of well-being to the *polis*.
7. The well-being of the *polis* depends on divine favor, and the gods must be appeased at all costs.

IV. Classical Athens saw the emergence of a new religious idea, that human beings were a part of the world of the gods.

A. Philosophers believed that a person's essence was reason and that each person's reason was a splinter of divine reason.
1. Human reason was a splinter of divine reason and, thus, the common element uniting human and divine existence.

2. The use of reason in philosophical contemplation could discern the intentions of the gods.
3. The Greeks believed that right behavior was an inevitable result of right knowledge; thus, the philosopher was the most virtuous man.
4. This meant that a person's way of life was the clearest indication of his or her knowledge of the good, the source of all virtue.
5. Trust in the virtuous person was specifically trust in that person's knowledge of right and wrong.
6. For most of the philosophers, the truest form of piety was the performance of right actions.

B. The height of classical culture in Athens was not based on human beings as individuals or as the proper focus of art, theatre, and philosophy.
1. Instead, the emphasis was on the glory of the Athenian *polis*, the common welfare, and the glory of the gods.
2. Divine glory and the glory of the *polis* were reflected in the beauty of buildings, crafts, and statuary and dramatic stories of violation and restoration.
3. Philosophy was intended to discern the divine will through the use of the divine element in humanity, the reason.

**Essential Reading:**

Robin W. Winks and Susan P. Mattern-Parkes. *The Ancient Mediterranean World: From the Stone Age to A.D. 600*, pp. 74–101.

Simon Price. *Religions of the Ancient Greeks*, pp. 1–88.

**Supplementary Reading:**

Sophocles. *The Three Theban Plays: Oedipus the King.*

E. R. Dodds. *The Greeks and the Irrational*, pp. 179–206.

H. D. F. Kitto. *The Greeks*, pp. 79–135.

**Questions to Consider:**

1. We often look to classical Athens as the model for our own ideals of government. How did Athenian democracy in the Classical era resemble and differ from our own?

**2.** Given the emphasis on rationality during the Classical era, why was theatre dedicated, on the one hand, to farcical comedy and, on the other, to tragedies based on traditional mythology? What purpose did such performances serve in Athenian society?

# Lecture Thirty-Three—Transcript
## The Classical Era in Greece

In our last session, we discussed different aspects of the divine feminine in great religious culture, in the persons of three specific goddesses: Athena, Demeter, and Aphrodite. In this session, we will consider the classical period in Greece—and especially, the chief city of Athens.

Now, the classical era in ancient Greece is usually defined as the end of the period of Greeks wars with the Persians, which comes in 481 B.C.E. and the death of Alexander the Great of Macedon in 322 B.C.E.

The Persian Empire was under Cyrus the Great, whom we've mentioned before, and he extended his power to western Asia Minor in the 540s B.C.E., and among the peoples they overcame at that point were the Greek coastal cities of Ionia.

In 499 B.C.E., the Ionians revolted against Persia, and they did so with some support from Athens, but the Persians were able to put down the revolt, and they exacted a vengeance against the city that had led the Ionian revolt, Miletus, and the city was severely punished by the Persians.

In 490 B.C.E., an army of 22,000 Persians advanced toward Athens because Athens was seen as sort of the center of resistance and Greek opposition to Persian hegemony, but this army of 22,000 Persians was met by an army that was half as large, an Athenian *hoplite* army of 11,000. The Athenian army encountered the much larger Persian army at Marathon, a plain about 26 miles from the city of Athens, and there, the Athenians routed the Persian forces.

To give the good news to the city of Athens itself, a messenger ran all the way from Marathon, the 26 miles, to the city of Athens, gave the good news of the victory, and promptly died from the exertion—thereby setting a model for all people who run marathons.

In the succeeding years, Athens devoted a good amount of its revenues to building and maintaining a naval fleet. This would be a naval fleet made up of *triremes*, large ships propelled primarily by oarsmen—although they also have sails—and this naval fleet of *triremes* was developed in order to protect the city from the sea.

Ten years later, in 480 B.C.E., the new Persian king, Xerxes, again moved into Greece with a large army. In this case, the Persian army was supported by a naval fleet of its own, a naval fleet that sailed along the coastlines in order to provide support and backup, shall we say, for the Persian army. As a result of these combined naval and army forces, many of the cities of Greece along the coastline surrendered, but others formed an alliance—an alliance that was formed under the authority of the Spartans—and under this alliance, the various cities assembled an army to meet the Persians.

Now, this army was defeated by the Persians at a place called Thermopylae, but in order to guard the retreat of the fleeing Greek armies, 300 Spartans remained to allay the Persians' pursuit, and, as a result, the Greek army was, for the most part, able to escape, reassemble, and re-marshal its forces—although, of course, the 300 Spartans died.

As a result of this encounter, as a result of the Persian victories, central Greece lay open to the Persian forces—so the Athenians felt it was wisest to abandon their city. At this point, the Greek navy came into play. This Greek navy was made up primarily of Athenian ships, and the navy attacked the Persians at Salamis, a narrow strait near the city of Athens, and naval forces of the Greeks soundly defeated the Persian navy. This established firmly the place of naval operations in the future defense of the Greek city-states, and it brought an effective end to the wars between Persia and Greece.

Now, in the aftermath of these wars against the Persians, Athens was one of the primary actors in both the military land offensives and defenses against the Persians, and as the predominant naval force of the Greeks, Athens became a dominant city-state, the dominant city-state, of Greece. During this period that we now call the "classical" period, Athens developed a unique political culture that ushered in what really was the height of Athenian and Greek civilization.

Somewhere around the year 400 B.C.E., Athens developed what we can call a "radical democracy," radical in the sense that it was democratic in its roots and in its branches. This was a democracy that opened full charges based in government and political debate to all

Athenian citizens. Most political offices at this point were filled by lot. This was to avoid the undue influence of the wealthier Athenians over the poorer Athenians. With offices being filled by lot, there was an element of chance, but it was also the element of fairness.

Moreover, a stipend was provided for those who filled these offices that were chosen by lot. This meant that there was no undue hardship for those who were poorer, if they were chosen to serve the government—thereby allowing poorer citizens to hold office without any kind of financial loss to themselves.

Most decisions in this radical Athenian democracy were made by majority vote of the established assembly of all citizens. The assembly met 40 times a year, and the usual attendance at an assembly was at least 6,000 Athenian citizens. You will note, however, that I keep referring to the term, "Athenian citizen." This body of citizens was now even more restrictive than it had been during the earlier days of the *polis* of Athens. It was now restricted to those freemen who were landowners and whose parents were both Athenians; other groups—women, foreigners, and slaves, of course, continued to be excluded from political power.

This, then, was the governmental, the cultural, social background to the classical age in Athens, but, of course, we usually pay much more attention to what we call "classical" culture, in the sense of art, architecture, drama, and philosophy. Generally speaking, classical culture in Athens is exemplified by a particular approach to art and architecture, as well as parallel tendencies in theater and philosophy.

This approach is often called *humanism*, and the name "humanism" reflects what is believed to be typical of these different expressions of Athenian culture at this time. Humanism was said to reflect a new sense of the importance of the individual, and the integrity of the individual, in the face of the gods and in the face of human society. So, "humanism" is the name given to the culture of classical Athens because it is seen to be based on the human, the individual, rather than on the gods, and rather than on society.

One example of this sort of humanism is the human form in classical sculpture, which at this point achieved a naturalism that was previously unknown in the ancient world—a naturalism that still, in many ways, sets the model for naturalistic art in the West.

This naturalism is said to show an emphasis on human person. Similarly, the evolution of Greek tragedy that focuses on the travails of the tragic hero and the group of forces beyond his or her control is said to grant the individual a new literary focus—as, now, literature focuses on individuals rather than on the grand sweep of epics, or the doings of nations.

Then, again, Greek philosophy dealt, now, with the duties of human beings and the meanings of the ideals that human beings adhered to as a source of their actions. Human beings appeal to various ideals that were examined by Greek philosophy—such as justice, truth, piety, love, some sense of the good.

All of these ideas, we are told, exemplify the *new humanism* of the classical era, the new importance of the individual, the new focus on individual men and women—primarily men. In fact, though, the Athens of the classical era was, in many ways, deeply foreign to us as modern people of the West—not least because its focus was, in fact, not on the individual, but rather on the *polis*, on the city-state.

Much of the political impulse that lay behind the development of radical Athenian democracy was a deep sense of the superiority of the Athenians as a people over other Greeks, and over foreigners. This superiority was supposed to be based on a kind of natural nobility that was typical of the Athenian citizen, and this is what made Athenian citizens in general fit to rule over themselves, while other Greek cities, who were not as blessed with the superior citizenry, had to depend on the leadership and rule of the elites. So, Athenians—because of their natural abilities, their natural talents— were fit to govern themselves, while other Greeks were only fit to be governed by certain members of their society.

Superiority was also believed to justify the narrowing of the definition of citizen at the same time that the responsibilities and rights of citizens were being expanded. The superiority of the Athenian justified the narrowing of the definition for Athenian citizen, since only citizen soldiers of true Athenian blood—that is, with two Athenian parents—could be trusted to have this sort of natural ability, this sort of natural nobility, that made them fit to govern themselves as well as other Athenian citizens.

The Athenians—they believed—had proven themselves superior to other Greeks, and to non-Greeks, as a result of the war against the Persians. They were able to defeat the Persians because of their strategic cleverness and their bravery, and also because the Persians were, after all, not Greek. The word that was used for those not Greek was "barbarian," which has, as its origin, the Greek word meaning, "babbler," people who don't speak Greek, and, therefore, all of the language just sounds like "bar-bar-bar-bar-bar." Thus, it meant "babblers" were all foreign people, and, "They're not like us. They're not like Athenians."

The focus of this virtue, though, the focus of this natural superiority, the focus was the Athenian state, the *polis*, and the worth of the individual was based on his worth as a servant of the Athenian state—in other words, what contribution I could make as a citizen to the common good. So, the individual who was most venerated was the individual who contributed the most of the common good of the *polis*—not an individual for his own integrity, not an individual for his own sake, but an individual as a supporter of the common good of the Athenian *polis*.

Here, we can look at the mythological story of Athena and Poseidon as rivals for patronage of the city of Athens. What was the contest? The contest was which god could make himself or herself the most useful to the Athenian *polis*. As we saw, Athena won by providing the olive tree as a source of the Athenian economy. It is the individual's usefulness to the *polis*, then, that determines his or her value as an individual.

Similarly, architecture was intended to present the glory of the Athenian *polis* through a building's proportion and its beauty. This was believed to reflect the sedate beauty of the divine order. As in other ancient Mediterranean religious cultures, the work of the gods was to impose order on the chaos that would otherwise threaten to overwhelm creation.

In Greece, that divine order was increasingly understood as a function of reason—that is, primarily the practical reason that enables a person to get things done. This is the sort of wisdom identified with Athena, and the reason that enabled a person to get things done included the science of numbers. In other words, order was represented by the beauty of proportion. Proportion was a function of mathematical reasoning, and mathematical reasoning was a divine science that was imparted to humanity as a gift from the gods.

Mathematics was a branch of philosophy because it was a part of knowledge, and, of course, philosophy is the love of wisdom—the love of knowing things, and investigating and contemplating things. Mathematics was intertwined with other philosophical investigations, both practical and not so practical.

The philosopher Pythagoras, from the 6th century B.C.E., was a mystical thinker, and he believed that numbers were the means of understanding creation—not in the sense of physics, as some moderns would postulate, but rather that numbers were the key to the thinking of the gods. Numbers were a divine gift that revealed something of the essential nature both only of the gods themselves, and of the creation.

Now, the Athenian buildings that are most often cited as examples of classical architecture were the temples of the Acropolis, buildings that were dedicated to glorifying the gods. The temples and other sacred buildings were intended to express the sense of order, the sense of proportion that was typical of the divine control of the cosmos, and also, of course, to express the sovereignty and the rational order of the Athenian state, the *polis*.

In fact, the image, as is often the case in politics, was more important than the reality. In some cases, the design and proportions of the buildings on the Acropolis had been modified from straight lines and consistent measurement to give the appearance of proportionality, rather than the reality.

As the cosmos itself was more likely to be thought of as a well-ordered, rational design that kept chaos at bay, the gods themselves were increasingly conceived of in terms of idealized rationality, and this began to create a tension, as you can imagine, to traditional mythology, as almost anything but rational, almost anything but temperate and thoughtful, in a way that the Athenians now thought of as the cosmos.

Then, there was art: In statuary, the focus on the human form was also arguably a manifestation of the divine order because the idealized human form was, itself, a divine creation. The gods had made humanity, and the gods had made human bodies beautiful and proportionate.

Now, Greek statuary had long taken stylized forms. One of these was the *kouros*, which depicted a naked young man in the standard pose, and the female equivalent was the *kore*, which depicted a young woman in a standard pose.

Now, these standardized forms were retained, even though sculptors began to create increasingly naturalistic images of the human beings in these standardized poses. The intention was less to represent individual human beings than to represent certain traditional images and certain traditional ideas; so, the emphasis on the individual human form and its naturalistic presentation was secondary. It was secondary to the idealization of the human form, which was in conformity with the prevailing ideas of human beauty for both men and women. So that even as the proportions and features of human beings were idealized, those same idealized human forms were used to represent the gods as literal embodiments of order and design and, again, they were captured in poses emblematic of their divine nature, as we have seen in the case of Aphrodite.

Again, what we have here is less an emphasis on the human form of the individual per se, than using the human form as a means of saying something about the gods, and about the divine order.

Another artistic expression of classical culture in Greece was theater, and theater in Greece had its origins and settings in the festival worship of Dionysius. Every spring, in March or April, came the great religious festival of the Dionysia—four days of performances of poetry, music, and dance—all in honor of Dionysus.

Dithyrambs, which were lyric hymns in praise of Dionysus, were performed by choruses of 50 men or 50 boys, and these choruses both sang and danced on a stage in an amphitheater—one of those semicircular, large outdoor theaters, but the stage, the floor of the amphitheater, may have originally been a threshing floor because the threshing floors were traditional sites for fertility rituals, as you can imagine, since the grain that was being threshed was the product of fertility, the gift of the gods. It appears that the threshing floor later evolved into the stage where the Dionysian celebrations took place.

Tragedies, of course, had a chorus of a somewhat smaller size, but in tragedies, their chorus augmented their singing and their dancing with individual actors, individual actors who performed in masks and took on the roles of specific characters in a dramatic story that was based on traditional mythology and, therefore, the course of whose plot was already known to the audience, an important point to remember.

Similarly, there were comedies, and comedies also presented individual actors and a chorus, but in this case, they were involved in a lighthearted and usually highly obscene story of human folly, and, of course, because it was a comedy, it would end happily.

Each of these sorts of performances involved not only interaction of human beings with one another, but the interaction of human beings and the gods. The gods in tragedy and comedy both act as interested parties in the unfolding action, even if the gods themselves are not depicted explicitly in the action.

The best-known tragedies are those of Aeschylus, whose dates are 525 to 456 B.C.E.; Sophocles, whose dates are about 496 to 406 or 405 B.C.E.; and Euripides, whose dates are about 485 to 406 B.C.E.—these tragedies reflect on individual actions, but within the context of the *polis*.

The leading characters in the surviving tragedies are often members of ruling families, and their actions have immediate consequences on the people of their cities and on the cities themselves, as well as the primary actors.

For example, Aeschylus's trilogy, *The Oresteia*, is about the family of Agamemnon. It centers first on the murder of Agamemnon by his wife, Clytemnestra, and then on the revenge taken by their son, Orestes—and then, finally, on Orestes's purification from the sin of matricide, in order to restore order, to restore divine order to the territory of Argos.

Similarly, Sophocles's *Oedipus the King*, probably the most famous Greek tragedy, concerns how Oedipus of Thebes seeks to remove a plague from his city, from the *polis* of Thebes, by punishing the person who has somehow offended the gods and brought the plague on the city. In the end, of course, Oedipus must be exiled himself because he discovers that it is he who has unwittingly committed the crimes that have brought the plague upon the city.

In one of his plays, *The Bacchae*, Euripides deals explicitly with Dionysus himself. He tells the story of how Pentheus, another king of Thebes, rejects the new worship of Dionysus and is punished by the god. Then, Pentheus's family is exiled from the city, restoring order to Thebes once again.

In most of these plays, the Chorus represents a voice of traditional wisdom and traditional piety, and, usually, the Chorus is found counseling submission to the will of the gods as the best action for all concerned to follow.

Now, not all tragedies follow this story arc of offense, discovery, retribution, and exile—but in many, the resolution is less about the fate of the characters, than it is about the restoration of the *polis* after a series of civic calamities—in other words, the individual having something happen to him or her that results, ultimately, in the restoration of order and the well-being of the city. The well-being of the *polis*, then, depends on divine favor—and all other considerations, such as the happiness of individuals, must take second place to appeasing the gods.

Now, the classical era in Athens also saw the emergence of a new religious idea among the philosophers and some others—that human beings were, in essence, a part of the divine world of the gods. Greek philosophers shared the conviction that the *psyche*, or psyche, the essence of a person, was primarily a matter of reason, primarily a thing of reason, we might say, and that reason that made up the essence of a person, *psyche*, was a small spark of divine reason. Human reason was a spark of the divine humanity, and so, *psyche* was what united human and divine existence.

This meant that the use of reason in philosophical contemplation was a means of participating in the divine world, by exercising that faculty that human beings and the gods had in common. So, the philosophical contemplation, then, is a means of understanding and discovering the intentions of the gods—and so, also a form of piety. It is exercising that faculty that is most godlike in human beings.

Since the Greeks universally believed that right behavior was the inevitable result of right knowledge, the philosopher was also the most virtuous of people because the philosopher always acted in accordance with the will of the gods, as revealed by the philosopher's proper use of reason, and this meant that *ethos*—that is, a person's way of life—was the clearest indication not only of that person's virtue, but also of that person's knowledge of the good because it was that person's knowledge of the good that was the ultimate and immediate source of virtue that determined the *ethos*, the way of life.

Trust, then, in a virtuous person in the classical era was explicitly trust of that person's knowledge of right and wrong—not trust in that person's character, as we might call it, but trust in that person's knowledge of right and wrong that would ensure that person's virtuous action in the future. So, you trust not their character—whatever that might be—or their *ethos* as such, but, rather, their body of knowledge that results in virtuous behavior in the present and, so, also will result in virtuous behavior in the future.

For most philosophers, the truest form of piety was not the performance of ritual actions, not the performance of sacrifices, or the celebration of festivals, or participation in processions—but the performance of right actions in dealing with other human beings and in venerating the gods.

We may see, then, that the height of classical culture in Athens was not based on human beings as individuals in their own right, nor was it based on human beings as individuals as the proper focus of art, or theater, or philosophy. Instead, the emphasis on the classical era was on the glory of the Athenian *polis*, the common character and welfare of all of its people as a group, as well as the glory of the immortal gods. The gods' glory was reflected in the beauty of buildings, crafts, and statuary that presented a natural but idealized version of the human form, which reflected the proportionate and beautiful work of the gods who created humanity.

Greek tragedy presented dramatic stories of how violations of the cosmic order disturbed the common peace of the *polis*, stories that were resolved by the restoration of the city's well-being and by the exile or the death of the offending person.

Finally, philosophy was intended to discern the will of the gods through the use of the divine element in the human person—that is, by the reason, and this was engaged in contemplation that would result in correct moral action, on the basis of the philosopher's knowledge of what is good.

Now, in our next session, we will look more closely at Greek philosophy in the sixth and fifth centuries B.C.E., considering philosophy specifically as a parallel to—and sometimes as a substitute for—religion.

# Lecture Thirty-Four

## Greece—Philosophy as Religion

**Scope:**
During the Classical era, many of the elite rejected mythology as unworthy portrayals of the gods and turned to philosophy as an alternative. Philosophers revered "the good" as the highest god. Pythagoras taught that the soul was a divine spark trapped in a mortal body, to be released through purification over many lifetimes. The most influential philosopher was Socrates, whose confession that he knew nothing of value led him to question others in pursuit of knowledge. His student Plato developed a philosophical system based on the premise that all knowledge is knowledge of the divine realm, of which this world is only a shadow. The Epicureans found reassurance in believing that the gods didn't care about humanity. The Stoics believed virtue consisted in keeping one's resolve aligned with the dictates of the divine will, while the Cynics were itinerant philosophers who challenged common assumptions and lived a life "according to nature."

## Outline

I.   The idea of knowledge as the root of virtue led to contemplation as a form of religious activity in the Classical era.

   A.  Greece had a deeply engrained mythology that was at odds with emerging principles of rational thought.
      1.  The "Greek enlightenment" included attempts at rationalistic explanation of traditional mythology.
      2.  Traditional mythological stories were considered unworthy of the true nature of the gods, who would never commit immoral acts.
      3.  Myths were dismissed as explanations of the world, as legends about historical people and events, or as a way of "naming" the forces of nature.
      4.  Philosophers derided some aspects of religious culture as mere superstition.

   B.  Generally, philosophers acknowledged the gods but rationalized them as abstract principles under the power of Zeus.

1. Zeus, or "the god," was understood in terms of "the good," source and summation of all good.
2. "The good" was the god of the philosophers who was best worshiped by living a rational life, pursuing knowledge and virtue.
3. Philosophical investigation was based on reason and observation to the exclusion of emotion.
4. Emotion was generally regarded among the Greeks as the ruling force in human actions.

C. One school that incorporated both philosophical and religious principles was based on the teachings of Pythagoras.
1. Pythagoras is known only through the writings of his followers and other commentators.
2. Pythagoras believed that numbers were the means of understanding the nature and rhythms of the cosmos.
3. Pythagoras believed that the *psyche*, the soul or human essence, was a spark of divine reason trapped in the body.
4. The duty of the rational person is to purify the soul from the corrupting influence of the body by self-denial.
5. Purification can take several lifetimes, because the soul leaves one body at death and enters another in a process called *metempsychosis*.
6. Purification of the soul was a process of acquiring the knowledge that enables one to lead a virtuous life.
7. Ascetic practices notably included abstention from the use of animal products.

II. The most influential figure in Greek philosophy was Socrates, who was claimed as an inspiration by later philosophical schools.

A. We know Socrates primarily through the writings of his student Plato, a philosopher in his own right.
1. Plato presents Socrates as an ironist who is also acknowledged to be the wisest of all human beings.
2. In Plato's dialogues, Socrates constantly pretends to be less wise than he really is, claiming to know nothing of value.

3. It is this claim of ignorance that makes Socrates the wisest person, because his ignorance drives him to seek wisdom.

**B.** Socrates in the *Apology* traces his philosophical mission to a pronouncement of the Delphic oracle.
   1. An *oracle* was a person empowered by a god to speak a revelation, or it can mean the revelation itself.
   2. The Delphic oracle was a person empowered by the god Apollo to give yes or no responses to specific questions.
   3. A friend of Socrates asked the oracle whether anyone was wiser than Socrates, and the oracle replied, "No."
   4. Because a question to the oracle would be answered yes or no, the question had to be phrased carefully.
   5. The oracle's reply puzzled Socrates, because he knew that oracles must speak the truth but also that he himself knew nothing of value.
   6. Socrates set out to question people reputed to be wise, hoping to find the meaning of the oracle's reply.
   7. In each case, Socrates discovered that those reputed to be wise knew nothing of value and were not aware of their ignorance.
   8. Socrates decided he was wiser than they, because he knew that he knew nothing of value.
   9. Socrates ultimately concluded that the oracle meant that the wisest are those who, like Socrates, know they know nothing of value.

**C.** The philosophical mission of Socrates was to engage in dialogue and ask searching questions in hope of discerning truth.
   1. Socrates's profession of ignorance and his desire to learn was invariably dismissed as irony by his opponents.
   2. Socrates collected followers, especially among the aristocratic young men of Athens.
   3. Socrates was put on trial for impiety and undermining the welfare of the state by corrupting the morals of his young male followers.
   4. Socrates was found guilty and condemned to death, a death he accepted with calm rationality.

**D.** Plato (427–347 B.C.E.) wrote dialogues featuring Socrates, but most of them expound Plato's own philosophy.

    **1.** Plato argued that our world is in a constant state of change and, thus, cannot be a source of knowledge.

    **2.** Knowledge derives from our inborn awareness of the "real," unchanging divine world.

    **3.** This world "participates" in the reality of the divine world and recalls to our minds what we know of the other reality.

    **4.** Plato explained this concept in the allegory of the cave, where prisoners see only shadows, and the philosopher is one who escapes the cave to see things as they really are.

    **5.** Plato emphasized the benefits of questioning and contemplation as a means of understanding the cosmos.

    **6.** Philosophical introspection leads to virtuous behavior based on knowledge of the good.

    **7.** Platonism formed the basic presuppositions for philosophical thought for several centuries.

**III.** Other philosophical schools emphasized instruction in virtue and peace of mind in the face of fate.

    **A.** Socrates was often at odds with the Sophists, itinerant teachers of the skills that led to a successful life.

        **1.** Sophists were teachers of rhetoric who could argue any side of an issue and endorsed accepted ideas of virtue.

        **2.** Sophists charged fees for their teaching, and some of them became famous.

        **3.** Sophists were not philosophers but similar to Near Eastern teachers of wisdom.

    **B.** Epicureanism found happiness in the peace of mind that comes from freedom of anxiety about the power of fate.

        **1.** Epicurus (341–270 B.C.E.) believed that anxiety arose from fear of offending the gods and fear of what happens after death.

        **2.** Epicurus offered two affirmations to banish these fears: The gods do not care about human behavior, and existence ends with death.

        **3.** Epicurus intended his philosophy to be a substitute for the "superstitions" of traditional Greek religion.

**4.** Happiness lies in the moderate pursuit of pleasure among good friends in a philosophical community.

**C.** Zeno, who taught in the *Stoa Poikile* (the colonnade) in 4th-century Athens, founded the school of Stoicism.
  **1.** Stoicism asserted that the divine exists in and through everything that exists, a position called *pantheism*.
  **2.** Stoics believed that a human being could control only the inner resolve that determined how he or she behaved.
  **3.** Stoics maintained that virtue was the result of keeping one's inner resolve in agreement with the divine reason.
  **4.** One must remain "detached" from external circumstances to keep one's inner resolve fixed on the divine reason.
  **5.** Stoic cosmology concluded that history is cyclical, repeating itself exactly as determined by the reduplication of astral phenomena.
  **6.** Stoics understood fate as the perfect legislation of the divine reason, the *logos*.

**D.** The Cynics were wandering ascetic philosophers who stood apart from society as its critics.
  **1.** Cynicism was founded by Diogenes of Sinope, who as a treasury official, felt a call to "change the currency."
  **2.** Diogenes understood this as a call to reject popular cultural values and social conventions.
  **3.** Diogenes believed a person should live according to nature by satisfying natural needs.
  **4.** This meant stripping life down to its barest essentials and being ashamed of nothing "natural."
  **5.** Diogenes's "shamelessness" earned him and his followers the nickname *kunikos*, "dog-like."
  **6.** Cynics were wanderers well known for their scruffy appearance and caustic polemics against society.
  **7.** The Cynics had no systematic doctrine but were deeply influenced by Stoic philosophy.
  **8.** Some of the milder Cynics filled an important function as personal counselors.

**E.** The philosophical schools widened the breach between the intellectual elite and the rest of Greek society.

1.  The persecution of "rationalists" reflected concern for maintaining religious values and instilling them in the young.
2.  The common charge against philosophers was that they were "atheists" whose unbelief endangered the state.

**Essential Reading:**

Plato. *Five Dialogues, Apology.*

Simon Price. *Religions of the Ancient Greeks*, pp. 126–142.

**Supplementary Reading:**

A. H. Armstrong. *An Introduction to Ancient Philosophy*, pp. 21–32, 114–140.

Walter Burkert. *Greek Religion*, pp. 305–337.

**Questions to Consider:**

1.  Which of the philosophies discussed in this session seem most similar to a religious system? Why? Which philosophies seem more of an alternative to religion? Why?

2.  The life and philosophical career of Socrates raise questions about the proper role of the philosopher in society. In what ways might the philosopher benefit society at large? In what ways might the philosopher undermine the common good?

# Lecture Thirty-Four—Transcript
## Greece—Philosophy as Religion

In our last session, we looked at the classical age in Greece from about 481 to 322 B.C.E. This was the era between the end of the Persian wars and the death of Alexander the Great. This period saw the fullest development of Greek culture in government, architecture, art, theater, and philosophy.

Now, in this session, we will discuss Greek philosophy in greater depth, in terms, especially, of how the philosophers understood the divine world and human duty towards the gods.

Now, the idea of knowledge as the root of character and behavior—this was the prevailing idea in ancient Greece. This led to contemplation as a form of religious activity. This happens in the growing rationalism of philosophy in the classical era, but it is sometimes called the "Greek enlightenment."

By the beginning of the classical era, Greece had a rich and deeply ingrained mythology; we've been talking about it over the last few sessions, but this mythology was at odds with emerging principles of rational thought. The Greek enlightenment of the classical era included many attempts at some sort of rationalistic explanation for traditional mythology, and that meant, at the same time, the debunking of superstitious practices.

For one thing, traditional mythology was considered unworthy of the true nature of the gods. The gods, in fact, the philosophers maintained would never commit immoral acts. They were dedicated to justice. They were higher beings with a higher standing in terms of morality. Nor would the gods ever reveal a lack of knowledge, as they do in the traditional mythology. The gods, after all, have the ability to see and understand all things.

Mythology, then, was sometimes dismissed as an attempt at an unthinking explanation of the conditions of the world, or sometimes it was understood as overblown legends of historical people and events that had taken on divine proportions, or it might be understood as the result of giving "names" to natural forces and anthropomorphizing those natural forces that are at work in everyday life—and thereby understanding them as somehow divine as gods.

These different methods of rationalizing or explaining traditional mythology were an attempt to bring reason to the realm of religious culture. On the other hand, philosophers derided some aspects of religious culture—that is, traditional Greek religious culture—as mere superstition—although, of course, the distinction between what we might call "religious ritual" on the one hand and superstition on the other is not always clear in the present, and certainly not always clear in the past.

Generally, the philosophers acknowledged the traditional gods, but they did tend to rationalize them as abstract principles—I think it's safe to say that—abstract principles—and thereby, to submit them to the overriding power of Zeus, who was seen as being the highest god—and, to a certain extent, the only god—so Zeus, or "the Good," was understood in terms of "the source of all goodness." Sometimes, he's even referred to merely as "the god."

Zeus, then, as "the Good" was the source and summation of all good, however it might be manifested throughout the cosmos. That good might be manifested in partial forms on earth, but those partial forms were merely one aspect—one facet—of the true, overwhelming, divine good that governed the cosmos, and "the Good"—or "the god"—was the god of the philosophers, a term we still hear used sometimes.

This was a god who was best worshiped by doing what was itself, good—in other words, honoring the god by imitating the god, or perhaps enacting the god. In other words, one on earth could please the god best by living a rational life, pursuing knowledge and, therefore, virtue—because virtue arises from knowledge of the good.

Philosophical investigation in classical Greece was based on reason and on observation, but it excluded emotion because emotion was felt to have no role in the sense of the created world. This is an important omission because emotion was often presented among the Greeks as the ruling force of human action. As a matter of fact, at this same time, in the classical era, emotion is seen as the ruling force of human actions in Greek tragedy—so there was a dichotomy here in the way that people understood what motivates human beings to act in the way that they do.

Now, one early school that incorporated both philosophical and what we might call religious principles was based on the teachings of Pythagoras, whom I have already mentioned. Pythagoras founded a school of philosophy in Italy around the year 532 B.C.E., so in the 6th century B.C.E.

Now, Pythagoras himself has left us no writings, and, as a result, he is known almost entirely, in fact, through the writings of his followers, and on the basis of the writings of other commentators as well. There is some material about Pythagoras that is clearly legendary—with no basis in the historical—but Pythagoras was both a religious teacher and a philosopher and, specifically, a mathematician.

Pythagoras believed that numbers were the means by which human beings could understand the nature and the rhythms of the cosmos. Pythagoras also believed that the *psyche*, or psyche, the soul, the human essence, was a spark of divine reason, and this divine reason was trapped in the physical body of each individual human being. He saw the *psyche*, the divine spark, as trapped in the human body in the same way that the corpse is trapped in a tomb, and, in fact, this led to a simple equation in Greek, "*Soma sema*," meaning "The body is a tomb," that is, a tomb for this divine psyche.

Now, the duty of the rational person was to purify the *psyche*, or the soul, or the divine essence, from the corrupting influence of the body that surrounded it. One did this by asceticism—that is, self-discipline enforced through various forms of self-denial, or what a colleague of mine calls "renunciation," and he calls ascetics "renouncers."

Now, this purification is not the business of a single lifetime. Pythagoras believed that at death, the *psyche*, the soul, left the body and then entered another body of either a human or an animal, or some other form, and this process was called "metempsychosis." After a long process of metempsychosis, as the *psyche* moved from one body, one material form, to another, eventually, *psyche* would be purified sufficiently to return to the realm of the gods.

Purification of the soul, then, was in part a process of acquiring knowledge because knowledge enabled one to live a virtuous life, but it also involved discipline of the material body by renunciation, and this renunciation included—especially in the case of Pythagoras's philosophy—abstention from the use of animal products, and that included not only meat, but also leather as well. The idea was that all souls in all animals and all human beings were all on a common journey back to the divine realm, and, therefore, to harm an animal was to harm a soul like one's own.

Now, the most influential, and certainly the most enigmatic, figure in Greek philosophy is Socrates, an Athenian whose dates are 469 to 399 B.C.E.

Socrates was claimed as an inspiration by almost all later philosophical schools in Greece, as well as some others. As with Pythagoras, we only know Socrates through the writings of others, but we know him primarily in our own age through the writings of his student, Plato. Plato was, of course, also a philosopher in his own right.

Plato presents Socrates primarily as an ironist—that is, someone who practices irony, and in the context within which Plato writes, we might understand the term "ironist" as a dissembling rascal, someone who presents not to be what he, in fact, is. At the same time that Plato presents Socrates as an ironist, he presents him as well as the best, the wisest, the most just of all human beings. So, Socrates is portrayed in Plato's dialogues as constantly pretending to be less wise than he really is, and Socrates claims, in fact, that he knows nothing of real value, but as Plato presents the case, it is precisely this claim of Socrates's, Socrates's claim of ignorance, Socrates's claim that he knows nothing of real value, that makes Socrates the wisest person. His ignorance, at least in theory, is what drives him on to seek out wisdom.

Now, in Plato's *Apology*, Socrates's self-defense against the Athenian assembly when charges were brought against him of impiety, Socrates, in his apology, traces both his claim of ignorance and his philosophical mission to a pronouncement of the Delphic oracle.

Now, the term "oracle" is rather difficult to understand. Sometimes, an oracle is a person—that is, someone who is empowered by the god in various ways to speak a revelation from the god. Sometimes, the oracle is the revelation itself—so we will talk about somebody "consulting" an oracle in some cases, and in other cases, "receiving" an oracle.

In the case of the Delphic oracle, it was a person empowered by Apollo to provide "yes" or "no" responses to particular questions, and Socrates, in Plato's *Apology*, claims his ignorance—his claim of ignorance—and his philosophical mission both trace back to a question put to the Delphic oracle. This was a question asked by Socrates's good friend, Chaerephon.

Chaerephon went to the oracle at Delphi and asked whether anyone was wiser than Socrates, and the oracle gave the answer, "No—that is, that no one was wiser than Socrates. This follows the standard approach to an oracle in the history of Greek consultation of oracles, as opposed to the legends about oracles, I should point out.

The standard approach was that one would ask an oracle a question that could be answered "yes" or "no." We will be reminded of other examples in Egypt, for example, where you seek a "yes" or a "no" answer from the god, but seeking a "yes" or a "no" answer from the gods means that one must be careful how the question is phrased.

In the case of Chaerephon's question to the Delphic oracle, I did not phrase his question very well. He asked whether anyone was wiser than Socrates. The oracle replied, "No," meaning "No one is wiser than Socrates."

Now, Socrates himself was puzzled by this response. On the one hand, he knew that the oracle always spoke the truth and the oracle could not lie because it was a divine oracle speaking on behalf of the god Apollo. On the other hand, Socrates knew that he, himself, knew nothing of real value, so to discover what the oracle meant by this answer to Chaerephon, Socrates set out to question people reputed to be wise. He hoped that he would discover, after questioning them, that they were wiser than he, so that he might challenge the reply given by the Delphic oracle, but he failed.

In each case, Socrates discovered that those were reputed to be wise, when he questioned them extensively, in fact, proved to know nothing of value, and worse, they were not aware of their own ignorance. In each case, then, Socrates decided that he was at least wiser than this person because although he knew nothing of value, at least he knew he knew nothing of value, and to that extent, he was wiser than those he questioned.

Socrates, therefore, ultimately concluded that what the oracle meant when the oracle indicated that no one was wiser than Socrates, was that there was a body of people who could be considered a "wisest," and the wisest people were those who, like Socrates, were aware that they knew nothing of value.

Now, as portrayed by Plato and other writers, Socrates's philosophical mission was to engage other people in this kind of investigative dialogue, almost an interrogation. He would ask them searching questions in hopes of discerning some facet of the truth—so in dialogue, Socrates was always careful to indicate his own ignorance. He always indicated that he was anxious to learn from others, and this was a practice that was invariably dismissed by those he talked with as mere irony because they felt that he was dissembling, that he was playing a game with them, that he was only pretending that he didn't know anything of value—although I would argue that, in fact, Socrates was being quite sincere.

Over time, Socrates collected a substantial body of followers, especially among the aristocratic young men of Athens, who seemed to find him endlessly intriguing, much as philosophers have throughout history.

Socrates, as I've indicated, was ultimately put on trial for impiety before the Athenian assembly. They tried him for impiety and for undermining the welfare of the Athenian state by corrupting the morals of Athens's young men—then, specifically, by encouraging them to act the way that Socrates did by engaging those reputed to be wise in this kind of interrogation.

Despite his own spirited defense that is re-created in Plato's *Apology*, Socrates was found guilty, and, ultimately, he was condemned to death. This was the death by poisoning. He was ordered to drink hemlock, and he met his death with his usual calm rationality.

Now, Plato wrote a series of dialogues featuring Socrates, but most of them expound, in fact, Plato's own philosophy—Plato's philosophy departed rather substantially from Socrates's own profession of ignorance.

Plato's basic premise was that our world, the world we live in on an everyday basis, is in a constant state of change. This was already established in Greek philosophy. Plato argued that since this world is in a constant state of change, it cannot be a reliable source of knowledge, because as soon as something is known, it changes and becomes different. So, even what we seem to know from experience is not a reliable source of knowledge because it is based on the experience of something that is constantly changing.

Plato, therefore, argued that all knowledge, in fact, derives from an inborn awareness that we all share of what exists in what he called the "real world"—that is, the unchanging divine world of the gods—and Plato believed that this world in which we live and act is merely a pale reflection of the real world, the divine world.

Now, we do understand and recognize things in this world, but we do so only to the extent that the things in this world resemble—Plato would say "participate"—in the reality of the divine world, and by the resemblance to the things in the divine world, the things in this world recall to our minds what we know of that other reality; so, there is not a direct knowledge of seeing something and saying, "That's a cat." Instead, it's a matter of saying, "There is something that reminds me of something I recall from the divine world, and that thing I recall from the divine world is a cat. Therefore, this must be a cat," so that it's a triangular process, if you will, rather than a straight-line process of immediate recognition.

We have knowledge of what is in this world, then, only to the extent of what it reminds us of what exists in the real world, the divine world, knowledge that we have inborn with us at the moment of our birth.

Now, Plato explains this concept in his famous allegory of the cave. He has this idea that there are chained prisoners who are able only to look at the wall of a cave. What they see, cast up by a fire behind them, are shadows, and these shadows are produced by little simulacra of things in the real world, so that what the prisoners see is a shadow of an imitation of reality, and this is the only knowledge we have in this world of the real world.

For Plato, the philosopher is the person who escapes from his chains, leaves the cave, and then goes out to see the real world as it actually is, to see things as they really are, and then he comes back to reveal that knowledge to those still in the cave.

Plato, therefore, emphasized the benefits of questioning and contemplation as a means of understanding the divine order of the cosmos, and again, he believed this knowledge was inherent in the mind—so that philosophical introspection leads not only to knowledge, but also to virtuous behavior that is based on knowledge of "the good," the divine. Additionally, this knowledge allows the philosopher to conform his own mind more closely to the divine mind that governs the cosmos.

By about 100 B.C.E., Plato's philosophy was widely disseminated in both Greece and Rome, and it pretty much formed the basic presuppositions for all philosophical thought for several centuries to follow. That's not to say that there weren't other philosophical schools at this time. There were other philosophical schools during the classical period, and during the Hellenistic period that followed it, and these other philosophical schools also looked to Socrates's example, but they emphasized different aspects of Socrates's personality and his philosophical mission. Therefore, they emphasized especially instruction in virtue and the benefits of peace of mind in the face of Fate.

Socrates often found himself in opposition to a group called the Sophists. Now, the Sophists were not philosophers as such, but itinerant teachers of the skills and knowledge that led to a successful life. The Sophists were preeminently teachers of rhetoric—that is, the art of persuasion—and they prided themselves on being able to argue any side of an issue, a skill that is now primarily exhibited by attorneys.

The Sophists generally endorsed accepted ideas of virtue. They didn't rock the boat very much. Sophists also charged fees for their teaching—something that, of course, now is entirely accepted—but it was something of a shock to the philosophers, and some of the Sophists became famous both for their rhetorical skills on the one hand, and for their teaching on the other, because their teaching was of the sort that enabled a man to find success in this life.

The Sophists, then, were therefore somewhat similar to the Near Eastern teachers of wisdom. That is, they shared the goal of helping their students gain material success, and therefore happiness in their lives.

Now, another school of philosophy was "epicureanism." This was a school that was also concerned with happiness in life, but instead of material success, the Epicureans found happiness in peace of mind, the peace of mind that comes from freedom from anxiety—specifically, freedom from anxiety over the blind power of Fate.

The school was founded by Epicurus, whose dates are 341 to 270 B.C.E. Epicurus believed that the anxiety that plagued most human beings arose from only two sources. On the one hand, people were afraid that they might offend the gods in some way, and by offending the gods, that they might provoke divine retribution, or *nemesis*.

The other fear that people had that caused them anxiety was fear of what might happen to them in Hades after they died. What kind of eternal punishment might be meted out to them?

In reply, Epicurus offered two basic affirmations that were intended to banish these fears. On the one hand, he said that the gods do indeed exist, but they are very happy; they are drinking their nectar and eating their ambrosia, and they don't really concern themselves with what human beings do, no more than we concern ourselves with the doings of insects.

In reply to the second concern, Epicurus said that life is entirely material phenomenon. Human beings are entirely material, made up of atoms, and when they die, the atoms that make them up disperse, and they cease to exist—so you need not worry about what happens to you after death because there is no you after death, so nothing happens to you after death.

Epicurus intended these two philosophical positions to be a substitute for the "superstitions" of traditional Greek religion, or what he styled as the "superstitions" of traditional Greek religion. He argued that true piety and true honor towards the gods were the imperturbability and the independence of the wise man, and that imperturbability, that independence, makes the wise man happy, and, therefore, happiness is pleasing to the gods.

Happiness, in fact, lies in the moderate—not the hedonistic—pursuit of pleasure, moderate enjoyment of what life has to offer for as long as it lasts—a very familiar refrain to us. This meant especially pursuit of moderate pleasure in the context of the philosophical community—that is, good friends united in companionable philosophical discussion, living together in a companionable community. This community was unusual, and it included both men and women.

Another school of philosophy concerned with the power of Fate was Stoicism. Stoicism was founded by Zeno of Citium, in Cyprus. His dates are about 333 to 262 B.C.E., and Zeno taught in the *Stoa Poikile*—that is, the piazza or the colonnade, in the fourth and third centuries B.C.E., in Athens. Stoicism, then, is not named after its founder, but after the place where he did his business of preaching his philosophy.

Stoicism stands out from traditional Greek religious culture by asserting that the divine exists in and through everything that exists. This is a position that we have previously defined as "pantheism," that the divine exists in and through all things that exist. Stoics believed that the only thing a human being could completely control in life was his or her own inner resolve, and it is the inner resolve that determines how a person behaves in any and all circumstances. Stoics maintained that virtue is the only good that exists, and, of course, virtue consisted of knowledge, but particularly of keeping one's inner resolve in agreement with the dictates of the *Logos*—that is, the divine reason that governs the cosmos. This required that a person remained "detached" from external circumstances—from earthly status, from earthly affections—because remaining detached from external circumstances kept one's inner resolve free to focus on the *Logos*—so freedom comes from detachment, or in Greek, *apatheia*.

The Stoic cosmology, their view of the cosmos, was based on observations of the cycles of the planets, and certain earthly phenomena as well, so the Stoics concluded that history was cyclical, and like the passage of the cosmic cycles, it follows a certain predictable pattern, and, therefore, history would repeat itself exactly over and over, because each time it happened, it would be determined by the reduplication of astral phenomena in each eon; since the same astral phenomena are in place, the same events transpire on earth.

Stoics believed only material existence is real, like Epicurus, and that astral phenomena determine Fate, but they understood Fate as the perfect legislation of the divine *Logos*, the divine mind that governs the cosmos, and, therefore, it's not something to be avoided or resisted, but it is something to be agreed to.

Similar to the Stoic philosophically was the Cynic. Cynics were wandering ascetic philosophers—that is, renouncers—who stood apart from society as its critics, as people like Socrates, who stood apart from society, and the Cynics modeled themselves on Socrates.

Cynicism was founded by Diogenes of Sinope in a place on the western coast of Asia Minor, and Diogenes dates are about 400 to 328 B.C.E. He was originally a treasury official, and during his time as the treasury official, he felt a call to "change the currency." Diogenes came to understand this as a call not to do something as a treasury official, but rather as a call to become a philosopher and reject popular values and popular conventions.

Diogenes believed a person should live according to nature, and by that he meant that human beings should devote themselves to satisfying natural needs, and that they should do so in the easiest and cheapest way possible. In practice, this meant stripping life down to its barest essentials especially with regard to personal comforts, and it also meant being ashamed of nothing that was natural; so, Diogenes's principle of shamelessness extended to such things as personal hygiene and sexual behavior. This "loose attitude," shall we say, earned Diogenes and his followers the nickname *kunikos*, which means "dog-like."

The Cynics were wanderers who became well known for their scruffy appearance, but also for their caustic polemics against accepted standards in Greek society. The Cynics had no systematic doctrine of their own, but they were deeply influenced by Stoic philosophy, and the Stoics, in turn, admired the Cynics and recognized them as philosophical brothers.

Some of the milder Cynics filled an important function as personal counselors, and this was notably the case with Crates, whose dates are about 365 to 285 B.C.E., who was one of the few married Cynics.

The philosophical schools, then—although they reflected religious ideas and religious sentiments—widened the breach between the intellectual elite and the rest of Greek society. The persecution of "rationalists" like Socrates was the result of agitation by religious professionals, and an increased concern for maintaining proper religious values and instilling those values in the young. The most common charge against philosophers was that they were "atheists." They did not recognize the traditional gods, and, therefore, by their neglect, they endangered the welfare of the state.

In our next session, we will discuss the birth of the Hellenistic world and the conquest of Alexander the Great, and the changes in Mediterranean religious culture that came as a result.

# Lecture Thirty-Five

## Religious Culture in the Hellenistic World

**Scope:**
After the Peloponnesian War, Greece entered a political and economic decline that led to submission to Philip of Macedon. His son Alexander campaigned against the Persian Empire, conquering its territories until his dominion extended from Greece to the Indus River. Macedonian rule was accompanied by the growth of Hellenistic culture, as key elements of classical Greek culture were imposed on the subject nations. Religious syncretism arose when gods, rituals, and mythology of one religious culture were combined with those of another. In the political and social upheaval of the early Hellenistic era, the primary concern was fate's control over human life. Anxiety over the power of fate led to new forms of religious community, as well as the impulse to resort to magical means of seeing into the future and asserting control over one's life. Theophrastus's sketch of the superstitious man portrays the religious anxiety that marked the early Hellenistic age.

## Outline

I.  The Peloponnesian War between Athens and Sparta (431–404 B.C.E.) weakened both cities, leading to conquest by the Macedonians.

   A.  The Peloponnesian War revealed some weaknesses in the Greek city-states and exacerbated others.

      1.  Athenian imperial ambitions led the *polis* to overreach militarily, losing a large part of its navy in an attempt to conquer Sicily in 415 B.C.E.

      2.  Political strife weakened the Greek economy, already suffering from a trade deficit and a lack of natural resources.

      3.  Greek armies became increasingly dependent on mercenaries as the ideal of the citizen-soldier declined.

   B.  At the same time, Macedonia was consolidating its power under Philip II.

1. Macedon had a self-sufficient economy, a citizen army, and a strong monarchy under Philip II (r. 359–336 B.C.E.).

2. Macedon had participated in Greek culture since at least the 5<sup>th</sup> century B.C.E.

3. Philip conquered Greek cities, made alliances, and quashed rebellions, becoming leader of a Pan-Hellenic alliance in 338 B.C.E.

4. With Greece united behind him, Philip planned a campaign against Persia, but he was assassinated in 336 B.C.E.

C. Philip was succeeded by Alexander III, who invaded Persia and became master of most of the known world.

1. As Alexander's armies moved east, the Persian Empire fell into his hands piece by piece.

2. Alexander's conquest of the Persian Empire with a small army was a tribute to his military genius but also to the reforms his father had brought to war.

3. Alexander crossed the Indus River into India, but his troops refused to fight any longer.

4. Alexander the Great died of fever in Babylon in 323 B.C.E., at age 33.

5. His young son soon died, leaving three of Alexander's generals to divide his empire among them.

II. The shape of Hellenistic culture, which prevailed through the early Roman Empire, was largely determined by Alexander himself.

A. Alexander wished not only to conquer but also to create a cosmopolitan culture that would unify his vast domains.

1. Alexander was a fervent Hellenist who intended to bring the blessings of Greek classical culture to his subjects.

2. The vast majority of his subjects lived under regional officials who were now subject to Greek-speaking Macedonians.

3. In Egypt, Alexander presented himself to his new subjects in the trappings of the pharaoh.

4. Alexander intended to bring the Persian aristocracy into partnership with its Macedonian masters.

5. His soldiers and officers rejected mixing conquerors and conquered, maintaining Greek superiority over the "barbarians."

**B.** In time, Alexander's conquests did result in a single cosmopolitan culture, at least among the upper classes.

1. *Hellenistic culture* was primarily Greek but included elements of the native cultures Alexander conquered.

2. The Macedonian kings of Egypt and Syria adopted traditional royal trappings of the native cultures.

3. They also established the institutions of Hellenic culture in their domains to assimilate native aristocracies.

4. A simplified version of classical Greek became the language of government administration and the *lingua franca.*

5. The Greek educational system indoctrinated native aristocrats, while constitutions established or remodeled conquered cities as Greek *poleis.*

6. Hellenistic culture spread Greek athletics, Greek ideals of intellectual culture, and Greek religious culture.

**C.** The new Hellenistic cosmopolitanism led to widely spread syncretism.

1. *Syncretism* is the synthesis of elements taken from distinct religious cultures into new forms and combinations.

2. This process might include reinterpretation of rituals and mythology to give them more universal significance.

3. Syncretism was often actively encouraged by Hellenistic rulers to legitimate their power and unite their subjects.

**D.** Syncretism resulted in the creation of new gods, as well as the reinvention of traditional gods as savior figures.

1. Apollo seems to become identified with the sun god only as a result of his identification with Amun-Rē.

2. The Hellenistic god Serapis is a synthesis of the Egyptian god Osiris and the Apis bull of Memphis.

3. Foreign gods tended to become "Hellenized" by being presented and worshiped according to Greek models.

4. The Hellenistic era also saw widespread worship of some traditional Greek gods, notably Demeter and Dionysus.

III. In the aftermath of Alexander's conquests, the irrational again became a major element in religious culture.

A. Greek rationalism reached a high point with Aristotle's founding of the Lyceum in 335 B.C.E.

1. Aristotle (384–322 B.C.E.), a student of Plato, was interested in observation, classification, and theory.

2. The Lyceum was more of a research center than a philosophical school.

3. Aristotle has left works in natural science, logic, mathematics, physics, ethics, rhetoric, and drama.

4. Aristotle's work demonstrates an attempt to submit natural and social phenomena to rational analysis.

B. Greek rationalism contributed to some extent to its own downfall, because it undermined faith in traditional religious culture.

1. The condemnation of Socrates reflected concern with traditional religious culture in a time of political uncertainty.

2. There was a growing breach between the intellectual elite and the rest of society, with popular opinion against the philosophers.

3. Public forms of religion declined, to be replaced by belief in fate as the determining factor in life.

4. This idea was always inherent in Greek religious culture, but events leading to Macedonian hegemony reinforced it.

C. Belief in the power of fate inspired philosophical and religious remedies but also practices pushing the bounds of religion.

1. The Epicureans, Stoics, and Cynics taught how a person might find peace of mind despite the power of fate.

2. Religious interest shifted to gods who were believed to have the power to save their devotees from the power of fate.

3. The gods who received the most attention were those closest to the concerns of the people.

4. The sanctuaries of Asclepius, the god of healing, combined therapeutic and religious methods for treating the ill.

D. Some people during the Hellenistic era turned to predicting or influencing the future.

1. There were various means of gaining insight into the future to determine what fate had in store.

2. Magical practices ranged from spells and rituals intended to gain control of cosmic powers to reliance on amulets.

3. Magical practices tended to focus on three goals: inspiring love, cursing, or turning aside curses.

E. Toward the end of the $4^{th}$ century B.C.E., Theophrastus created a portrait of the superstitious man.

1. The portrait is part of a series of 30 depicting people dominated by various faults.

2. The superstitious man is particularly concerned with religious purity.

3. He is scrupulous about religious ritual, both around the house and elsewhere.

4. He takes countermeasures against bad omens and seeks advice from dream analysts.

5. He favors religious actions over practical ones.

6. He's particularly wary of crossroads, common sites of religious pollution.

7. This portrait gives a sense of the forms religious anxiety might have taken in the Hellenistic era.

8. It also provides a context for investigating the new religious groups and practices that became popular during the Hellenistic age.

**Essential Reading:**

Robin W. Winks and Susan P. Mattern-Parkes. *The Ancient Mediterranean World: From the Stone Age to A.D. 600*, pp. 101–117.

Luther H. Martin. *Hellenistic Religions: An Introduction*, pp. 3–15, 35–57.

## Supplementary Reading:

Theophrastus. *Characters*.

A. H. Armstrong. *An Introduction to Ancient Philosophy*, pp. 66–86.

## Questions to Consider:

1. Alexander's conquests united the eastern Mediterranean into a single Hellenistic culture, based on the Greek language and Macedonian rule. What were the advantages and disadvantages of a single dominant general culture for the subjects of his empire?

2. Syncretism involves the combination of the elements of one religious culture with those of another. What might be the advantages and disadvantages of syncretism, specifically in Hellenistic culture?

# Lecture Thirty-Five—Transcript
## Religious Culture in the Hellenistic World

In our last session, we discussed philosophy as an alternative to religion, as a means of gaining insight into the divine world, and bringing human behavior in line with the divine will. In this session, we will look at the rapid political and cultural changes that accompanied the ascent of the power of Macedon, the anxieties those changes produced, and the solutions sought to some of those anxieties.

Now, Athens's imperial ambitions led to the Peloponnesian War with Sparta, in the period between 431 and 404 B.C.E. This war weakened both cities, but Athens and Sparta, in fact, left Greece open to conquest by the Macedonians.

The Peloponnesian War also revealed some weaknesses in the situation with the Greek city-states, and it created—or in some cases, exacerbated—others. Athenian imperial ambitions led the *polis* to overreach militarily, probably most notably when a large part of its navy was destroyed in an attempt to conquer the island of Sicily in 415 B.C.E.

Political strife also weakened the Greek economy, while the lack of natural resources and a trade deficit with impoverishment of the middle class had already weakened the Greek economy, even as the Greek population was growing and the armies of the various *poleis* became increasingly dependent not on citizen-soldiers, but on mercenaries—those who fought for pay—because the ideal of the citizen-soldier declined. This happened to the detriment of the cities' cohesiveness.

At the same time, above the Greek peninsula, above Thessaly to the north, was Macedon. Macedon, at this time, was consolidating its power under a powerful king, Philip II. Macedon, unlike Greece, had a self-sufficient economy. It had a strong citizen army, and it had a powerful monarchy at this point under Philip II, who reigned from 359 to 336 B.C.E. It was Philip II who had united the nation of Macedon and reformed its army, a very important thing that he did.

Now, Macedon had participated in Greek culture since at least the 5<sup></sup>th century B.C.E. Macedon's language was a cognate, a connected language with Greek, a cognate of Greek. Philip, the king of Macedon, wished to present himself as essentially Greek.

Through a combination of skillful warfare and canny statesmanship, Philip was able to gain control over a number of Greek cities. He then made alliances with others, and he also managed to out-maneuver an attempt at a rebellion against his power. As a result, Philip II of Macedon became leader of a Panhellenic—that is, an all-Greek—alliance in the year 338 B.C.E.

With Greece united behind him, Philip planned a campaign against Persia for its 5th-century invasion of Greece, which we have already discussed, but Philip's plans came to nothing when he was assassinated in 336 B.C.E. at the age of 46.

Philip, however, was succeeded by his son, Alexander III, who at this point was only 20 years old, and it was Alexander who carried out Philip's plans to invade Persia. In the process, Alexander made himself the master of most of the known world and earned himself the title, "Alexander the Great." As Alexander's armies moved east, various pieces of the Persian empire fell into his hands: first, Asia Minor; then, Egypt; then, Syria-Palestine; then, Mesopotamia; and, finally, Persia itself.

Alexander set out to conquer the Persian empire with a relatively small army, and his conquest was a tribute to his own military genius, but it was also a tribute to the reforms that Alexander's father, Philip II, had made when he changed the nature of the Macedonian army—and, as a result, changed the nature of ancient war.

Alexander ultimately crossed the Indus River and fought some battles in India, but his own troops rebelled against him and refused to fight any longer. Alexander retired back into Babylon, and he died in Babylon of a fever in the year 323 B.C.E. when Alexander was only 33 years old, and yet, master of most of the known world.

Alexander left a young son as his successor, but his son soon also died, and it was three of Alexander's generals who divided his empire among them.

Now, the shape of what is called "Hellenistic culture," the culture that prevailed throughout Alexander's domains—this Hellenistic culture prevailed throughout the time of Alexander's conquests, and through the early centuries of the Roman empire. The character of Hellenistic culture was largely determined by Alexander himself.

You see, Alexander himself was an imperialist in the classic sense. That was, he did not only wish to conquer new territories, but he also wanted to create a single cosmopolitan culture throughout his vast domains that would unify his various subjects under his own rule, in a single cosmopolitan culture.

Although not himself a Greek, Alexander was a fervent Hellenist—that is, a fervent supporter of the Greek way of life—and he wanted to bring the blessings of Greek classical culture to all the former subjects of the Persian kings. Of course, for the vast majority of his new subjects, the change in national leadership did not mean a lot. For one thing, they were mostly still beholden to regional officials, and the regional officials were subject to higher regional officials—but those, in turn, were subject now not to Persian officials, but to Greek-speaking Macedonians. In other words, they now had to answer to Greek-speaking Macedonians instead of Aramaic-speaking Persians. For the average person, though, for the vast majority of the subjects of this new empire, the change didn't mean much, at least not initially.

Now, in Egypt, Alexander had been careful to present himself as a ruler on the traditional model of the Egyptian Pharaoh. He not only presented himself to his new subjects in Egypt in the trappings of a Pharaoh, but he also established his legitimacy by claiming that he had been declared to be a son of Amun by an Egyptian oracle.

Alexander also intended to bring the Persian aristocracy into partnership with their Macedonian masters, and so—there, too—in Persia, he adopted the royal trappings of a Persian king. He also married into the Persian nobility, and he intended to incorporate Persian soldiers into his Macedonian army, but once again, he was opposed by his own troops. Alexander's soldiers, as well as his own officers, rejected any idea of mixing the conquerors with the conquered because most of his soldiers, and most of their officers, believed that the conquest of Persia was proof of Greek superiority over the "barbarians," the superiority of those united under Alexander over those other peoples who opposed him.

Now, in time, it was the case that Alexander's conquests did result in a single cosmopolitan culture throughout his domains, at the very least at the upper levels, and this happened primarily through a process of assimilation.

What we call "Hellenistic culture" was promulgated by Alexander as well as his successors. This is a culture that was primarily Greek, but it also included elements of many of the native cultures that the Macedonians had conquered; so we cannot call this a "Hellenic" culture—that is, a Greek culture—but rather, a "Hellenistic" culture—that is, a Greek-like culture. It is not Greek, then, but it's like Greek culture—Greek-like culture that combines elements of Greek culture primarily with elements of various other cultures that Alexander had conquered.

Now, for example, the Macedonian king of Syria and the Macedonian king of Egypt—these were two of the major territories divided by the generals of Alexander; Syria, for example, included Mesopotamia.

These Macedonian kings legitimized themselves as Alexander had done, by adopting the traditional royal trappings of the native cultures. So we find that the Pharaohs of the Hellenistic era, for example, are represented in late Egyptian art in much the same way as the earlier Pharaohs were, even though these later Pharaohs were Macedonian in their national origin, rather than Egyptian.

However, the Macedonian kings also established the dominant institutions of Hellenic culture in their domains—that is, dominant Greek institutions that conveyed the essence of Greek culture. For example, this was a means of assimilating by language, by education, by practice, all the different peoples of the Hellenistic empires.

The kings, for example, attempted to assimilate native aristocracies and make them their supporters through the Greek educational system. The Greek educational system indoctrinated the sons of the native aristocracies by teaching them the Greek language, and by teaching them according to the Greek style.

The Greek language was common in the Hellenistic empire, and it was a somewhat simplified version of classical Greek called *Koine*; this became, first, the language of government administration, but in time, it became the *lingua franca* of the Hellenistic empire—that is, every citizen's first or second language, that allowed them to communicate with each other and with imperial officials.

Greek style city constitutions also transformed many of the cities of the Hellenistic empire by remodeling them on the form and the constitution of a Greek *polis*. In other words, constitutions established new cities in the Greek style, or they re-established existing cities in the Greek style, remaking them as Greek *poleis*, as Greek cities.

Along with these changes came the spread of reverence for athletics and the institutions that went along with that reverence, the Greek ideals of intellectual culture, Greek religious culture, and Greek mythology.

What was probably the most influential change arising from the Macedonian conquest was in this last category, religious culture, because this new cosmopolitan culture, this new Hellenistic culture, led to a widespread syncretism. Now, I have talked about syncretism as a religious phenomenon before. Syncretism is the synthesis of various elements from different religions into new forms and combinations—and that means gods, it means rituals, and it means mythologies—taken from distinctive religious traditions, and brought together and then re-expressed in new forms and the new combinations.

Of course, this process often included reinterpretation of existing rituals, reinterpretation of existing mythology, to give them a more universal significance that befitted the citizens of this new universal empire.

Most notably, this happened in the case of fertility rituals. Fertility rituals, for reasons that may be obvious, tended to be reinterpreted as rituals of death and rebirth, and this happened particularly in connection with what are called the "mystery religions," which I will be discussing in the next session.

Syncretism, then, was a powerful influence on Hellenistic religious culture, and, in fact, syncretism was actively encouraged by Hellenistic rulers to legitimize their power and to unite their subjects in a common religious culture. This is the case, for example, of Alexander's going to an Egyptian oracle, consulting that oracle, and then afterward, announcing to the people that the oracle had named him as a son of Amun. He used an Egyptian religious tradition to establish his own legitimacy as ruler over the Egyptians.

Syncretism also resulted in the creation of new gods, new gods who combined the attributes of several other gods and, occasionally, as well, the reinvention of traditional gods as more powerful and more pervasive savior figures.

For example, we find that Apollo, who was, of course, a Greek god, and who was originally a pastoral god that is, a god of the countryside—and an agricultural god—that is, a god of the farmers; his origins lie in Asia Minor; there are reasons why he supports Troy in the Trojan War.

He later was identified with Helios, the sun god, only very late, and the identification between Apollo and Helios appears to arise from Apollo's identification with the Egyptian god Amun-Re because Apollo shared many other attributes with Amun-Re and gained the additional attribute of being also thought of, then, as a sun god. Although we think of that as a primary attribute of Apollo, it's apparently in reality quite a late attribute of Apollo.

As far as new gods were concerned, there was a Hellenistic god named Serapis, and Serapis was a synthesis of the Egyptian god Osiris and the Apis bull of Memphis. The Apis bull was the physical manifestation of the *ba*—that is, the sacred essence of the god Ptah. When the sacred bull died, it was mourned with great ceremony until a new Apis bull was found; so when the Apis bull died, it became, in death, Osiris, and at that point was referred to as "Apis-Osiris."

Serapis appears to be based on these two gods, Osiris and the Apis bull of Ptah. Serapis was a god of the underworld, and he was worshiped with Greek rituals in a temple called Serapium, in Alexandria—Alexandria itself a new city established on the Nile delta by Alexander the Great.

Foreign gods, then, tended to become "Hellenized" and remained on the Greek model, and this happened as a result of being presented and worshiped according to Greek models. This way, their foreignness was not an obstacle to being worshiped by members of the Hellenistic empire, but, instead, their foreignness became primarily an indication of their ancient origins, and in some cases, of their universal appeal. Of course, the longer the god had been worshiped, the more proper and the more powerful were the associations of those gods.

The Hellenistic era also saw the widespread worship of some traditional Greek gods, notably Demeter and Dionysus, but now, these traditional Greek gods were understood in a new way, as universal gods who controlled the power of life, death, and rebirth, because of their original associations with fertility.

Now, in the aftermath of Alexander's conquest, the irrational, again, became a major element in Greek religious belief, and in Hellenistic religious belief, and expression and religious action, and—ultimately—this gave free rein to what we identify as superstition and magical practices.

Now, as we have seen, Greek rationalism was on the ascendancy throughout the classical period, and it reached something of a climax with Aristotle and his founding of the Lyceum in 335 B.C.E. Aristotle's dates are 384 to 322 B.C.E. He was a student of Plato, but Aristotle's interest was more in observation, classification, and theory, rather than in metaphysical speculation of the sort that Plato indulged in.

The Lyceum, then, was more of a research center, as we might call it, than a philosophical school on the model of Epicurus or of Zeno. The Lyceum had a large library, and it had associates of Aristotle at work in their own fields of interest.

Aristotle has left works in natural science, in logic, in mathematics, in physics, in ethics, in rhetoric, and in drama—in other words, things that can be observed, discussed, and analyzed.

Of course, an even larger part of Aristotle's work has been lost. Some of it survives in fragments, and some of it appears to have been the result of collaboration with others, but—in general—Aristotle's work demonstrates an attempt to submit natural and social phenomena to rational analysis, the apparent belief that human reason was capable of understanding all aspects of the natural world, but also the human world, and did so by means of observation and analysis.

However, the Greek rationalism exemplified by Aristotle contributed, to some extent, to its own downfall, because this new rationalism undermined faith in traditional religious culture, and it did this as a means of battling uncertainty.

Socrates, as we've seen, was convicted of impiety and corrupting young Athenians—in other words, with undermining the welfare of the Athenian state by raising religious questions and deviating from religious traditional practice.

This reflects a concern with traditional religious culture in a time of growing political uncertainty. There was a growing breach between the intellectual elite and the rest of society, and popular opinion was most often against the philosophers. The rich heritage of Greek religious culture continued to shape and influence thought and influence expression, even as public forms of religion declined. Instead, they were replaced by a belief in Tyche, or Fate, and many people came to believe that Fate alone was the determining factor in the course of one's life.

To some extent, this idea was always inherent in Greek religious culture because, of course, the gods, as well as humanity, were subject to the dictates of Fate, but events that led to the Greeks' submission to Macedon during the early Hellenistic era appear to have reinforced the belief in the blind power of Fate, and to have set Fate apart as the single determining factor in the course of human life.

This belief in the dominant power of Fate inspired a number of philosophical and religious remedies in reaction, as well as practices that—at least in our eyes—began to push against the proper boundaries of religion. We have already seen that a major point of emphasis in the philosophical schools of the Epicureans, the Stoics, and the Cynics was how a person might find peace of mind, peace of mind that would endure despite the power of Fate in one's life for good or for ill.

At the same time, religious interest shifted to gods who were believed to have the power to save their devotees from Fate and its blind dictates. Usually, this meant the god of the cult, the god of the religion, became a patron to the devotee or worshiper. As was always the case, the gods who received the most attention were those closest to the daily concerns of the people who worshiped them, but those concerns were now more and more likely to involve protection from disease or injury, or from the power of fate, so we find, for example, that the healing cult of the god Asclepius was particularly popular.

Asclepius had sanctuaries that combined therapeutic techniques with religious methods for treating the ill, and dormitories for sick people with temples, and a devotee could go to one of these temples and sleep there and hope that he or she would receive a revelatory dream from the god, and hope in that dream, there would be some indication of how a person might be cured.

Now, some people during the Hellenistic era chose to take what we might call a more active part in protecting themselves from the power of Fate, and they turned to predicting—or in some cases, influencing—the future, and thereby, the course of their lives.

Now, there were various means of gaining insight into the future, to determine what Fate had in store for a person, and that meant that that person could take preventative measures. Magical practices promised to grant a person some degree of control over their personal destiny, and magical practices included rituals that ranged from elaborate spells, elaborate rituals of various kinds that were intended to gain control over the cosmic powers, and then went all the way down to reliance on amulets and charms as a means of turning away evil.

In fact, the concerns of those who resorted to magical practices— some of these practices being very ancient—their concerns tended to focus on three goals. They either wanted to inspire erotic love in another person, or they wanted to curse another person, or they wanted to turn aside the curse set against them by another person. I will be discussing this at greater length in another session.

Now, towards the end of the 4th century B.C.E., Aristotle's pupil and successor as head of the Lyceum was a man named Theophrastus. Theophrastus created the succinct *Portrait of the Superstitious Man.*

This portrait was one of 30 that depicted people dominated by various common faults, and these ranged from absent-mindedness on the one hand to bad taste on the other.

As far as we can tell, Theophrastus's character sketches were intended to be merely entertaining, but Theophrastus does provide us an insight into the beliefs and practices of the superstitious man, or what we might call "the hyper-religious man."

The superstitious man, Theophrastus tells us, is particularly concerned with religious purity, with making himself pure from various contaminating influences—so he sprinkles water on himself continually, or cleansing herbs, and he does this after any encounter that might contaminate him or might appear to portend bad fortune.

The superstitious man is very scrupulous about the performance of religious ritual, and he's very scrupulous about religious ritual around the house, but also elsewhere, and he finds himself running off many times a day to the temple, to perform particular rituals, but Theophrastus notes that his wife, generally, is too busy to go with him—so he has to take a slave along, instead. Honestly, the wife has better things to do than to spend all day running back and forth to the temple.

The superstitious man takes countermeasures after a weasel crosses his path. Apparently weasels were the black cats of the ancient Mediterranean world. He takes countermeasures if he finds a snake in his house. He seeks advice from a dream analyst or a prophet if he seems to have a dream that has some deeper meaning.

When he finds that mice have gotten into his sack of provisions, his first impulse is to go to a seer, to find out what he should do, and he rejects the more sensible alternative of going to work to mend the sack that the mice have destroyed.

The superstitious man is particularly wary of crossroads, because crossroads are common sites of religious pollution, and so, he performs small rituals at each crossroads he encounters, but if he sees someone at a crossroads who is wearing garlic to ward off evil influences, the superstitious man runs away because that sight convinces him that things must be worse than he had thought.

Now, this portrait provides an exaggerated type, honestly, the sort of exaggerated type found in comedies, but it does give a sense of some of the forms of religious anxiety that we might find during the Hellenistic era, the kind of hag-ridden fear that an individual might experience in the face of the anxieties of the Hellenistic era.

It also, fortunately, provides us with a context for investigating various new sorts of religious groups and practices that became popular during the Hellenistic age and might give us some clues to their popularity.

In our next session, we will look at mystery religions as characteristic expressions of religious yearning in the Hellenistic era, and some of the distinctive features that set the mystery religions apart from other forms of ancient religious communities.

# Lecture Thirty-Six

# Mystery Religions in the Hellenistic World

**Scope:**
The Hellenistic era saw a return to the worship of earth-based deities in mystery religions. These were religious groups with secret rituals that included initiation rites. The gods of the mystery religions, whether Greek or foreign, were generally fertility deities whose mythology was reinterpreted as stories of death and rebirth. A person chose to join a mystery religion on the basis of religious experience and, by so doing, became a devotee of the god, who in turn, became the devotee's patron. The "salvation" provided by the mystery religion was specifically salvation from the blind power of fate, because the god would ensure the devotee's welfare in all circumstances. Demeter was worshiped in a mystery cult at Eleusis and elsewhere, based on her daughter Kore's descent to Hades and return. The cult of Dionysus, the god of wine and ecstasy, focused on the god's life-giving power, celebrated in ritual banquets.

## Outline

I.   Mystery religions were so called because the central rituals were secret, that is, "mysteries."

  A.  The Hellenistic era saw a renewed worship of earth-based (*chthonic*) deities, as their fertility rites were reinterpreted as salvation rituals.

    1.  The power of these deities was based on their association with the cycle of fertility and all aspects of dynamic life.

    2.  Myths originally associated with the fertility cycle were reinterpreted as myths about death and rebirth.

    3.  The deity controlled the cycle of fertility and, thus, the cycle of life, death, and rebirth.

  B.  Mystery religions included secret initiation rituals as a prerequisite to membership.

    1.  These rituals were expensive and time-consuming and represented the devotee's sincerity.

    2.  First, there was a ritual of purification and a vigil.

    3.  There was usually a sacrifice to the god, most often a pig whose blood ran into the earth.

4. This was followed by a confession of faith, when the devotee expressed the desire to become an initiate into the cult.

5. The initiation apparently culminated in a revelatory vision of the central cultic symbol.

**C.** Public rituals and ceremonies publicized the mystery religion and attracted new initiates.

1. Public celebrations included processions accompanied by music, singing, and dancing.

2. Celebrations often included a recital or reenactment of the central myth of death and resurrection or rebirth.

**D.** The mystery religions offered their devotees a personal relationship with the cult's deity.

1. A person became a follower of a mystery religion by choice on the basis of some sort of religious experience.

2. The mysteries emphasized the bond between the deity and the initiate.

3. The "salvation" offered by the mystery religions was salvation from the blind power of fate.

4. Just as the god in the cultic mythology overcame adversity, so he or she would protect the devotee and bring him or her "home."

5. The mysteries forged a patron/client relationship of worship and protection between the initiate and the god.

6. A person might be an initiate into several different mystery religions at once.

**E.** Although mystery religions achieved new popularity during the Hellenistic era, many of them were ancient in their origins.

1. Most gods of the mysteries were "foreign," and this emphasized the antiquity and universality of their cults.

2. Some goddesses of the mysteries retained a specifically "foreign" identity.

3. Others became thoroughly Hellenized and cosmopolitan, to the extent they became identified with Greek gods.

4. This is the case with Isis, who is identified with several Greek goddesses.

**5.** Mystery gods were explicitly deities for the entire world, and their devotees were also missionaries.

**II.** Demeter was a goddess of the Greek pantheon whose worship evolved into a mystery religion.

    **A.** The Eleusinian mysteries were based on the myth of Kore's abduction and rape by Hades.

        **1.** Demeter was plunged into despair by Kore's disappearance and served the king of Eleusis as a nurse.

        **2.** The earth lay fallow until Zeus sent Hermes to demand that Hades return Kore to Demeter.

        **3.** Kore could return to earth for only a part of each year before returning to Hades.

        **4.** This myth is typical of stories explaining the fertility cycle that easily become stories of death and rebirth.

    **B.** Demeter's primary sanctuary was in Eleusis, where a temple was built at her command when Kore returned to her.

        **1.** Eleusis was the site of an early festival celebrating the sowing of grain and, later, the *Thesmophoria*, mourning Kore's annual return to Hades.

        **2.** The Eleusinian mysteries seem to have evolved out of these celebrations, reinterpreted as festivals of rebirth.

        **3.** At Eleusis, both men and women worshiped, although elsewhere, only women celebrated the Eleusinian mysteries.

        **4.** The worship space in Eleusis could hold several thousand worshipers.

        **5.** Priests of Eleusis served as advisors in the institution and reform of other mystery religions.

    **C.** After Eleusis was conquered by Athens, the "greater mysteries" were celebrated with a procession from Athens to Eleusis.

        **1.** On the first day, sacred objects and chests were carried from Eleusis to Athens.

        **2.** On following days, a herald excluded criminals and barbarians; initiates sacrificed and bathed in the sea.

      **3.** Finally, a procession along the Sacred Way from Athens to Eleusis returned the sacred objects to the hall of initiation to cries of "Iacchos!"

   **D.** Some written and graphic evidence survives indicating what the ceremonies of Demeter might have included.

      **1.** There were three sorts of activities in the Eleusinian mysteries: "things recited," "things shown," and "things performed."

      **2.** The public aspect of the ritual is parodied in *The Frogs* by Aristophanes.

      **3.** Initiation reportedly included fasting, drinking a mixture of barley meal and mint, and manipulating sacred objects.

      **4.** The ultimate revelation is believed to have been a head of grain that revealed the essential nature of life.

**III.** Dionysus, the god of wine and ecstasy, also became the god of a mystery religion.

   **A.** Worship of Dionysus forms something of a complement to the worship of Demeter.

      **1.** Demeter's grain must be made into bread to provide food, just as grapes must be made into the wine of Dionysus.

      **2.** Dionysus was a son of Zeus and the mortal Semele, who was struck dead during her pregnancy.

      **3.** Zeus took her unborn child and sewed him into his thigh until he was ready to be born.

      **4.** Dionysus was later entrusted to nymphs of Mount Nysa, who raised him.

      **5.** Dionysus discovered wine and traveled throughout Greece to share it.

      **6.** He was ultimately included in the company of the gods after rescuing Semele from Hades.

   **B.** Various stories tell about those who refuse to recognize the divinity of Dionysus and suffer the consequences.

      **1.** The most well known story is told in Euripides's *The Bacchae*, when Pentheus, king of Thebes, imprisoned Dionysus.

**2.** Dionysus inspired the women of Thebes to join his followers and persuaded Pentheus to spy on them, but the Bacchae discovered Pentheus and tore him to pieces.

**3.** Such stories reflect Dionysus's chthonic identity that runs counter to the official religious culture.

**C.** Such stories tell us about the god's power and the effects he was believed to have on his worshipers.

    **1.** Dionysus was originally a rustic deity associated with the rural gods Pan, Silenus, and Priapus, as well as with satyrs, fauns, and nymphs.

    **2.** Dionysus sometimes appears as a bull but more usually as an effeminate young man with long curls.

    **3.** Dionysus was believed to cause ecstasy and madness in human beings.

    **4.** In Euripides's play, the Bacchae eat raw flesh as a means of feeding on Dionysian power in the animal.

    **5.** The intention of Dionysian worship was to ingest the intoxicating power of the god and to exhibit divine possession.

    **6.** Rituals of Dionysus involved eating and drinking wine; banquets in his honor appear to have included sexual activity.

    **7.** Sexual activity and secrecy led the Roman Senate to severely restrict the worship of Dionysus in 186 B.C.E.

**D.** Dionysus was identified with Osiris and associated with death and rebirth.

    **1.** Dionysus's rescue of Semele from Hades, with his identity as the god of the power of life, made him a potent mystery deity.

    **2.** Dionysus appears to have promised his devotees an afterlife of enjoyment of the sensuous appetites his presence inspired on earth.

## Essential Reading:

Marvin W. Meyer, ed. *The Ancient Mysteries*, pp. 1–45, 61–109.

Luther H. Martin. *Hellenistic Religions: An Introduction*, pp. 58–72, 90–98.

**Supplementary Reading:**

Sarah Iles Johnston, ed. *Religions of the Ancient World: A Guide*, pp. 98–111.

**Questions to Consider:**

1. What seem to be the most valuable characteristics of the mystery religions? How did they contrast in that respect with the traditional religions of the Hellenistic era?

2. What characteristics do the gods and goddesses of the mystery religions seem to have in common? How are these characteristics reflected in the mystery religions themselves?

# Lecture Thirty-Six—Transcript
# Mystery Religions in the Hellenistic World

In our last session, we considered the political and cultural changes that accompanied the conquests of Alexander the Great and ushered in what we call the "Hellenistic world." In this session, we will look at one form of religious practice in a community that promised "salvation" from the power of Fate. These are the Hellenistic mystery religions. Now, mystery religions, I should indicate right away, are called "mystery religions" because their central rituals were secret—that is, they were "mysteries."

Now, as we've seen, the Hellenistic era saw the return to ancient earth-based—that is, chthonic—deities. The fertility rituals associated with these chthonic deities were reinterpreted during the Hellenistic era's salvation rituals. The power of these deities, usually goddesses, in fact, was based on their association with the cycle of fertility—that is, an association that often broadened, as we have seen, into control over all of the cycles of life, as well as cosmic cycles, cosmic rhythms, and all aspects of dynamic life.

Now, the mythology originally associated with the fertility cycle—such as the myth of Hades abducting Kore, the daughter of Demeter, and then her periodic return to her mother, Demeter—establishes the cycle of fertility; this sort of mythology was reinterpreted as stories about death and rebirth during the Hellenistic era. Thereby, the goddess concerned gains control not only over the cycle of fertility, but also over the cycle of life, death, and rebirth.

Now, the "mysteries" in the mystery religions were secret initiation rituals that were a prerequisite to membership in the mystery religion, and these rituals themselves represented a death, but this was a death to one's old way of life, and rebirth as a devotee of the goddess of the mystery religion. These kinds of secret initiation rituals were apparently both very expensive and very time-consuming, and, to a certain extent, one's willingness to undergo this process was taken as an indication of the sincerity of the devotees—that is, his or her sincerity in seeking to become a worshiper of the goddess of the mystery religion.

First, there was a period of personal preparation for the initiation, and this would include some sort of ritual purification, presumably to make one fit to face and enter the company of the god. It included new clothing and, often, a vigil the night before the initiation. We can compare this initiation ritual to the preparations for being entered into the roles of knighthood during the medieval era, or we can compare it to preparation for ordination, in the Christian tradition.

As part of the initiation ritual, there was usually a sacrifice the day beforehand to the god or goddess of the mystery cult. In the case of chthonic deities, the sacrifice was often a pig, and the blood of the pig, after it was sacrificed, was allowed to run down into the earth, and therefore to make contact with this earth-based goddess.

This was followed by a more or less public confession of Fate—that is, the devotee would have the opportunity to express publicly his or her desire to become an initiate into the cult of this particular goddess, and the initiation process would, apparently, culminate in a secret ceremony that included, at its center, a revelation, a vision of the central cultic symbol, which was seen as an expression of the deity's essential nature.

In addition to these secret initiation rituals, the mystery religions also had a distinctive public face. This was a means of performing public rituals and ceremonies in such a way as to publicize the religion, and so also to gain new initiates. These sorts of public celebrations took place in a festival atmosphere. They included processions. They were accompanied by music, singing, and dancing. They would have the cultic priest carrying sacred objects associated with the mystery religion, and a core of devotees would be arrayed in special colorful costumes. You can imagine the kind of stir this would cause in the city. It would be like having a Shriner's parade in the middle of your daily work—or something more elaborate, perhaps.

Such celebrations also included a recital of the central myth of the mystery religion, or even a reenactment of the central mythological story of the death and resurrection of the god or goddess associated with the primary deity. This would both remind the devotees of the cult of the central mystery of their own experience of initiation, and it would proselytize new recruits and encourage them to become initiates themselves.

Now, it was not just this public expression of the festival carnival atmosphere of the mystery religions that attracted people to them. The appeal of the mystery religions was that they offered their devotees more than traditional Hellenistic religious culture was able to offer. This was a personal relationship with the deity of the mystery religion—that is, the kind of relationship where the individual and the god formed a personal bond, a bond similar to that of a patron and client, the devotee being a supporter and client of the god, who takes on a form of protection and concern for the devotee, much like that of a patron for a client.

A person became a follower of a mystery religion, then, by choice—usually on the basis of some sort of religious experience, and the mystery religions emphasized the bond between the deity and initiate. This was, again, a personal bond, and it was based on the initiate's inward devotion toward the god, which was then expressed in outward demonstrations of that devotion.

Now, these were groups that offered salvation. The mystery religions offered salvation, but the "salvation" they offered was not salvation from death. It was salvation from the blind power of Fate. Initiation would bring the devotees into the patronage of a powerful deity, and then that powerful deity would act as a patron and provide the devotee with protection against the buffets of Fate. The hope was that just as the goddess of the cult herself, in the mythology of the cult, overcame adversity, and eventually regained her loved one, and returned home in peace, so the goddess would also protect her devotee during life's wanderings and bring the devotee home in peace—in this case, home to the goddess.

Although the mystery religions formed a patron/client relationship in this way and established a personal bond between the worshiper and the god, the relationship established in the mystery religion was not an exclusive one. This is rather surprising to us as moderns, but it appears to be that one could be a devotee and initiate in several different religions at one and the same time, and he or she could form this close personal bond with a number of patron gods and goddesses.

Although the mystery religions achieved a new popularity during the Hellenistic era, many of them were quite ancient, and most worshiped gods that had long histories. In fact, most of the gods who were worshiped in the mystery religions were not native to Greece, with the notable exceptions of Demeter and Dionysus, and often their "foreign" character emphasized the antiquity of their cult. They were worshiped someplace other than Greece for a long time and only gradually came to the awareness of the Greek people, but also indicated the universal scope of their power and worship. Not only were they worshiped here in Greece, but they were worshiped in their own nation as well—indicating, again, the breadth and depth of their power.

Some of the goddesses in the mysteries retained a specifically "foreign" identity. This is relatively rare, and that foreign identity makes them suspicious in the eyes of some observers; one of these quite ostentatiously foreign deities was Cybele, also known as "The Great Mother." Another was Atargatis, who was known as "The Syrian Goddess," as if there was no other.

On the other hand, other foreign deities became thoroughly Hellenized, thoroughly Greek-like, and to the extent that they became Hellenized, they became cosmopolitan; so, as a result, they lost much of their foreign character, and they became identified with traditional Greek gods in the thoroughgoing form of syncretism. They were also presented in the form and along the design of the Greek gods.

We may see this at work in the list of attributes and names of Isis, the Egyptian goddess, a list of attributes and virtues found in Syme, in Asia Minor. This is where the goddess enumerates her achievements and her divine titles.

In this list of attributes and names, the goddess claims to have invented letters, and also written laws. She claims to direct the course of the stars, to unite male and female, to overthrow tyrants, and to control nature. She calls herself Queen of Rivers, Queen of the Wind and the Sea, Queen of War, Queen of the Thunderbolt, Queen of Navigation, Lawgiver, and surprisingly, Lord—a male title—Lord of Rainstorms. All of these titles and attributes Isis claims for herself in this document.

This demonstrates the sort of accumulation of attributes, accumulation of powers, and accumulation of associations that come to the gods of the mystery religions. These mystery gods and goddesses were explicitly deities for all the world, and, to some extent, their devotees became missionaries, because they would carry the worship of their patron deity with them wherever they traveled in the Hellenistic world.

Now, Demeter, the goddess of grain and agriculture in Greece, was one of the goddesses of the traditional Greek pantheon whose worship evolved into a mystery religion. This happened during the classical period, and after.

Her mystery religion was called the "Eleusinian Mysteries," named after Demeter's sanctuary in the city of Eleusis. They were based on the myth of Demeter's daughter, Kore, who was abducted and raped by Hades, the god of the underworld. We recall that Demeter was plunged into despair by Kore's abduction. We remember that she wandered the earth in mourning, during which time the earth lay fallow, and, for a while, Demeter was a nurse to Triptolemus, son of King Celeus, in Eleusis.

The earth remained fallow until Zeus sent Hermes to Hades, to demand that Hades return Kore to her mother, but Hades tricked Kore, now called Persephone, into eating pomegranate seeds, a symbol of marriage. As a result, Persephone could only return to her mother on earth for a period of time, a part of each year, for two-thirds of the year, when crops grow and flourish, and then, of course, Persephone had to return back down to the underworld—and to her husband, Hades.

This myth is typical of stories explaining the fertility cycle. We can compare the story of Inanna and Dumuzi, which also includes going down to the underworld, and these easily become stories of death and rebirth because, of course, the metaphor for the fertility cycle is based on images of death and rebirth.

Now, Demeter's primary sanctuary was in Eleusis. Eleusis is about 12 miles west of Athens, near the sea, and this is where a temple was, according to the mythology, built at Demeter's command when Kore had been returned to her.

Eleusis was apparently an early site of a cultural cult, and this included a festival celebrating the sowing of the grain. Later, in Eleusis, there was a ceremony called the *Thesmophoria*, a festival celebrated solely by married women. This took place for three days in early October, and during this festival, the Thesmophoria, they mourned Kore's return to the underworld.

The Eleusinian Mysteries seem to have evolved, then, out of this celebration, with the annual return of the growing season reinterpreted as a time of rebirth of all life; so, when Kore goes down to the underworld, there is a time of mourning, a time of fallowness, but when she returns in the spring, that is a time of rebirth not only for the agricultural year, but for all life, after the fallow times of winter.

At Eleusis, both men and women joined in the worship of the goddess Demeter, but elsewhere, the "greater mysteries" of Demeter were celebrated exclusively by women. Now, the worship space in Eleusis was quite large. It's a very large temple sanctuary, and the worship space there could hold several thousand worshipers, and the priests of Eleusis were preeminent among the priests of mystery religions. In fact, they would often be hired out as advisers in the institution of other mystery religions, and in the reform of the ceremony of other mystery religions.

Now, Eleusis was conquered by the city of Athens around 400 B.C.E, and after that time, the "greater mysteries" of Demeter were celebrated by a procession from Athens to Eleusis in September or October. These were known by the title, the Greater Mysteries of Demeter. On the first day, sacred objects and chests were carried by young Athenian men from Eleusis to Athens, and once they arrived in Athens, these objects and chests were stored in the temple of Demeter, in Athens.

On the following days, a herald would announce exclusion of criminals and barbarians from the festivities because criminals and barbarians had no place in these rites that were devoted to the Athenians. Initiates at this point would sacrifice a pig to Demeter, and they would bathe in the sea as a form of purification. Finally, there would be a festive procession along the Sacred Way that extended from Athens to Eleusis, and this procession would return the sacred objects and chests to the hall of initiation at Eleusis, called the "Telesterion."

As the procession progressed, there would be frequent outcries of, "Iacchus!" Presumably, this was the name of a god sometimes identified with Bacchus, but it's not quite clear what the meaning is. It could just be an outcry of joyous fervor.

Now, some bits of written and graphic evidence have survived to allow us a glimpse at the private ceremonies Demeter might have included. According to the sources, there were apparently three sorts of activities involved in the Eleusinian Mysteries.

There were *legomena*, "things recited"; there were *deiknymena*, "things shown"; and there were *dromena*, "things performed"— although, really, that's not very helpful information. They said things; they looked at things; and they did things—although, I suppose, it's nice to have that verified.

Now, the public aspect of the rituals associated with Demeter find a parody in Aristophanes's comedy, *The Frogs*. In *The Frogs*, Dionysus and his slave, Xanthias, meet a procession of Demeter's initiates down there. The initiates make a series of execrations, a series of curses, aimed at particular people—similar to those execrations of the criminals and the barbarians excluded from the festivals of Demeter.

In this case, however, the execrations are aimed at corrupt officials, people who like bad jokes, the enemies of Athens, and perhaps significantly from Aristophanes, those who demand fees from poets, among others.

The devotees of Demeter in *The Frogs* invoke Demeter, and then they invoke Iacchus, and they combine these invocations with requests for success in making the audience laugh, and they hope to do that with attacks on citizens and, of course, by their salacious comments.

We also have a witness to the Mysteries of Demeter from the 3rd century of the Common Era, and this is the Christian writer Clement of Alexandria. He noted that the Eleusinian initiation included a fasting, but also the drinking of a particular beverage called *kykeon*. This was a watery mixture of barley meal and mint, and he also confirmed that the initiation included the manipulation of sacred objects. There was, therefore, fasting, as well as the drinking of the *kykeon*, this particular beverage, and, again, the manipulation of sacred objects as things done, presumably.

The ultimate revelation that completed the initiation into the mystery religion of Demeter is believed to have been a head of grain. The ultimate revelation is a head of grain, but this is a head of grain that is observed in silence, and it is understood in the context of the initiation to reveal the essential nature of all life; so the ritual not only initiated the new member into the cult, but also enlightened the new member into the cult. The initiate saw all things in a new way, from a new perspective, because of his or her initiation into the rites of Demeter.

Now, we might compare this, in our own time, to a newly baptized Christian. We are told for newly baptized Christians that all things are now new, and, typically, they understand their situation in life from an entirely different perspective, certainly not a phenomenon restricted to our own time and to our own religious culture.

Now, another traditional god of Greek religious culture who was also honored with a mystery religion was Dionysus. Dionysus was the god of wine and the god of ecstasy, and he also became the god of a mystery religion that grew out of the diverse forms of worship that were offered to Dionysus throughout the Greek world.

Now, of course, the worship of Dionysus forms something of a natural complement to the worship of Demeter, who is the goddess of grain, the goddess of agriculture, and the goddess of the plowed earth. Both gods represent the fruit of the earth as it is remade by human industry. After all, Demeter represents grain. Grain must be plucked; it must be crushed; it must be made into bread to provide the food that human beings require. So the grape must also be picked; it must be crushed; it must be allowed to ferment to create the wine of Dionysus for human beings to drink. So, they are not a god and goddess of a natural product, but a natural product that is transformed by human industry—perhaps indicating the alliance between the gods and human beings.

Now, Dionysus was a demigod, originally. He was the son of Zeus and the mortal woman Semele. He lost his mother while she was still pregnant with him. Hera, the wife of Zeus, became jealous of Semele, who was carrying Dionysus, the child of Zeus, and Hera urged Semele to ask Zeus for the favor of seeing him as he truly was in all his divine glory.

Zeus had promised to grant her any request, and he, of course, tried to dissuade her from this particular one, but she insisted, and when she saw him in all his divine glory, of course, the overpowering sight killed her, essentially annihilated her—which, of course, was Hera's intention from the start.

Zeus took her unborn child and sewed Dionysus into his own thigh until Dionysus was ready to be born, and then after his birth, Zeus entrusted Dionysus to the nymphs of Nyssa, who were the ones who raised him.

Dionysus made an important discovery in his youth. He discovered wine, and he traveled throughout Greece to share this gift with human beings, and he was ultimately included in the full company of the gods after rescuing his mother, Semele, from Hades.

Now, there are various stories about those who refuse to recognize Dionysus's divinity, and, therefore, they suffer the effects of the god's wrath as a result. The best-known of these stories is told in Euripides's *The Bacchae*, titled after the followers of Dionysus. In this story, Pentheus, the young king of Thebes, imprisons Dionysus, who has disguised himself as one of his own devotees because Pentheus is attempting to suppress the worship of Dionysus.

However, Dionysus inspires Pentheus's mother and other women of Thebes to join his female followers, the group of the Bacchae. Dionysus also persuades Pentheus to spy on the Bacchae while he himself is disguised as one of them. He does this largely by preying on Pentheus's prurient interest, but the Bacchae discover Pentheus, and under the delusion that he is a lion, they tear him to pieces.

This and similar stories appear to reflect Dionysus's ancient chthonic identity that runs counter to the official religious culture of classical Greece, an earth-based deity whose worship is not entirely consistent with the traditional religious culture of classical Greece.

Now, we know very little about the Dionysian Mysteries, but stories like this that Euripides tells in *The Bacchae*, tell us something about the god's power and the effects that he was believed to have had on his worshipers.

Dionysus was originally a deity of the countryside. He was a rustic deity associated with such rural gods as Pan, Salinas, and the ithyphallic Praipus, but also with satyrs, fawns, nymphs, and other woodland creatures. Sometimes, Dionysus appears in the form of a bull, a familiar image to us from our studies, but more commonly Dionysus appeared in the form of an effeminate young man. He wore long curls, and he carried a *thyrsus*, a staff crowned with ivy or vine leaves.

Dionysus was believed to cause ecstasy and madness in human beings, and, of course, this attribute probably derives from his association with wine. Euripides, at least, credits the devotees of Dionysus with feats of strength and acts of magic while in one of their inspired frenzies.

In Euripides's play, the Bacchae tear animals to pieces and eat the raw flesh in an act called "homophagia." This was a means of feasting on the Dionysian power present in the wild animal, and, in fact, the intention of much of Dionysian worship appears to be to ingest the intoxicating power of the god, to be filled with the divine spirit, and to exhibit divine possession and various acts of ecstasy, and the ecstatic state itself.

Given such actions and the basic nature of the god, it is perhaps not surprising that the rituals of Dionysus involve eating and drinking, especially the holy gift of wine, and the banquets in honor of Dionysus appear, at least in some cases, to have included rampant sexual activity. It is this kind of rampant sexual activity that is usually associated with the Festival of Bacchanalia, at least as traditional attributes, and it is both sexual activity and the secrecy that lies behind mystery religions, especially the mystery religion of Dionysus that led the Roman Senate to severely restrict the worship of Dionysus in Roman territories, beginning in 186 B.C.E. Apparently, they were not afraid of suffering the same fate as Pentheus.

Dionysus was, in some cases, identified with Osiris, and in this capacity, he appears to be associated with death and rebirth in a way that complements his role as a god of fertility. Dionysus did, after all, rescue his mother, Semele, from Hades, and, of course, he himself is reborn, we might say, as a god at the end of his wanderings.

This combines with Dionysus's identity as a god of the surging power of life and of ecstatic frenzy to make him, in fact, the potent deity for the kind of worship we find in the mystery religions. Dionysus also appears to have promised his devotees a blessed afterlife, although that afterlife would probably be thought of as primarily the continuing enjoyment of the sensuous appetites that Dionysus's divine presence inspired on earth.

Now, in our next session, we will consider other mystery religions, especially those that concern Isis, the Queen of Heaven, and we will look at these mystery religions as they are illustrated by Apuleius's *Metamorphoses*, a novel also known as *The Golden Ass*.

# Map

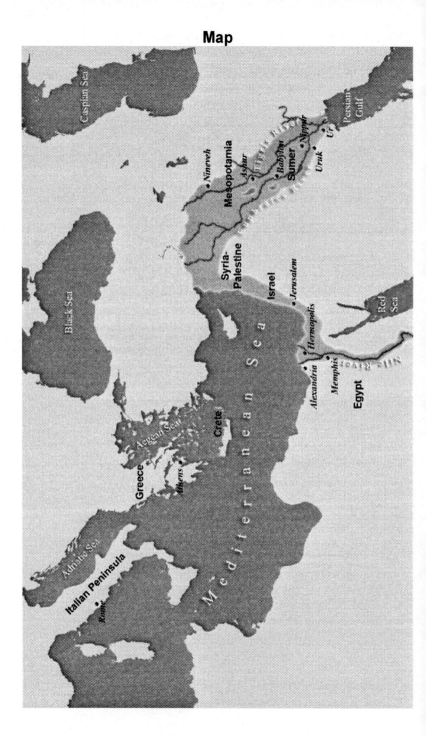

©2005 The Teaching Company Limited Partnership

# Timeline

| | |
|---|---|
| 2,000,000 years ago–c. 17,000 B.C.E. | Paleolithic era (Old Stone Age) |
| 130,000–30,000 years ago | Neanderthals appear, flourish, and decline |
| 70,000–30,000 years ago | Middle Paleolithic era, Mousterian material culture |
| 30,000 years ago–c. 17,000 B.C.E. | Paleolithic era |

**B.C.E.**

| | |
|---|---|
| c. 17,000–c. 8300 | Mesolithic era (Middle Stone Age), Natufian material culture in Syria-Palestine |
| c. 8300–c. 4000 | Neolithic era (New Stone Age) |
| c. 3500–1450 | The Aegean: Minoan civilization in Crete |
| c. 3000–2670 | Egypt: Archaic era— Dynasties 1 and 2 |
| c. 2900 | Mesopotamia: Amorites settle to the north of Sumer |
| c. 2670–2198 | Egypt: Old Kingdom— Dynasties 3–6 |
| 2654–2635 | Egypt: Djoser; career of Imhotep, later deified as god of medicine |
| 2571–2548 | Egypt: Khufu (Cheops) |
| 2334–2279 | Mesopotamia: Sargon the Great of Akkad |
| c. 2200–1200 | Middle and Late Bronze Ages |
| c. 2198–1938 | Egypt: First Intermediate Period—Dynasties 7–11 |

c. 2111...................................................Mesopotamia: Ur-Nammu establishes Third Dynasty of Ur

2081–2065 .............................................Egypt: Inyotef I

c. 1938–1759.........................................Egypt: Middle Kingdom— Dynasty 12

1938–1909 ............................................Egypt: Amenemhet I

1919–1875 ............................................Egypt: Senwosret I

1792–1750 ............................................Mesopotamia: Hammurabi, first great king of Babylon

c. 1759–1539.........................................Egypt: Second Intermediate Period—Dynasties 13–17

c. 1630–1522.........................................Egypt: the Hyksos— Dynasties 15 and 16

c. 1600–1200.........................................The Aegean: Mycenaean civilization in Greece

1595–1157 ............................................Mesopotamia: Kassites rule Mesopotamia

c. 1539–1075.........................................Egypt: New Kingdom— Dynasties 18–20

1353–1336 ............................................Egypt: Amenophis IV/Ankhenaten

1279–1213 ............................................Egypt: Ramesses II

1244–1208 ............................................Mesopotamia: Tukulti-Ninurta, king of Assyria

c. 1200–800..........................................The Aegean: Dark Age in Greece

1115–1077 ............................................Mesopotamia: Tiglath-Pileser I, king of Assyria

c. 1075–664..........................................Egypt: Third Intermediate Period—Dynasties 21–25

| | |
|---|---|
| c. 1020................................................ | Syria-Palestine: establishment of the Israelite monarchy under Saul |
| 1000–961 ............................................. | Syria-Palestine: David, king of United Monarchy of Israel and Judah |
| 922 ...................................................... | Syria-Palestine: Israel and Judah divide into two kingdoms |
| 883–859 ............................................... | Mesopotamia: Assurnasirpal II, king of Assyria |
| 882–871 ............................................... | Syria-Palestine: Omri, king of Israel |
| c. 871–851............................................ | Syria-Palestine: Ahab, king of Israel |
| 858–823 ............................................... | Mesopotamia: Shalmaneser III, king of Assyria |
| c. 851–850............................................ | Syria-Palestine: Ahaziah, king of Israel |
| 842–814 ............................................... | Syria-Palestine: Jehu, king of Israel |
| 800–480 ............................................... | The Aegean: Archaic age in Greece |
| 786–758 ............................................... | Syria-Palestine: Uzziah, king of Judah |
| 785–749 ............................................... | Syria-Palestine: Jeroboam II, king of Israel |
| 758–742 ............................................... | Syria-Palestine: Jotham, king of Judah |
| 753 ...................................................... | Rome: Traditional founding date of the city of Rome |
| 744–727 ............................................... | Mesopotamia: Tiglath-Pilescr III, king of Assyria |

| | |
|---|---|
| 742–726 | Syria-Palestine: Ahaz, king of Judah |
| 740–732 | Syria-Palestine: Rezin, king of Aram-Damascus |
| 735–731 | Syria-Palestine: Pekah, king of Israel |
| 726–697 | Syria-Palestine: Hezekiah, king of Judah |
| 721–705 | Mesopotamia: Sargon II, king of Assyria |
| 697–642 | Syria-Palestine: Manasseh, king of Judah |
| 669–627 | Mesopotamia: Assurbanipal, king of Assyria |
| 604–562 | Mesopotamia: Nebuchadnezzar II, king of Babylon |
| 556–539 | Mesopotamia: Nabonidus (Nabu-naid), king of Babylon |
| 559–530 | Persia: Cyrus II ("the Great"), king of Persia |
| 525–456 | The Aegean: Aeschylus, Greek tragedian |
| 510 | Rome: Establishment of the Roman republic |
| c. 496–406/5 | The Aegean: Sophocles, Greek tragedian |
| 486–465 | Persia: Xerxes, king of Persia |
| c. 485–406 | The Aegean: Euripides, Greek tragedian |
| 481–322 | The Aegean: Classical era in ancient Greece |

106–48 ................................................Rome: Pompey (Gnaeus Pompeius Magnus), general and statesman

100–44 ................................................Rome: Julius Caesar (Gaius Julius Caesar), general, statesman, and dictator

c. 82–30.............................................Rome: Marc Antony (Marcus Antonius), general and statesman

69–30 ................................................Egypt: Cleopatra VII, queen of Egypt 51–30 B.C.E.

63 B.C.E.–14 C.E................................Rome: Augustus Caesar (Gaius Octavius), first emperor

c. 4 B.C.E.–c. 30 C.E. .........................Syria-Palestine: Jesus of Nazareth, Jewish religious reformer

c. 4 B.C.E.–after 96 C.E.......................Roman Empire: Apollonius of Tyana, Pythagorean philosopher

**C.E.**

9–79 ...................................................Roman Empire: Vespasian (Titus Flavius Vespasianus), emperor 69–79 C.E.

c. 10–c. 64 ...........................................Roman Empire: Paul of Tarsus, Christian missionary and author

c. 20...................................................Roman Empire: birth of Cornutus (Lucius Annaeus Cornutus), Stoic author

37–68 ................................................Roman Empire: Nero (Nero Claudius Caesar), emperor 54–68 C.E.

| | |
|---|---|
| 131–135 ............................................ | Roman Empire: Bar Kochba revolt against Rome in Judaea |
| 145/46–211 ....................................... | Roman Empire: Septimus Severus (Lucius Septimus Severus), emperor 193–211 C.E. |
| c. 150–211/16.................................... | Roman Empire: Clement of Alexandria (Titus Flavius Clemens), Christian theologian |
| 161–192 ............................................ | Roman Empire: Commodus (Lucius Aelius Aurelius), emperor 180–192 C.E. |
| c. 170–245/49.................................... | Roman Empire: Flavius Philostratus, Sophist and author |
| 205–269/70 ....................................... | Roman Empire: Plotinus, Neoplatonic philosopher |
| 208/9–235 ......................................... | Roman Empire: Alexander Severus, emperor 222–235 C.E. |
| 235–238 ............................................ | Roman Empire: Maximinus (Gaius Julius Verus), emperor |
| 244–249 ............................................ | Roman Empire: Philip the Arab (Julius Verus Philippus), emperor |
| 249–251 ............................................ | Roman Empire: Decius (Gaius Messius Quintus), emperor |
| c. 250–311........................................ | Roman Empire: Galerius (Gaius Galerius Valerius Maximianus), emperor 305–311 C.E. |

253–260 ...............................Roman Empire: Valerian (Publius Licinius Valerianus), emperor

253–268 ...............................Roman Empire: Gallienus (Publius Licinius Egnatius), Caesar 293–305, Augustus 305–311 C.E.

284–305 ...............................Roman Empire: Diocletian (Gaius Aurelius Valerius), emperor (Augustus)

c. 285–337...........................Roman Empire: Constantine (Flavius Valerius Constantinus), Augustus 306–324, sole emperor 324–337 C.E.

308–324 ...............................Roman Empire: Licinius (Valerius Licinianus), emperor (Augustus)

# Glossary

**Achaeans**: The people of mainland Greece who made war against Troy.

*agora*: Greek, public space, open marketplace.

**Akkadian**: Semitic language, dominant in Mesopotamia from the 19th century B.C.E.

**Amorites**: Semitic peoples from the west who settled to the north of Sumer c. 2900 B.C.E.

*ankh*: Egyptian symbol of eternal life.

**anthropomorphic**: In human form.

**Anunnaki**: Sumerian, the gods of earth and the underworld.

**apocalyptic reversal**: The vindication of the poor and the outcast over the rich and powerful at the end of the age.

**apocalypticism**: The expectation that God will directly intervene into human history to save and vindicate his people.

**Aramaeans**: Ethnic group of nomads appearing in Genesis.

**Aramaic**: Alphabetic Semitic language, dominant in Mesopotamian from the 12th century B.C.E.

**Archaic Age in Greece**: 800–480 B.C.E.

**Archaic era**: Era in Egyptian history, Dynasties 1 and 2, c. 3000–2670 B.C.E.

**aretology**: A list of titles and attributes of a god and often rites and locations sacred to him or her.

*asheroth*: Hebrew, poles or trees sacred to the Canaanite goddess Asherah.

*atê*: Greek, madness or self-delusion.

**audition**: An ecstatic experience that is primarily aural.

**augurs**: Roman priests who oversaw auspices to determine whether a sacrifice was accepted.

**auspices**: A form of divination involving birds.

***ba***: Egyptian, a person's activity or spiritual presence perceivable in what he or she does.

**Bacchae**: Ecstatic female worshipers of Dionysus (sing. Bacchante).

**Bacchanalia**: Festival in honor of Dionysus.

***bamoth***: Hebrew, "altars," "high places," national shrines.

**barbarians**: Greek, "babblers," those who don't speak Greek, non-Greeks.

**B.C.E.**: Before the Common Era.

***Bel Matati***: Akkadian, "Lord of the World."

**benben**: Egyptian, a primeval hill shaped like a pyramid.

**calends** (new moon): A Roman division of the month.

**canopic jars**: Containers for a mummy's internal organs.

**Capitoline temple of Jupiter**: The primary temple of Jupiter, on the Capitoline hill in Rome

**C.E.**: Common Era, the current era, theoretically reckoned from the birth of Jesus.

**cenotaph**: A memorial stone.

**Chaldeans**: A Semitic people who established the Neo-Babylonian empire.

***charismata***: Greek, "spiritual gifts."

***chresmologos***: An oracle-monger with large collections of oracles to provide clients.

**chthonic deities**: Earth-based gods and goddesses.

**Classical era**: In ancient Greece, 481–322 B.C.E.

**Coffin Texts**: Instructions for the dead painted inside Middle Kingdom coffins in Egypt.

**consul**: One of the two chief magistrates of the Roman Republic.

**"Cyclopean" walls**: Fortifications made of unworked boulders or blocks of stone.

**dactyl**: Metrical unit consisting of a long syllable and two short ones.

*daimons*: Supernatural creatures that combine characteristics of the spiritual and physical.

**Dark Age**: In Greece, c. 1200–800 B.C.E.

**Day of the Lord**: The day when the Lord acts decisively to deliver and vindicate his faithful people.

*deiknymena*: Greek, "things shown."

**deities**: Self-conscious controllers of numinous power.

*Deshret*: Egyptian, "the red land," the Egyptian desert.

*dingar*: Sumerian, "god," "one of heaven."

**dithyrambs**: Lyric hymns in praise of Dionysus.

*droît du seigneur*: From French, "right of the lord," a lord's prerogative to deflower virgin brides before they marry.

*dromena*: Greek, "things performed."

*dromos*: Greek, a walkway; long tunnel leading to a Mycenaean burial chamber.

**duality**: The idea that all that exists is an expression of one or the other of two equal, opposed, and contrasting realities.

**ecstatic phenomena**: What is experienced in a state of mind when one "stands outside" one's self, and one's normal perception of reality is temporarily interrupted.

**effective cursing**: Using access to the spiritual world to call wrath down upon one's enemies.

**Ennead**: Greek, "group of nine," the nine principal gods of Egypt.

**epic poem**: Story about a historical hero who undertakes a series of adventures lived out in conscious relationship to the divine world.

*ethos*: Greek, a person's way of life.

**Etruscans**: Neighboring people to the Romans who sometimes ruled over them.

**execration texts**: Names of enemies on clay vessels that are then smashed, effectively breaking the enemy's power.

**fauns**: Young men with the horns and legs of a goat, attendants of Dionysus.

**fetials**: Roman priests who undertook rituals to initiate a war and ensure that it was "just."

**fetish**: An object made by human skill, venerated for its spiritual power.

**First Intermediate Period**: Era in Egyptian history, Dynasties 7–11, c. 2198–1938 B.C.E.

*Galli*: Self-castrated transvestite priests of Cybele (sing. *gallus*).

*genius*: Latin, the male spiritual essence of the man.

**Gnosticism**: A form of Christian teaching that emphasized esoteric knowledge as the means of salvation.

**"God-fearers"**: Gentiles who were sympathetic to Judaism and observed most of its tenets but rejected circumcision and full conversion.

**guild prophets**: Prophets who lived and prophesied in groups, usually under a leader.

*haruspicia*: Latin, "looking at entrails," finding omens in the entrails of animals sacrificed to the gods.

*Hashem*: Hebrew, "the Name."

**Hellenic**: From Greek, *Hellas* ("Greece"), "Greek."

**Hellenistic**: From Greek, *hellenistikos*, "Greek-like."

**henotheism**: A religious culture devoted to worshiping one god out of the many gods that exist.

*hieros gamos*: Greek, "sacred marriage."

**history**: A realm of discourse concerning what can reasonably be surmised to have happened in the past on the basis of historically acceptable data and analysis.

*hoc est corpus meum*: Latin, "this is my body."

*Homo sapiens:* the species of modern human beings.

*hoplite*: Greek, an armored soldier armed with a spear and short sword and carrying a large round shield, a *hoplon*.

**humanism**: A literary and artistic movement reflecting the importance of the individual in the face of the gods and human society.

**HWY**: Hebrew, "to be."

**Hyksos**: West Asian rulers of Egypt in Dynasties 15 and 16.

**"Iacchos!"**: Cry of the festival procession to Eleusis, presumed to be the name of a god.

**ides** (full moon): A Roman division of the month.

**Igigi**: Akkadian, the (10) great gods.

*ilu*: Akkadian, "god," "one of heaven."

*imperator*: Latin, the holder of the *imperium*.

*imperium:* Latin, the full sovereign power of the Roman Senate.

**inaugural experience**: A vision or audition (something seen or something heard) that first calls the prophet to prophesy.

**independent prophets**: Individual prophets who speak on the Lord's behalf without royal authority.

**ironist**: A "dissembling rascal" who pretends to be less than he really is.

*juno*: Latin, the female spiritual essence of the woman.

*ka:* Egyptian, the interaction of the mind and the body as a person.

*Kemet:* Egyptian, "the black land," the Nile Valley.

*koiné*: Greek, "common," the Greek of Hellenistic culture.

*kunikos*: Greek, "dog-like."

*kykeon*: A watery mixture of barley meal and mint.

*Lares*: The ancestral spirits of a Roman clan or family.

**Latin tribes**: The early core of the Roman people.

*legomena*: Greek, "things recited."

*lingua franca* (Italian, "Frankish tongue"): the common (second) language of a people.

*logos*: Greek, "word," "reason"; divine reason.

*ma'at*: Egyptian, divine harmony or balance.

**mana**: Spiritual power.

**"martyr"**: From the Greek *marturein*, meaning "to bear witness."

**material culture**: The physical remains of a human culture, discovered through archaeology.

*Matralia*: Festival of the goddess Dawn on June 11.

*Matronalia*: Festival in honor of women, especially mothers, on March 1.

*matzeboth*: Hebrew, "sacred pillars."

*m e*: Sumerian, "authority," "supernatural power."

*megaron*: Greek, a large room; a circular room with an open hearth at the center and four supporting columns.

**"men for sacred actions"**: First 2, later 10, men who kept the Sibylline books in Rome.

**Mesolithic era**: The Middle Stone Age, c. 17,000–c. 8300 B.C.E.

**Mesopotamia**: Greek, "between the rivers."

**messiah**: From Aramaic *mesiach*, "anointed one" (= Greek *christos*), the Lord's designated agent for a particular purpose on earth.

*metempsychosis*: Greek, the transmigration of the soul from one body to another at death.

**Middle and Late Bronze Ages**: c. 2200–1200 B.C.E.

**Middle Kingdom**: Era in Egyptian history, Dynasty 12, c. 1938–1759 B.C.E.

**Middle Paleolithic era**: 70,000–30,000 years ago.

**Middle Platonism**: A form of Platonic philosophy current from the 1st century B.C.E. to the early 3rd century C.E.

**Minoan civilization**: The civilization of Bronze Age Crete, c. 3500–1450 B.C.E.

**Mishnah**: A collection of rabbinic commentary on the teachings of Torah compiled c. 200 C.E.

**Mithraea**: Sanctuaries of Mithras (sing. Mithraeum).

*Monad*: Greek, "unity"; God as an indivisible unity, absolutely simple and perfect.

**monism**: The assertion that all that exists is based in and an expression of a single reality manifested in myriad forms.

**monotheism**: A religious culture reflecting devotion to the one and only god believed to exist.

**Mousterian culture**: The material culture of the Middle Paleolithic era.

**Mycenaean civilization**: A civilization of Bronze Age Greece, c. 1600–1200 B.C.E.

**mystery religions**: Religions devoted to "savior gods," with secret initiation rituals.

**myth**: A realm of discourse involving any idea of what motivates or drives history, the supernatural, or what lies behind or above history.

**mythology**: Legendary accounts of gods and heroes.

**natron**: Hydrated sodium carbonate ($Na_2CO_3.10H_2O$), used in mummification.

**Natufian culture**: The material culture of Syria-Palestine during the Mesolithic era.

**"natural" religious communities**: Religious communities coextensive with a social community.

*Navigium Isidis*: Latin, "Isis's Sea Journey," a festival recalling Isis's voyage to Byblos.

**Neanderthals**: Early human beings, fl. between 130,000–30,000 years ago.

**necromancy**: The summoning up of the spirits of the dead to gain insight into the present or foresee the future.

**Neolithic era**: The New Stone Age, c. 8300–c. 4000 B.C.E.

**New Kingdom**: Era in Egyptian history, Dynasties 18–20, c. 1539–1075 B.C.E.

**nome**: Small territories under military leaders in early Egypt.

**nones** (first quarter of the moon): A Roman division of the month.

*Nones Caprotinae*: A festival celebrated by free and slave women on July 7.

*numen*: All-pervasive spiritual power.

**Nun**: Egyptian, the dark waters of the limitless depths.

**Ogdoad**: Greek, "group of eight," four pairs of primeval Egyptian gods and goddesses.

**official prophets**: Professional prophets who worked within the context of the royal court or the shrine.

**Old Kingdom**: Era in Egyptian history, Dynasties 3–6, c. 2670–2198 B.C.E.

*omophagia*: Greek, the eating of raw flesh.

**Paleolithic era**: The Old Stone Age, began about 2 million years ago, ended c. 17,000 B.C.E.

**panentheism**: The idea that deity is not only present in all things but expresses itself and grows in the processes of natural and human history.

**pantheism**: The idea that deity suffuses the cosmos and that all its creatures are extensions and expressions of the divine.

*pater familiaris*: Latin, "father of the family," the head of the household.

**patricians**: Influential families who formed the senatorial aristocracy in the Roman Republic.

*Penates*: The household deities of a Roman clan or family.

**pharaoh**: The Egyptian king, from *Per Ao*, "great house."

**plebeians**: The commoners who sought greater power during the Roman Republic.

*polis*: Greek, the regional city-state ruled by a council of citizens.

**polytheism**: A religious culture with many gods.

*pontifex maximus*: Latin, "highest priest," the chief office of the college of pontiffs.

**pontiffs**: Roman priests who oversaw sacrifices and served as the guardians of sacred law.

*principiate:* Latin, "rule of the chief of state [*Princeps*]," the emperor's rule.

*prophetes:* Greek, "forth-teller," "proclaimer"; a prophet.

**prophetic action**: A particular behavior enacted by a prophet as part of the prophetic message.

*psyche*: Greek, the essence of a person, "soul."

**Pyramid Texts**: Egyptian religious inscriptions in the chambers of Old Kingdom pyramids.

*Rabshakeh*: Hebrew, "chief officer," an emissary of the Assyrian king to Hezekiah.

*religio licta*: Latin, a legitimate non-conforming religious culture within the empire.

**Sabine women**: Women from a territory neighboring Rome taken as wives by early Romans under Romulus.

**sacred, the**: That which permeates, influences, and relates to material reality, yet is recognized as part of another reality not subject to the limitations of the material.

*šā mūti*: Akkadian "bread of death."

*šāmūti*: Akkadian, "bread of heaven."

**sanctuary**: The sacred space devoted to worship, including temple, altar, and associated buildings and space.

*Saturnalia:* A festival of misrule celebrated December 17–23.

**satyrs**: Part-animal attendants of Dionysus.

**Second Intermediate Period**: Era in Egyptian history, Dynasties 13–17, c. 1759–1539 B.C.E.

**shamans**: Spiritual adepts who are believed to commune with the spirit world while in a trance.

**Sibylline Oracle**: An oracle of the gods located at Cumae in Campania.

*si deo, si dea*: Latin, "whether god or goddess."

**sistrum**: A type of musical rattle.

*soma sema*: Greek, "the body is a tomb."

**Sophists**: In the classical world, itinerant teachers of the skills and knowledge that led to a successful life.

*soter*: Greek, "savior."

**spondee**: Metrical unit consisting of two long syllables.

**sub-apostolic period**: About 70 to 130 C.E.

**suzerainty treaty**: A treaty in which a subject people accepts a king as its sovereign, with stipulations placed on both sides.

**syncretism**: The synthesis of elements taken from distinct religious cultures into new forms and combinations.

**Tanakh**: The Hebrew scriptures, the Christian Old Testament.

*taurobolium*: The ritual slaying of a bull in the mystery religion of Cybele.

*tauroctony*: Greek, a bull-slaying scene.

**Telesterion**: The hall of initiation at Eleusis.

**tetrarchy**: Greek, "rule of four," form of government with four co-rulers.

*theios aner*: Greek, "divine man," a man endowed with spiritual power manifested in supernatural wisdom and miracle-working.

**theodicy** (Greek, "god is in the right"): Showing a god is in the right in taking particular actions despite appearances to the contrary.

**theophoric element** (Greek, "god-bearing"): A god's name appearing as part of a person's name.

*Thesmophoria*: Festival of Demeter at Eleusis celebrated three days each October.

**Third Intermediate Period**: Era in Egyptian history, Dynasties 21–25, c. 1075–664 B.C.E.

*tholos*: Greek, dome; a "beehive" tomb.

**tribune**: A plebian magistrate who could cancel the actions of the other magistrates.

**trireme**: A large battleship powered by oarsmen, with a bronze ram at the prow.

*tyché:* Greek, "fate."

*Tychē Agathē*: Greek, "Good Fortune."

**Ubaidians**: Neolithic settlers in southeastern Mesopotamia.

**Upper Paleolithic era**: 30,000–17,000 years ago.

**Urim and Thummin**: An apparatus to discover the Lord's will, part of the high priest's apparel.

*ushebtis*: Egyptian, "answerers," tomb models of male and female slaves.

**Vestal Virgins**: Women who guarded the flame of Vesta on the "hearth" of the city.

**vision**: An ecstatic experience that is primarily visual.

**"voluntary" religious communities**: Communities one chooses to join as a result of conversion.

**Yahweh**: Vocalization of YHWH, the name of the Lord of Israel.

**YHWH**: Hebrew, the name of the Lord of Israel.

**ziggurat**: Massive pyramidical brick building intended to represent the sacred mountain.

# Biographical Notes

**Alexander III ("the Great") of Macedon** (356–323 B.C.E.). The son of Philip II of Macedon, Alexander succeeded him as king in 336 B.C.E. He crossed the Hellespont in 334 B.C.E. with an army of 40,000 to challenge the Persian Empire. Alexander gradually gained supremacy over Persian holdings in the west, then defeated the Persians to take Babylon and the Persian capitals. Ultimately, his empire stretched from Greece and Macedon in the west to the Indus River in the east and from Bactria in the north to Egypt in the south. Alexander brought his domains not only Greek forms of government and the Greek language but Hellenistic culture. Alexander's domains fostered a cosmopolitan religious culture characterized by syncretism, the synthesis of gods and rituals from different national traditions. Alexander died of a fever in Babylon at age 33, leaving his empire to his young son. It was soon divided among Alexander's commanders into separate kingdoms, but the territories of his empire remained essentially Hellenistic in language and culture until the Muslim conquest.

**Amenophis IV/Ankhenaten**, king of Egypt (1353–1336 B.C.E.). A pharaoh of Dynasty 18 during the New Kingdom, Amenophis IV sparked a religious and cultural revolution during his reign. Devoted to the solar god Aten, originally a manifestation of Rē-Horakhty, Amenophis built a temple for the Aten at Karnak with decoration that ushered in a new artistic era. The king replaced the traditional representations of the gods with the image of the sun disk radiating beams that terminated in hands bringing blessings to Egypt. Amenophis changed his name to Ankhenaten and built a new capital in Middle Egypt, Akhetaten, now known as Tell el-Amarna. Ankhenaten ordered the systematic obliteration of the names and images of Amun and other gods throughout his kingdom in favor of the sole depiction and glorification of Aten. The reign of Ankhenaten was a blow to the deeply traditional Egyptians, and he imposed his will with shows of force. Despite his efforts, his theological and cultural revolution was gradually reversed during the reign of his eventual successor, Tutankhamun.

**Apollonius of Tyana**, philosopher (c. 4 B.C.E.–after 96 C.E.). Apollonius was born in Cappadocia in Asia Minor and began to follow the life of a philosopher at an early age. Through his devotion to the ascetic life of a Pythagorean philosopher, he lived a life of simplicity and gentle wisdom, although he could be stern with his opponents or scoffers. He traveled widely, including in India, and was reputed to have the power to work miracles. He was subject to persecution under both Nero and Domitian but, in both cases, escaped condemnation. The most extensive account of his life was written by the Sophist Flavius Philostratus at the behest of the empress Julia Domna at the beginning of the $3^{rd}$ century C.E. Philostratus is far from reliable, and there are only scattered references to Apollonius elsewhere, although the satirist Lucian of Samosata dismissed him as a libertine and a charlatan.

**Augustus Caesar (Gaius Octavius)**, Roman emperor (63 B.C.E.–14 C.E.). The son of the niece of Julius Caesar, Octavius was Caesar's adopted son and chief heir after his death. He managed to make allies among the leading citizens of Rome and, through military and political skills, gained the status of senator and consul and later became a member of a triumvirate that also included Marc Antony. His growing power in Italy led to a confrontation with Antony and Cleopatra in Egypt. Octavius emerged victorious and unopposed, ultimately acquiring the *imperium*, or power to rule, from the Senate in 27 B.C.E., as well as the title Augustus. As emperor, Augustus placed himself under the patronage of Apollo and the god Julius, his deified adoptive father. He was a traditionalist and undertook a campaign to restore the glory of Rome after a generation of civil war but, in the process, also consolidated and institutionalized his own power. He built new temples in Rome and rebuilt old ones, ordered a definitive collection of the Sibylline oracles, and placed himself and the imperial family in the center of Roman religious culture. Within a month of his death, Augustus was declared a god.

**Constantine (Flavius Valerius Constantinus)**, Roman emperor (c. 285–337 C.E.). Constantine was the son Constantius Chlorus. When Constantius became part of the tetrarchy ruling the empire, young Constantine was sent to the court of Diocletian in Nicomedia. Constantine showed promise as a commander and became a member of the tetrarchy after his father's death in 306. In 313, Constantine and his co-emperor Licinius issued the Edict of Milan, ending persecution of Christians in the empire and granting them certain rights. Through a series of alliances and battles, Constantine gained sole control over the empire in 324. He oversaw an overhaul of the imperial administration, issued new coinage, and established a new capital in Byzantium on the Bosporus, named Constantinople in his honor. Both traditional Roman and Christian rituals solemnized the city's founding. Among Constantine's building projects in the new capital were many churches, including the Church of the Holy Wisdom, but no temples of the traditional gods. Christians regarded Constantinople as the "Christian Rome." Constantine's own religious ideas are far from clear, but he intervened in Christian doctrinal disputes, most notably at the Council of Nicea in 325. The emperor was finally baptized a Christian in 337 on his deathbed.

**Cyrus II ("the Great")**, king of Persia (559–530 B.C.E.). Cyrus was originally a ruler over part of Iran and a vassal to the Medes, but he slowly consolidated power in the surrounding territories. The Babylonians under Nabonidus (556–539 B.C.E) asked for Cyrus's assistance against the Medes, and by 550 B.C.E., Cyrus was ruler of both Persia and Media. Cyrus compounded one military success with another, conquering Lydia in 546 B.C.E. and Babylonia in 539 B.C.E. Cyrus soon ruled over an empire of unprecedented size. His policy toward his subject people was remarkably enlightened for its time. He allowed those peoples the Babylonians had exiled to return to their native lands and to observe the customs of their own religious cultures, provided they prayed to their gods for the well-being of the Persian king and his empire. It was during his reign that many of the exiles of Judah returned to Jerusalem, taking with them much of the Temple furniture that the Babylonians had seized. Isaiah 45:1–3 portrays Cyrus as a deliverer of God's people and refers to him as God's anointed one, or *messiah*.

**David**, king of Israel (1000–961 B.C.E.). The son of a Moabite mother and a father from the Jebusite city of Bethlehem, David first became associated with Israel by serving its first king, Saul, as a military commander. David's military successes led to a break with Saul, and David was, for a time, a mercenary commander for the Philistines. He later became king of Judah, with his capital in Hebron. After Saul's death, David fought against Saul's son and successor, Ishbaal. After Ishbaal's death, David became king over Israel by virtue of a covenantal agreement made with its leading citizens. David ruled over the united kingdoms of Israel and Judah and greatly increased their territories, becoming the strongest and most influential of the kings of Judah and Israel. His later years were taken up in part by rebellions arising from dissension among several of his sons over the succession. In spite of a challenge from his son Adonijah, at David's death, his kingdom passed peacefully to Solomon.

**Diogenes of Sinope**, Greek philosopher (c. 400–328 B.C.E.). Diogenes reportedly came to Athens as an exile after serving as a treasury official and being accused of "changing the currency." This became his philosophical mission, as he flouted conventional ideas of morality and propriety in an attempt to make life as simple and, therefore, as happy as possible. He believed happiness consisted in living "according to nature," in the sense of doing what satisfied basic human needs without regard to public opinion or social conventions. The public shamelessness of Diogenes and his followers led the public to compare them to dogs and brand them *kunikos*, or "dog-like," the origin of the name *Cynic*. Diogenes and other Cynics lampooned popular standards and opinions in public diatribes. The distinguishing characteristics of the Cynics were their simple clothing, their staff and bag, and their brusque and offensive manner.

**Epicurus**, Greek philosopher (341–270 B.C.E.). Epicurus was born the son of a teaching master in the Greek colony of Samos. He studied philosophy in Athens at the Academy and became familiar with the atomistic theories of Democritus. He established philosophical schools in the eastern Aegean before returning to Athens in 307 or 306 B.C.E., when he bought a house and garden that became the setting for his philosophical community. Epicurus believed that the best thing for a human being to do was to enjoy the pleasures of life in moderation and to live without anxiety. He identified the primary sources of anxiety as fear of offending the gods and fear of what comes after death. He argued that the gods exist but have no interest in human beings and, thus, cannot be offended by them; on the other hand, at death, the atoms that make up the body are dispersed and consciousness ends, so there is nothing to fear after death. Epicurus and his followers lived a quiet life of contemplation. His school was famous—or notorious—for including women among its members, and this, as well as the school's supposed hedonism and atheism, made Epicureans the subject of popular disdain.

**Hammurabi**, king of Babylon (1792–1750 B.C.E.). Hammurabi inherited from his father, Sin-muballit, a relatively small domain centered in Babylon and surrounded by larger, more powerful kingdoms. Within a few years, he enlarged his territory considerably by military conquest and eventually united most of Mesopotamia under his own royal rule and the authority of Babylon. He reformed the Babylonian administration and created the first major written law code. The *Code of Hammurabi* shows concern both for individual rights and the demands of justice. During his long reign, Hammurabi presided over a flourishing of the arts and literature, established Babylon as the capital and principal city of Mesopotamia, and granted divine preeminence to Babylon's patron god, Marduk.

**Jesus of Nazareth**, Jewish religious reformer (c. 4 B.C.E. – c. 30 C.E.). Jesus, a native of Nazareth in Galilee, was an associate of John the Baptist who, after John's imprisonment, began his own ministry. His message was the approaching kingdom of God, and the need for repentance to obtain God's forgiveness in anticipation of the new era. Jesus collected a body of followers who shared his travels and proclaimed his message. Jesus had a reputation as a miracle-worker, and aroused opposition among the Jewish authorities in both Galilee and Judaea because of his criticism of their policies and practices. While in Jerusalem to celebrate Passover, Jesus was arrested by the Temple police and handed over to the Roman authorities, who crucified him. His followers claimed Jesus was alive again a few days after his execution, and continued to spread his message, initially as a sect within Judaism, but later as an independent religious movement.

**Moses**, leader of Israel (early to mid-13th century B.C.E.). A member of the people of Israel born in Egypt, Moses rose to a position of authority in the Egyptian government, most likely in connection with the forced labor provided by his people for building projects in the eastern Nile Delta during the reign of Ramesses II. He left Egypt and lived among the Midianites and, during that time, married. He later returned to Egypt, where he became a leader of his people in their attempts to gain their freedom, both from forced labor and from Egypt. After a successful escape from Egypt, the people of Israel looked to Moses as their chief lawgiver and religious mediator. He oversaw construction of the Tabernacle, the portable sanctuary for sacrificial ritual, and installed his brother Aaron as high priest.

According to tradition, Moses led Israel in the wilderness for 40 years and died on Mt. Nebo in Moab shortly before his people entered Canaan.

**Nebuchadnezzar II**, king of Babylon (604–562 B.C.E.). Nabû-kudurri-usur (Nebuchadrezzar) campaigned against the Egyptians while still crown prince under his father, Nabopolassar, and successfully drove them from Syria-Palestine. At his father's death, he returned to Babylon to be crowned king. He mounted campaigns in Syria-Palestine on a regular basis to keep the Egyptians in check and to ensure loyalty among his vassals. When Jehoiakim of Judah stopped paying tribute, Nebuchadnezzar captured Jerusalem in 597 B.C.E. and exiled the king, his court, and other leading citizens to Babylon. Ten years later, Nebuchadnezzar's chosen client king in Judah, Zedekiah, also rebelled, and once again, Babylonian armies moved against Jerusalem, taking the city in 587 B.C.E. Another exile of leading citizens from Judah to Babylon followed, although some of the people sought refuge in Egypt instead. Nebuchadnezzar established peace throughout his domains by extensive and effective use of force but was unable to eliminate the forces that led to the fall of Babylon less than a quarter-century after his death.

**Nero (Nero Claudius Caesar)**, Roman emperor (37–68 C.E.). Nero was adopted as a son by the emperor Claudius after Claudius married his niece, Nero's mother, Agrippina. Nero displaced Claudius's son Britannicus, who died—and was, perhaps, murdered—soon after Nero became emperor in 54. Agrippina dominated Nero at first, but he soon exerted his own will and, in 59, had his mother murdered. Nero had artistic ambitions, but his pursuit of vanity and his ruthless use of power turned the Roman public against him. After a suspicious fire destroyed half of Rome in 64, Nero placed the blame on the city's Jews, who in turn, shifted the blame to the followers of Jesus. Nero's persecution of the followers of Jesus in Rome included grotesque forms of execution, inspiring fear and disgust toward the emperor and pity for his victims among Roman citizens. Conspiracies against the emperor arose as conditions worsened in the empire. When the Praetorian Guard finally turned against Nero to support Galba as emperor, Nero committed suicide at the age of 30.

**Paul of Tarsus**, Christian missionary (c. 10–c. 64 C.E.). Paul, a native of Tarsus in Cilicia in southeastern Asia Minor, received a typical education for a Jew of his time, including study with a rabbi and training in rhetoric. Paul made a living as a tentmaker and leatherworker but also worked for the Jewish authorities in Jerusalem in the attempt to suppress the Jesus movement. While engaged in this work, Paul experienced a vision of the risen Jesus. As a result, he became a member of the Jesus movement and, some years afterwards, a missionary. Paul had his greatest success among Gentiles allied with Jewish synagogues who would not undergo circumcision and full conversion. Paul welcomed such people into the Jesus movement, prompting a reaction from those who thought of the movement as a sect within Judaism. In response, Paul developed the idea that salvation was a free gift of God's grace appropriated by those, Jews or Gentiles, who trusted in his promises. Paul founded congregations in several prominent cities and wrote a number of letters expounding his theology and encouraging his congregations to live a moral life. He apparently died in Rome in 64 C.E. during Nero's persecution of Jesus's followers.

**Plato**, Greek philosopher (427–347 B.C.E.). Plato was an Athenian of good birth who became a follower of Socrates. After Socrates's death, Plato traveled extensively before returning to Athens and there founded a philosophical school, the Academy, around 385 B.C.E. He devoted the rest of his life to philosophical teaching and writing, producing around 25 dialogues. Although his early dialogues are believed to bear the stamp of the historical Socrates to some extent, Plato's interests and willingness to theorize went far beyond what Socrates had taught. His interest in politics and his creation of the "philosopher-king" led to his involvement with political affairs in Syracuse. The Academy survived Plato's death and continued as a center of philosophical inquiry until the school was finally closed by the Byzantine emperor Justinian in 529 C.E.

**Ramesses II**, king of Egypt (1279–1213 B.C.E.). A pharaoh of Dynasty 19 during the New Kingdom, Ramesses II is often identified as the pharaoh of the Exodus. His 66-year reign was notable for massive building projects, including the city of Pi-Riamsese in the eastern Nile Delta. Initially through combat and later through diplomacy, Ramesses came to an accommodation with the Hittites, Egypt's long-time rival for hegemony in Syria-Palestine. The treaty led to a long period of peace, freeing Ramesses to devote his attention to his building projects, many of which included colossal representations of the king. In addition to his harem, Ramesses had 2 official wives, and produced more than 50 children. Ramesses II was succeeded by his son Merneptah (1213–1203 B.C.E.). A stele commemorating a campaign into Syria-Palestine by Merneptah includes the first mention of Israel as a people.

**Sargon II**, king of Assyria (721–705 B.C.E.). Sargon was the successor of Shalmeneser V, although it is unclear whether he was a son of the royal house or a usurper. Assyria's enemies Egypt and Elam fostered rebellions among Sargon's vassals, and Sargon devoted much of his attention to maintaining control of his empire. He was able to assert his authority over most of the rebellious territories, including Babylon and the nations of Syria-Palestine. Sargon captured Samaria, the capital of the northern kingdom of Israel, and deported its leading citizens, replacing them with a foreign aristocracy that served as provincial administrators under Sargon's authority. Sargon built a new capital, Dûr-Sharrukîn near Khorsabad, 24 kilometers northeast of the traditional Assyrian capital, Ninevah, but died in battle a year after the city was completed.

**Socrates**, Greek philosopher (469–399 B.C.E.). Socrates served as a hoplite in the Athenian army but devoted his life to philosophy early on. He was primarily concerned with ethics, the right way to live one's life, and conducted his philosophical investigations through dialogue, cross-examining his interlocutors in pursuit of truth. The Delphic oracle, in reply to a question from Socrates's friend Chaerephon, proclaimed that no one was wiser than Socrates. Socrates was puzzled by this answer and saw his subsequent philosophical career as a way of determining what the oracle meant by her reply. In 399 B.C.E., Socrates was tried before the Athenian council on a charge of introducing strange gods and corrupting Athenian youth. His self-defense before the council is the substance of Plato's early work *Apology*. Socrates was found guilty and sentenced to death by poison, a death he accepted with good grace. After his death, Socrates's example continued to serve as the model of the ideal philosopher appealed to by many different philosophical schools.

**Zeno of Citium**, Greek philosopher (c. 333–262 B.C.E.). Zeno came to Athens about 313 B.C.E. and studied at the Academy. He sampled several philosophical schools before finally developing his own philosophy, Stoicism, named after the *Stoa Poikile*, or painted colonnade, where he taught. Zeno maintained that the only thing a person can truly control is his or her inward disposition, which should at all times be aligned with the dictates of the *logos*, or divine mind, that governs the cosmos. In order to keep one's inner resolve in agreement with the *logos*, it was necessary for a person to distance the self from the influence of emotions and relationships. Such lack of feeling (*apatheia*) allowed the inner resolve to dictate the Stoic's actions with no other intention than conforming to the will of the *Logos*, leading to a virtuous life. Zeno's system included logics and physics, but the most influential aspect of his philosophy was the proposition that virtue is the only good, and virtue depended only on the Stoic's determination to conform his or her will to the dictates of the *logos*.

# Bibliography

**Essential Reading:**

## Egypt

Baines, John, Leonard H. Lesko, and David P. Silverman. *Religion in Ancient Egypt: Gods, Myths, and Personal Practice*. Edited by Byron E. Shafer. Ithaca, NY: Cornell University Press, 1991. An excellent survey of the primary components of Egyptian religious culture, both official and popular.

Foster, John L., ed. and trans. *Ancient Egyptian Literature: An Anthology*. Austin, TX: University of Texas Press, 2001. A collection of texts from ancient Egypt, including hymns, wisdom literature, love poetry, and *The Tale of Sinuhe*, in clear, readable translations.

Gahlin, Lucia. *Egypt: Gods, Myths and Religion*. New York: Barnes and Noble, 2002. A beautifully illustrated, accessible survey of Egyptian religious culture, incorporating color photographs and helpful charts.

Hornung, Erik. *History of Ancient Egypt: An Introduction*. Translated by David Lorton. Ithaca, NY: Cornell University Press, 1999. An authoritative short history of Egypt from the prehistoric era to its incorporation into the Persian Empire in the 4th century B.C.E.

Redford, Donald B., ed. *The Ancient Gods Speak: A Guide to Egyptian Religion*. New York: Oxford University Press, 2002. A reliable resource for information about ancient Egyptian religious culture presented in dictionary form; well suited to the needs of general readers.

## Mesopotamia

Black, Jeremy, and Anthony Green. *Gods, Demons and Symbols of Ancient Mesopotamia: An Illustrated Dictionary*. Austin, TX: University of Texas Press, 2003. A guide to Mesopotamian religious culture from its beginnings to the turn of the age, presented in dictionary form, with a variety of helpful illustrations.

Bottéro, Jean. *Religion in Ancient Mesopotamia*. Translated by Teresa Lavender Fagan. Chicago: University of Chicago Press, 2001. A brief, authoritative account of the history of Mesopotamian religious culture that places it in the context of religious study in general and traces its influence on other ancient Mediterranean religious cultures.

Dalley, Stephanie, ed. and trans. *Myths from Mesopotamia: Creation, the Flood, Gilgamesh, and Others*. Oxford World's Classics. Rev. ed.. New York: Oxford University Press, 1989. A collection of the primary religious texts from ancient Mesopotamia, in translations that convey the sense without disguising some of the difficulties the current state of the texts presents; includes useful notes.

Roux, George. *Ancient Iraq*. 3rd ed. New York: Penguin, 1992. A comprehensive history of ancient Mesopotamia from the prehistoric era to the Hellenistic age, intended for general readers.

Wolkstein, Diane, and Samuel Noah Kramer. *Inanna, Queen of Heaven and Earth: Her Stories and Hymns from Sumer*. New York: Harper & Row, 1983. A collection of texts from ancient Sumer intended to portray the "history" of Inanna, with translations that demonstrate an admirable frankness and clarity. Includes helpful commentaries on Sumerian history and the problems presented by the sources.

## Syria-Palestine

Blenkinsopp, Joseph. *A History of Prophecy in Israel: From the Settlement in the Land to the Hellenistic Period*. Rev. ed. Philadelphia: Westminster John Knox, 1996. A history of the phenomenon of prophecy in ancient Israel, set in its larger historical and cultural context in the ancient Near East

Flanders, Henry Jackson, Jr., Robert Wilson Crapps, and David Anthony Smith. *People of the Covenant: An Introduction to the Hebrew Bible*. 4th ed. New York: Oxford University Press, 1996. A textbook intended for use in college courses, including a thorough introduction not only to the Hebrew Bible but also to the history of Israel in the ancient Near East and the critical methods used by modern scholars to make sense of the biblical texts.

Herrmann, Siegfried. *A History of Israel in Old Testament Times*. 2nd ed. Philadelphia: Fortress, 1981. A readable history of Israel from the ancestors to the beginning of Roman rule that offers reasonable interpretations of its subject's many problems.

## Greece

Cashford, Jules, trans. *The Homeric Hymns*. Introduction and notes by Nicholas Richardson. New York: Penguin, 2003. A sound introduction to these important religious texts in elegant translations.

Guthrie, W. K. C. *The Greeks and Their Gods*. Boston: Beacon, 1985. First published in 1950 "to serve as a kind of religious companion to the Greek classics" and now a classic itself as an introduction to the primary ideas at work in Greek religious culture.

Hesiod and Theognis. *Hesiod: Theogony, Works and Days*; *Theognis: Elegies*. Translated by Dorothea Wender. Penguin Classics. New York: Penguin, 1973. An intelligent translation of the archaic Greek poems, intended to convey both the style and the content of the originals, with a helpful introduction and notes.

Homer. *The Iliad*. Translated by Robert Fagles. Introduction and notes by Bernard Knox. New York: Penguin, 1990. This and the following entry are Homer's two great epic poems, in what are arguably the best translations for the modern reader.

———. *The Odyssey*. Translated by Robert Fagles. Introduction and notes by Bernard Knox. New York: Penguin, 1996.

Plato. *Five Dialogues: Euthyphro, Apology, Crito, Meno, Phaedo*. Translated by G. M. A. Grube. Indianapolis: Hackett, 1981. A good, readable translation of the Platonic dialogues that focus on the events leading up to the death of Socrates.

Price, Simon. *Religions of the Ancient Greeks: Key Themes in Ancient History*. New York: Cambridge University Press, 1999. A scholarly introduction to Greek religious culture from the 8th century B.C.E. to the 5th century C.E., addressing a number of subjects with data from an array of sources.

**The Hellenistic Era**

Martin, Luther H. *Hellenistic Religions: An Introduction*. New York: Oxford University Press, 1987. A brief, comprehensive overview of the religious cultures of the Greco-Roman world from the 4th century B.C.E to the 4th century C.E.

Meyer, Marvin W., ed. *The Ancient Mysteries: A Sourcebook: Sacred Texts of the Mystery Religions of the Ancient Mediterranean World*. San Francisco: HarperCollins, 1987. A well-chosen collection of texts relevant to mystery religions of the ancient Mediterranean world, intended to give the modern reader a view of the mysteries through the eyes of those familiar with them.

## Rome

Apuleius. *The Golden Ass*. Translated by Robert Graves. New York: Farrar, Straus and Giroux, 1998. A clear and witty translation of Apuleius's novel by the author of *I, Claudius*, with proper appreciation for its notes of humor, pathos, and religious solemnity.

Beard, Mary, John North, and Simon Price. *Religions of Rome*. Volume 1: *A History*. Volume 2: *A Sourcebook*. New York: Cambridge University Press, 1998. A revisionist approach to the religious cultures of the Roman world, the result of carefully chosen texts and other forms of evidence and a convincing analysis. The second volume provides most of the texts and other sources referred to in the first volume.

Kraemer, Ross Shepard. *Her Share of the Blessings: Women's Religions among Pagans, Jews, and Christians in the Greco-Roman World*. New York: Oxford University Press, 1992. A survey of the forms taken by women's religious activity in the Greco-Roman world, including surveys of the mystery religions, the traditional religious culture of Rome, Judaism, and the early Jesus movement.

Lucian of Samosata. *Lucian*. Translated by A. M. Harmon. Loeb Classical Library. Volumes 4 (*Alexander the False Prophet*) and 5 (*The Passing of Peregrinus*). Cambridge, MA: Harvard University Press, 1925, 1936. Scholarly, readable translations of Lucian's work, with introductions and notes; the Greek text and the English translation appear on facing pages.

Ovid. *Metamorphoses*. Translated by Mary M. Innes. Penguin Classics. New York: Penguin, 1955. An excellent translation for the general reader of Ovid's Latin retelling of the myths that formed part of the Greek religious inheritance of early imperial Rome, as well as the founding myths of Rome and the empire itself.

Turcan, Robert. *The Gods of Ancient Rome: Religion in Everyday Life from Archaic to Imperial Times*. Translated by Antonia Nevill. New York: Routledge, 2001. A brief traditional introduction to the religious cultures of the Roman world, covering the religious beliefs and actions associated with the family and the land, the city, and the empire.

## Christianity

Chadwick, Henry. *The Early Church*. Penguin History of the Church. Rev. ed. New York: Penguin, 1993. A standard history of the early Christian movement from its beginnings to the end of the ancient period; intended for general readers.

Ehrman, Bart D. *A Brief Introduction to the New Testament*. New York: Oxford University Press, 2004. A short textbook intended for use in college courses, including an introduction to the books of the New Testament, their historical and cultural context, and the methods used to study them, reflecting the most recent scholarship.

Keck, Leander E. *Paul and His Letters: Proclamation Commentaries*. 2nd ed. Philadelphia: Fortress, 1988. An excellent short companion to the genuine letters of Paul, with major sections devoted to the "historical" Paul, the gospel message Paul proclaimed, and the primary concerns that motivated Paul's evangelical mission and the controversies with his opponents.

Pagels, Elaine. *The Gnostic Gospels*. New York: Vintage: 1989. An award-winning study that uses Gnostic texts from the Nag Hammadi library to illuminate the diversity of earliest Christianity.

Powell, Mark Allan. *Jesus as a Figure in History*. Philadelphia: Westminster John Knox, 1998. An excellent review for the general reader of recent scholarly attempts to identify the "historical Jesus," with a clear explanation and careful analysis of each of the "portraits" that results.

**General**

*The Concise Oxford Companion to Classical Literature*. Edited by M. C. Howatson and Ian Chilvers. New York: Oxford University Press, 1993. Primarily a companion to Greek and Roman classical literature and its authors, including brief sketches of the gods and other characters appearing in myths, with helpful information about figures from Greek and Roman history, as well.

Winks, Robin W., and Susan P. Mattern-Parkes. *The Ancient Mediterranean World: From the Stone Age to A.D. 600*. New York: Oxford University Press, 2004. A brief history of the ancient Mediterranean world, from the prehistoric era to the end of the ancient period, with helpful maps, charts, and illustrations; intended for the general reader.

**Supplementary Reading:**

**Prehistory**

Cunliffe, Barry, ed. *The Oxford Illustrated History of Prehistoric Europe*. Oxford Illustrated Histories. New ed. New York: Oxford University Press, 2001. An illustrated overview of the prehistoric era in Europe by a number of scholars, intended to reconstruct as accurately as possible the full range of the lives of prehistoric people.

## Egypt

Assmann, Jan. *The Search for God in Ancient Egypt*. Translated by David Lorton. Ithaca, NY: Cornell University Press, 2001. A specialized investigation and analysis of the full realm of Egyptian religious culture in terms of the categories of religious scholarship.

Hart, George. *Egyptian Myths: The Legendary Past*. Austin, TX: University of Texas Press, 1990. A review of primary themes in Egyptian mythology, with clear retellings and explanations of different myths.

Ray, John. *Reflections of Osiris: Lives from Ancient Egypt*. New York: Oxford University Press, 2002. A selection of biographical sketches of figures from more than 2,000 years of Egyptian history, illustrating both the familiarity and the strangeness of the Egyptian world.

Traunecker, Claude. *The Gods of Egypt*. Translated by David Lorton. Ithaca, NY: Cornell University Press, 2001. A comprehensive introduction to conceptions of the divine in Egyptian religious culture, in a clear and systematic presentation.

## Mesopotamia

Bottéro, Jean. *Everyday Life in Ancient Mesopotamia*. Translated by Antonia Nevill. Baltimore: Johns Hopkins University Press, 2001. A collection of essays by Bottéro and others on a variety of subjects, from cuisine to astrology, to love and sex, to the role of women in ancient Mesopotamia, helping to make its peoples and civilizations more real for the modern reader.

Jacobsen, Thorkild. *The Treasures of Darkness: A History of Mesopotamian Religion*. New Haven, CT: Yale University Press, 1976. A history of Mesopotamian religious culture, focusing on literary evidence and the controlling metaphors for each era of Mesopotamian religious history.

Kramer, Samuel Noah. *The Sumerians: Their History, Culture, and Character*. Chicago: University of Chicago Press, 1963. A scholarly but accessible history of all aspects of ancient Sumer, by one of the leading authorities on the subject.

———. *Sumerian Mythology: A Study of Spiritual and Literary Achievement in the Third Millennium B.C.* Rev. ed. Philadelphia: University of Pennsylvania Press, 1972. A scholarly retelling and assessment of Sumerian mythology, with discussion of the problems surrounding the present state of the texts.

———. *History Begins at Sumer: Thirty-Nine Firsts in Recorded History.* 3$^{rd}$ ed. Philadelphia: University of Pennsylvania Press, 1981. A popular account of Sumerian civilization, organized by historical "firsts," such as "The First Case of 'Apple-Polishing'" and "The First 'Farmer's Almanac.'"

Mitchell, Stephen. *Gilgamesh: A New English Version.* New York: Free Press, 2004. A literary translation meant for the general reader, with an introduction and notes.

Nemet-Nejat, Karen Rhea. *Daily Life in Ancient Mesopotamia.* Peabody, MA: Hendrickson, 2002. An account for general readers of the history, society, and culture of ancient Mesopotamia.

Oates, Joan. *Babylon.* Rev. ed. New York: Thames & Hudson, 1986. A history of Babylon and its peoples from its beginnings until the Hellenistic era, including the city's archaeological history and the influence of the Babylonian empires on the surrounding peoples.

## Syria-Palestine

Cross, Frank Moore. *Canaanite Myth and Hebrew Epic: Essays in the History of the Religion of Israel.* Cambridge, MA: Harvard University Press, 1973. A collection of scholarly essays on the development of Israelite religion, focusing on its context among the other religious cultures of Syria-Palestine.

Hayes, John H., and J. Maxwell Miller, eds. *Israelite and Judaean History.* Old Testament Library. SCM 1977. A scholarly history of Israel and Judah by primary periods, with a review of the available sources and possible historical reconstructions preceding the history of each period from the ancestors to the Roman era.

Koch, Klaus. *The Prophets.* Volume 1: *The Assyrian Period*, Volume 2: *The Babylonian and Persian Periods*. Philadelphia: Fortress, 1983, 1984. A good introduction to the prophets of the Hebrew Bible, both those of the historical books and those credited with books of prophecy, dealing with each of the major prophets in turn.

# Greece

Armstrong, A. H. *An Introduction to Ancient Philosophy*. 3$^{rd}$ ed. Lanham, MD: Littlefield Adams Quality Paperbacks; original edition, 1957. A brief history of Greek, Hellenistic, and Roman philosophy, continuing into Christian thought to the end of the ancient period; intended for general readers.

Bremmer, Jan N. *Greek Religion*. Greece & Rome: New Surveys in the Classics 24. The Classical Association. New York: Oxford University Press, 1994. Intended as a supplement to Walter Burkert's *Greek Religion*, concentrating on developments in the field after the appearance of Burkert's original German edition in 1977.

Burkert, Walter. *Greek Religion*. Translated by John Raffan. Cambridge, MA: Harvard University Press, 1985. A comprehensive and authoritative scholarly introduction to all aspects of Greek religion.

———. *Homo Necans: The Anthropology of Ancient Greek Sacrificial Ritual and Myth*. Berkeley: University of California Press, 1987. An authoritative examination of the practice of animal sacrifice in ancient Greece, with ramifications for the notion of blood atonement in other religious cultures, both ancient and modern.

Dodds, E. R. *The Greeks and the Irrational*. Berkeley: University of California Press, 1951. A classic work on the role of the primitive and the irrational in the history of Greek thought, including the "rationalism" of the classical era in Athens.

Easterling, P. E., and J. V. Muir, eds. *Greek Religion and Society*. New York: Cambridge University Press, 1985. A collection of scholarly essays on specific aspects of Greek religion understood in the context of ancient Greek society, including the influence of religious ideas in Greek poetry, art, and education.

Kitto, H. D. F. *The Greeks*. Rev. ed. New York: Penguin, 1991. A brief overview of the history and culture of ancient Greece to the decline of the city-states; first published in 1950.

Sophocles. *The Three Theban Plays: Antigone, Oedipus the King, Oedipus at Colonus*. Translated by Robert Fagles. Introduction and notes by Bernard Knox. New York: Penguin, 1982. An excellent translation of Sophocles's tragedies, capturing the subtleties of his wordplay and presenting his work as stage plays fully suitable for modern performance.

## Hellenistic Era

Graf, Fritz. *Magic in the Ancient World*. Translated by Franklin Philip. Revealing Antiquity 10. Cambridge, MA: Harvard University Press, 1997. A scholarly investigation of magic among the Greeks and Romans, from the 6th century B.C.E. to end of the ancient period, including the presentation of magical practices in literary works.

Konstan, David. *Friendship in the Classical World*. Key Themes in Ancient History. New York: Cambridge University Press, 1997. An examination of the concept of friendship in the Greco-Roman world from Homer to the 4th century C.E., including its role in larger social, political, and religious contexts.

Theophrastus. *Characters*. Herodas. *Mimes. Sophron and Other Mime Fragments*. Edited and translated by Jeffrey Rusten and I. C. Cunningham. Loeb Classical Library. Cambridge, MA: Harvard University Press, 2002. A scholarly translation with introductions and notes; the Greek text and the English translation appear on facing pages.

## Rome

Philostratus. *Life of Apollonius of Tyana*. Translated by F. C. Conybeare. Loeb Classical Library. 2 vols. Cambridge, MA: Harvard University Press, 1950. A scholarly translation with introductions and notes, in two volumes; the Greek text and the English translation appear on facing pages.

Turcan, Robert. *The Cults of the Roman Empire*. Translated by Antonia Nevill. The Ancient World. Oxford: Blackwell, 1996. A scholarly account of the multiplicity of religious cultures within the Roman Empire, focusing on the mystery religions.

Virgil. *The Aeneid*. Translated by Robert Fitzgerald. Vintage Classics. New York: Vintage, 1990. A faithful poetic translation for the modern reader of Virgil's incomplete epic of the travels of Aeneus, with a glossary and a thoughtful postscript.

## Christianity

Aune, David E. *Prophecy in Early Christianity and the Ancient Mediterranean World*. Wipf & Stock Publishers, 2003. A comprehensive scholarly account of the phenomenon of prophecy in the Greco-Roman world in the early years of the Jesus movement, including a definitive treatment of the nature of prophecy among the earliest followers of Jesus.

Ehrman, Bart D. *Lost Christianities: The Battle for Scripture and the Faiths We Never Knew*. New York: Oxford University Press, 2003. A review and analysis of the variety of competing visions of the Jesus faith that vied for supremacy in the first four centuries of the Christian movement's history.

Hopkins, Keith. *A World Full of Gods: The Strange Triumph of Christianity*. New York: Plume, 2001. A clever, lighthearted attempt to recreate for the modern reader the Greco-Roman world at the turn of the age, the better to understand the triumph of Christianity over traditional Greco-Roman religious cultures.

Stark, Rodney. *The Rise of Christianity: A Sociologist Reconsiders History/How the Obscure, Marginal Jesus Movement Became the Dominant Religious Force in the Western World in a Few Centuries*. New York; HarperCollins, 1997. A clear, compelling examination of the reasons for Christianity's ultimate triumph over traditional Roman religious culture, based on contemporary studies of the growth of religious movements.

## General

Aharoni, Yohanan, and Michael Avi-Yonah. *The Macmillan Bible Atlas*. 3$^{rd}$ rev. ed. New York: Macmillan, 1993. An excellent reference for better understanding events in the history of Israel, later Judaism, and the early Jesus movement.

Coogan, Michael D., ed. *The Oxford History of the Biblical World*. New York: Oxford University Press, 1998. A detailed, accessible history of Syria-Palestine from the prehistoric era through the end of the ancient period, written by leading experts in the subjects covered.

Holland, Glenn. *Divine Irony*. Selinsgrove, PA: Susquehanna University Press, 2000. A discussion of irony as the result of looking at human events from the divine point of view, drawn on examples from the Tanakh and Greek religious culture, with special attention to Socrates and the letters of the apostle Paul.

Johnston, Sarah Iles, ed. *Religions of the Ancient World: A Guide*. Cambridge, MA: Belknap/Harvard University Press, 2004. A comparative overview of the religious cultures of the ancient Mediterranean world produced by a number of distinguished scholars, incorporating introductory materials on each religious culture and a series of comparative surveys on such topics as sacrifice, divination, deities, rites of passage, death and the afterlife, and mythology.

Livingston, James C. *Anatomy of the Sacred: An Introduction to Religion*. 5th ed. Upper Saddle River, NJ: Pearson/Prentice Hall, 2005. An introduction to the various issues involved in the study of religion, focusing primarily on modern and contemporary religious cultures, with helpful case studies illustrating particular phenomena.

*The New Larousse Encyclopedia of Mythology*. Crescent Books, 1987. A classic presentation of world mythologies, profusely illustrated in a large format, with an introduction by Robert Graves.